HISPANIC CLASSICS
Golden Age Drama

Tirso de Molina

TAMAR'S REVENGE

(*La venganza de Tamar*)

Translated with an Introduction and Notes
by

John Lyon

ARIS & PHILLIPS — WARMINSTER — ENGLAND

Spanish text © Cambridge University Press 1969. Reprinted from *Tirso de Molina 'La venganza de Tamar'* by A.K.G. Paterson by permission of Cambridge University Press.

British Library Cataloguing in Publication Data
Tirso, de Molina
    Tamar's Revenge. - (Hispanic Classics)
    I. Title   II. Lyon, J. E.   III. Series
    IV. La venganza de Tamar. English & Spanish

ISBN 0 85668 323 X (cloth)
ISBN 0 85668 324 8 (limp)

The publishers gratefully acknowledge the financial assistance of the Dirección General del Libro y Bibliotecas of the Ministerio de Cultura de España with this translation.

Printed and published in England by Aris & Phillips Ltd, Teddington House, Warminster, Wiltshire.

CONTENTS

The illustrations are taken from "The Drawings of Rembrandt", Otto Benesch, 1957.

For BAB and KEN

PREFACE

I would like to thank Cambridge University Press for their permission to reprint the text of *La venganza de Tamar* established by Alan Paterson in his 1969 edition of the play. I have made some minor adjustments to the Spanish text as follows:

Act I,   l.122 second half of the line spoken by Amón
                         l.471 *que la hue* amended to *que ella hue*
                         l.565 *asaltando* amended to *Asaltando*
                         l.606 *aunque su esfuerzo presuma* amended to *aunque en su esfuerzo presuma*

Act II,   l.179 *y no saben* amended to *y no sabe*
                         l.625 *de en día en día* amended to *de día en día*
                         l.1016 *los mismo* amended to *lo mismo*

Act III,   l.32 *lame* amended to *lama*
                         l.953−6 punctuation has been amended here: semi−colon inserted after *convite* and a full stop changed to comma after *ingrato*.

These alterations, for which I take full responsibility, were made in cases where there appeared to have been omissions or printing errors in the Cambridge text and after correlation with the texts printed in the *Biblioteca de Autores Españoles* edition and that of Blanca de los Ríos in the Aguilar edition of Tirso's *Obras dramáticas completas*. I would also like to make a general acknowledgement of my debt to Professor Paterson's excellent edition of *La venganza de Tamar* which first aroused my interest in this play.

My thanks are also due to William Croft of Chichester Theological College for his prompt and enthusiastic responses to my naive queries on matters relating to the Old Testament, though I hasten to add that any blunders committed in this area are mine alone. I am grateful to Rosemary Jenkins for her patience in typing the manuscript and, as always, to my wife Elizabeth for her help and support at all stages of the work.

J. E. Lyon, Bristol 1988

Drawing of Tirso de Molina by Anthony Stones

INTRODUCTION

1. Tirso de Molina and his time

Fray Gabriel Téllez, who wrote under the pseudonym of Tirso de Molina, may be considered as a bridge between the primitive cloak—and—dagger comedies of the early Lope de Vega and the *comedia* as a form capable of moral and philosophical depth perfected by Calderón in his maturity. Tirso's contribution to the *comedia* was not primarily a technical one, since his construction tends more towards the instinctive improvisation of Lope than to the intellectual rigour of Calderón. His importance was that he invested this popular form of theatre with a moral vision, which, despite the variety of subject—matter, gives cohesion and unity to his work.[1] It is a vision which, despite its ideological orthodoxy, has the flavour of an individual personality behind it. Lope echoed collective aspirations to social harmony and Calderón affirmed the importance of the individual conscience and will. Tirso's attitudes were less systematic and categorical than those of Calderón and more morally aware than Lope's. He is as vehement as the former in his condemnation of pride and egocentricity but less clinical in his judgements, which are tempered by humour and a sympathetic understanding of human weakness.

Little is known about Tirso's life and even his date of birth is uncertain. The most probable year seems to be 1580 or 1581.[2] What is certain is that he became a friar in the Mercedarian order in 1600, took his vows a year later, and served in this order until his death in Almazán (near Soria) in 1648. This order had originally been founded for the humanitarian purpose of raising funds for the ransoming of Christian prisoners from the hands of the Moors, though it later developed into a teaching order. Tirso's work as a dramatist reflects both these aspects of his order, revealing a humane moralist and a cultured mind. Since drama was commonly used as a didactic vehicle, it is probable that Tirso began his dramatic career by writing plays on the lives of saints, though he quickly extended his range into other forms of theatre, religious and secular. His earliest work seems to date from about 1610,[3] although the chronology of his plays, like his life, is shrouded in uncertainty. This has made any serious attempt to trace his artistic development impossible and most critics have settled for classification of his theatre either according to subject—matter or dramatic treatment. Apart from plays on the lives of saints, Tirso wrote light comic intrigues of love and jealousy, plays on serious moral and religious issues, historical and chronicle plays, biblical plays and allegorical drama. Some eighty plays in all have been reliably ascribed to his name. Yet the categories constantly merge and overlap. History overlaps with hagiography, broad farce appears in the middle of serious moral, heroic or historical drama, psychological realism fuses with allegory and parable, cloak—and—dagger intrigue finds its way into biblical situations. Such classifications and divisions should never be allowed to overshadow the essential unity of moral emphasis and personality that emerges from Tirso's work as a whole.

Tirso's most intensive period of literary activity, between 1618 and 1625 in Madrid, coincided almost exactly with an equally intensive period of social reform, much of which was directed at the theatre. During the first half of the 1620s the long—running debate between the defenders of the popular theatre and its critics came to a head.[4] This had been a complex debate involving not only literary and aesthetic but also moral and political issues. From the last decade or so of the previous century, Lope de Vega had been developing, virtually single—handed, his anti—classical *comedia nueva*, a fast—moving dramatic style which involved many elements of Roman comedy and showed scant respect for the 'purist' school of Aristotelian drama. He streamlined the cumbersome five—act form into three, ignored the classical restrictions on theatrical time and space and, most important of all, advocated a mingling of the serious and the comic, noble and plebeian, within the same play, thus disturbing all the long—held assumptions about artistic and social decorum. Lope's cheerful defence of his practice is to be found in his *Arte nuevo de hacer comedias* ('New art of making plays'), published in 1609, in which he claims that theatre (he ironically reserves the word 'art' for those who follow the 'rules') should imitate nature in all its variety.

The controversy between the supporters of Lope's *comedia nueva* and its opponents entered its most intensive phase from about 1616.[5] Opposition came both from the Aristotelian critics, who were incensed by what they saw as Lope's disrespect for classical precepts, and from the voices of moral reform in the Church, who saw the spread of popular theatre as a dangerous social development. There had been a natural alliance between Aristotelians, the Church and the more conservative element at court ever since Thomas Aquinas had synthesized Christian doctrine and Aristotelian philosophy in his *Summa Theologica*. Consequently any thought which ran contrary to Aristotle had the smell of heresy about it. Literary opposition to the *comedia* became confused with a general attack on the theatre as a degrader of morals and with a more political unease with the theatre as a possible threat to the established values.[6] There was no clear demarcation between the attitudes towards theatre as a social phenomenon and the more technical debates between purists and popularizers. The majority of Aristotelian critics in their condemnation of the new genre failed to distinguish between moral and aesthetic categories. Support for the cause of the *comedia nueva* would therefore have had an air of moral subversion about it, and it is against this background that Tirso's forthright defence of the new style should be viewed.

For its critics the *comedia* was associated at worst with licentious example, both in the plays themselves and in the private lives of the actors, at best with triviality; and it must be said that neither of these accusations was entirely without foundation. It has been argued that the demand for a more exemplary kind of theatre did in fact result in a raising of moral and aesthetic standards of plays in the 1620s. The Aristotelians may not have won the battle for a return to classical precepts and decorum, but it seems the climate created by the controversy led eventually to a more responsible attitude on the part of dramatists to their work and to an awareness that the *comedia* form could be used for serious moral comment. Dramatists who had at first thought of themselves as purveyors of popular and ephemeral entertainment began to publish collections of their plays and carefully correct their texts. Ruth Lee Kennedy[7] argues that the plays written, produced and published in the early 1620s, generally speaking, have a greater seriousness of purpose and refinement of workmanship than those of the early 1600s, a trend which culminates in the meticulous craft of Calderón. The new mood of moral seriousness is evident in the plays written by Tirso in or around this period. There are a number of plays which explore the conscience and responsibilities of kings, plays which allude under historical guise to the evils of the institution of *privanza* or royal favourites, and plays which critically examine such national attitudes as the *pundonor* or code of honour. Paradoxically, it seems to have been Tirso's increased seriousness in his examination of the morality of those in power rather than his alleged incitement to evil conduct which led to his banishment in 1625.

Tirso would have been about forty years of age when he was transferred to the house of the Mercedarian order in Madrid in 1620 or 1621. After his years of study of the Arts in Salamanca (1601−1603), of Theology in Toledo, Guadalajara and Alcalá (1603−1610), some five−years' residence in the quiet atmosphere of Toledo (1611−1616), and a spell of duty on the Caribbean island of Santo Domingo (1616−1618), the intensely conflictive and politicized atmosphere of the capital must have been a disturbing though, judging by his output in the early 1620s, exhilarating experience. Tirso was already the author of a substantial body of work, but he now found himself in close contact with the literary élite and the manipulators of political power. In the preface to the *Primera Parte* of his plays (published in 1627 in Seville) and on other occasions, Tirso refers to an atmosphere of hostility towards the theatre in general and envy towards his own in particular. At the root of all this tension was the ambitious and all powerful *privado* or favourite of the young Philip IV, the Count−Duke of Olivares, who practised institutionalized nepotism and imposed divisive measures on the country. Since artists and writers were inevitably dependent on political patronage at court, Olivares' policies of selective favouritism created an atmosphere of intense rivalry and envy amongst the galaxy of literary stars in the capital. Ruth Kennedy's intricate researches show how Tirso's conflicts with Olivares and with those self−seeking poets of his entourage eventually culminated in Tirso's troubles with the *Junta de Reformación*, a commission set up by Olivares to act as a political, social and moral watchdog to safeguard the crumbling realm against the threat of subversion. It was this committee that in March 1625 strongly censured Tirso for writing 'profane plays which incited to evil conduct and set bad examples' and forbade him, under pain of excommunication, to write any more plays of profane verse, recommending that he be removed from his Madrid post to one of the remoter houses of the Mercedarian order. [8] In view of Tirso's well−documented antipathy towards Olivares and the number of plays which portray young princes corrupted by ruthless and ambitious courtiers, with clear allusions to the *privado* himself, it is reasonable to speculate that there may have been some political motivation behind this decision. (Ruth Kennedy attributes it to the immediate influence of Antonio Hurtado de Mendoza, a mediocre court poet protected by

Olivares).[9] Although there is evidence that some of Tirso's plays were written or modified for publication after 1625, the Junta's decision virtually marks the end of his career as an active dramatist. In 1626 he was transferred to Trujillo in Extremadura for a period of three years and from that time until the year of his death in 1648 applied most of his literary energies to prose works of a devotional nature, including a voluminous history of the Mercedarian order.

2. Tirso and the *Comedia*

In the polemics over the theatre, Tirso's stance was that of an enthusiastic apologist for the Lopean *comedia nueva* both on moral and aesthetic grounds. There is an eloquent defence of the theatre in a passage intercalated (in 1620 or 1621) into his early work *El vergonzoso en palacio (The Shy man at Court)*[10] and a considered appraisal of the *comedia nueva* in his miscellany *Los cigarrales de Toledo (The Country Houses of Toledo)* (1624). The Serafina speech in *El vergonzoso*[11] is clearly aimed at those critics who saw nothing but triviality and licentious examples in the theatre. It characterizes the theatre as a compendium of life in all its variety, created by the dramatist in the imagination of his audience, and in addition, as a vehicle for thought and a means of nourishing the intellect. In *Los cigarrales* Tirso's defence of his departure from classical precept is set out with greater coherence and intellectual rigour than Lope's somewhat offhand and loosely—argued treatise. His succinct exposé makes clear something that had been only vaguely implied in the *Arte nuevo*: that Aristotle's central principle of unity of conception is, generally speaking, respected by the *comedia*, in spite of its multiple scene changes and the elasticity of its time—scale. Tirso realized that the so—called 'unities' of 'time and place were accessories to this central tenet — i.e. something perceived by Renaissance critics as the logical consequence of Aristotle's thinking — and were therefore not inviolable. Referring to his play *El vergonzoso en palacio*, he defends the extension of the action beyond the twenty—four hour limit on the grounds that, for an action to be complete in the Aristotelian sense with a beginning, middle and end, a longer imaginary time—span is often necessary. That is, for certain subjects such as love and jealousy, there is not time in one day for emotions to be conceived and developed and for dramatic consequences to ensue. How, he asks, can the virtue of loyalty be shown within twenty—four hours? Tirso argues that the time—span must be more or less consistent with the events portrayed and that the 'unity of time' principle must sometimes be sacrificed to the more important Aristotelian requirement: a complete action. By artificially limiting the time the 'rules' frequently militate against the verisimilitude they were intended to safeguard.

Tirso's challenge to the 'unities' is also founded on the general principle that art, and especially theatre, necessarily depends on the imaginative participation of the spectator. He draws an analogy between a play on stage and a painting. Just as a painting may depict great distances in three dimensions within a small two—dimensional area of canvas, so a play may depict a variety of scenes within the framework of a stage and two and half hours of performance. He also quotes the example of a reader's experience of a story, which may move from one place to another over a period of many months or years but which the reader absorbs in a few hours without moving from his chair. Tirso here transcends the literal interpretation of 'imitation' or 'truth to nature' by accepting that art and life are separate and operate according to different principles and that art is essentially an illusion which must count on the cooperation of a reader's or spectator's imagination and his willing suspension of disbelief.

Tirso's challenge to the authority of the classics is more an attack on slavish and uninformed imitation than on the validity of the precepts themselves. The originators of an art, he claims, deserve our admiration for having overcome the initial difficulties, but it is the duty of their successors to develop and build on their discoveries, while remaining true to the original principles. Artistic forms must be modified in the light of conditions and experience. What was suitable for ancient Greece is no longer appropriate for seventeenth—century Spain. Again arguing by analogy, Tirso is able to reconcile the idea of evolution and change with fidelity to a principle or identity. Those who discovered the principle of music would not expect later generations to continue exclusively with a hammer and an anvil as their instruments. In the sphere of horticulture the diversification of a species into different sub—species is not inconsistent with a general family identity.

Apart from claiming that the forms of art must vary according to the time, nationality and local conditions, Tirso defends the artist's right to *induce* change, to experiment. He quotes the horticultural example of 'grafting', in which the blending of two separate species — a sweet fruit and a sour one — produces an entirely new variety. By this analogy Tirso justifies the mixing of styles — high and low, noble and plebeian, serious and comic. It would be difficult to reconcile this particular development of the *comedia* with the principles of Aristotle, for whom the separation of styles was a basic assumption, especially since Tirso carried this practice much further than his mentor, Lope de Vega. Lope rarely goes further than juxtaposing the two elements, interspersing farcical scenes into an otherwise serious context. In Tirso, the tragic (or serious) and the comic sometimes become indissolubly fused into a new and separate substance. *La venganza de Tamar (Tamar's revenge)* provides an excellent example of precisely this process.

3. Humour, irony and paradox in Tirso's theatre.

This serio—comic view of life constitutes a powerful unifying force in Tirso's theatre. His plays are the product of a serious yet arch and mischievous mind. For Tirso, humour was not merely the result of plot complication or the sole prerogative of the lower classes and comic servants. It was a fundamental dimension of his outlook which surfaces even in his historical works, plays on the lives of saints and sombre tragedies such as *La venganza de Tamar*. His works — at least the best of them — are unusual in the Golden Age in that they reveal what one might call a serious use of humour, evidence of his realization that humour does not necessarily trivialize, that it can serve a totally serious argument. His early play *Santo y sastre (The Tailor Saint)* is an example of how Tirso allows the trivialities of mundane, everyday experience to blend with elevated religious feeling and faith. The play was probably written to order for the tailors' guild in honour of their patron Saint Homobono. The last act concludes with the conventional feature of miracles attributed to the saint, but the first two contain a great deal of humour and even broad farce. This is created not merely by the character of the *gracioso*, Pendón, but by Tirso's sense of irony and paradox. Dorotea, who has been for most of her life a mercenary gold—digger, is made to fall in love with Homobono's virtue. She pursues him with the highly honourable object of marriage, aided and abetted by Homobono's father who has noted the size of Dorotea's fortune. The future saint himself is a gauche and ingenuous character whose ineptitude in amorous situations creates much of the humour. Many of his pious statements at this stage of the play cannot fail to appear priggish and pretentious and are robustly deflated by the comments of the *gracioso* or by the farcical situations in which Tirso places him. Ridiculous as many of these episodes are, Homobono's simple piety ultimately emerges with dignity. With all its conventional miracles, *Santo y sastre* shows Tirso as a dramatist with a comic view of life which is able to embrace the unheroic and ludicrous elements without losing sight of the dignity and humanity of the character. Again in his play *Antona García*, Tirso injects humour into a basically serious and heroic conception. This derives not only from the scenes of rustic stereotypes which commonly leavened the heroic element in Golden Age plays, but from the protagonists themselves and the incongruous situations in which they find themselves. One of the best scenes of the play is between the folk heroine Antona herself and the Conde de Penamacor in which we witness the discomforting of a court dandy by the formidable Antona, who ironically deflates his amorous vanity by forcing him into a discussion on politics![1 2] The comic potential of this scene is further reinforced by the fact that Antona, as a recently married woman, is trying to repress her naturally forthright and aggressive tendencies and conform to the image of a dutiful wife. The picture that the amorous count sees — that of a pretty peasant and presumably easy conquest engaged in the archetypally feminine activity of dressing flax — contrasts humorously with what the audience already knows of Antona's virile strength and determination.

Tirso's sense of ironical paradox frequently takes the form of this inversion of male and female roles, especially in the lighter comedies where much of the humour stems from the confrontation of diffident men and forceful women, perhaps hinting at the paradox that men, with all their independence and freedom of action, were the passive element in love and that women, despite the restriction of society, were the active element. His comedy, *Don Gil de las calzas verdes (Don Gil of the Green Stockings)* is an anti−Tenorio play which portrays the discomfiture of a Don Juan figure at the hands of one of his discarded conquests, who, by winding a web of intrigue around her former seducer, reduces him to a state of total confusion and abject surrender.

The two plays for which Tirso is best known — *El burlador de Sevilla (The Trickster of Seville)* and *El condenado por desconfiado (Damned for Despair)*[13] — contain no inversion of sexual roles but provide other examples of how the author's sense of irony can illuminate his moral vision.   One of the basic themes of *El burlador* is that of sin and retribution.   Tirso's original Don Juan is a man who lives by deceit and treachery and dies by the same token at the hands of the stone statue, who uses the same gesture as Don Juan had used to deceive others: the proffering of his hand as a symbol of faith and trust.   The moral theme of 'as you sow, so must you reap' is not restricted to Don Juan and the statue.   It is typical of Tirso's ironic perspective that he echoes this theme, in a minor key, in Don Juan's victims.   Each of the seductions is in some sense a retribution for some fault — pride, presumption, bad faith — either in the victim or someone closely associated with the victim.   In his theological drama, *El condenado por desconfiado*, Tirso dramatizes the theme of faith in the teasing paradox of the criminal who is saved and the pious hermit who is damned.   Apart from the obvious contrast between the trusting criminal and the doubting hermit, the play offers some ironic contrasts and parallels with *El burlador*, in the author's treatment of the hermit, Paulo, and Don Juan.   Paulo is condemned for a lack of trust and confidence in God's mercy, which springs from his fundamental egoism.   He wishes to receive cast—iron guarantees of his own salvation.   Don Juan is condemned for his over—confidence not so much in God's mercy as in his own ability to judge the time allotted to him for repentance.   *El burlador de Sevilla* could well have been entitled *El condenado por confiado* or 'Condemned for over—confidence'.

Tirso's ability to create individual characters has sometimes been overstated.   There are no Celestinas, Shylocks or Falstaffs in his theatre; his characterisation is generally too sketchy for that.   Rather, he was sensitive to the need for character contrast and to the dramatic possibilities of incongruity.   What Tirso gives us is contrast *between* characters — light and shade — which makes for meaningful and interesting interaction.   His comedy *El vergonzoso en palacio*, for instance, is built round contrasting attitudes to love.   The Madalena—Mireno relationship is an encounter between an impulsive, sensual woman and a shy nervous man, the former the daughter of a duke and the latter believing himself to be the son of a shepherd.   This is set alongside the relationship between Antonio, a hot—blooded extrovert, determined, resourceful, flamboyant in his language, and the duke's other daughter, Serafina, who is cold, inward—looking and icily narcissistic. Antonio's energy contrasts with Mireno's diffidence and Madalena's impulsiveness with Serafina's calculated reserve. The two relationships are carefully counterpointed and the ironic contrasts skillfully highlighted. The one is a relationship of two rogues trying to exploit one another, the other of two people genuinely trying to reach one another across a social and temperamental divide.

This dramatic instinct for paradox, incongruity and the fusing of serious and comic responses sometimes takes the form of an internal contradiction within Tirso's central characters. The most elementary examples are the numerous female protagonists who for one reason or another take on an assumed role, women who disguise themselves as young men, ladies who disguise themselves as peasants. Tirso achieves delightful comic effects by occasionally allowing the real personality to penetrate the disguise, the noble lady showing through the peasant garb in Doña Violante in *La villana de Vallecas (The Girl from Vallecas)*, the real profane objectives piercing through the professed religious fanaticism in *Marta la piadosa (Pious Martha)*. In some cases the character is made to be unaware of the reasons for this duality in his make—up. Mireno in *El vergonzoso*, unaware of his noble birth, is unable to explain the shafts of arrogant ambition that occasionally break through his diffidence and timidity. At its best, however, this tendency in Tirso reflects an interest in the real ambivalence of human motives or an exploration of conflicting values. This is the case of *El rey don Pedro en Madrid*. Although many critics deny Tirso's authorship of this play, it contains several features of his style and thematic preoccupations. The typical shape of the *comendador* type of play, in which the King brings a wayward baron into line, is here complicated by the ambiguous character of the King.[14] The King is the fount of justice and the instrument of the well—deserved retribution that the baron, Don Tello, suffers, yet he himself is the victim of the same overweaning pride we see in Don Tello. His justice is vitiated by his need to prove his prowess and superiority as an individual, as well as inspiring fear by his authority as a King. *El rey don Pedro en Madrid* explores one of Tirso's favourite themes, which is the conflict between justice and mercy. In *La venganza de Tamar*, King David finds himself confronted with this stark choice after the rape of Tamar by Amnon. He is placed in a tragically impossible dilemma. Don Pedro's case is somewhat different in that he is shown as a character in whom the passion for justice is linked to personal pride and in whom the quality of mercy can only operate once that pride is satisfied. In trying to redress his reputation for cruelty in the eyes of the people, he is determined to press for justice on the baron, Don Tello, but, in the very pursuit of justice, falls into vindictive retribution. Don Pedro is only persuaded to exercise mercy when begged to do so by Don Tello's victims and after he has demonstrated his personal superiority over the baron.

In an article entitled 'Some Baroque Aspects of Tirso de Molina', Myron A. Peyton[15] quotes such contradictions in human values and schisms in the human personality as examples of how life 'disintegrates' in Tirso's plays, as evidence of a fundamental scepticism which is uncompensated by a positive belief in any value other than that of 'conscious aspiration' and the will. Karl Vossler, on the other hand, sees his detached irony as the serenity of an intimately austere and religious man, secure in his own beliefs, who has come to terms with the contradictions of the world.[16] Certainly, Tirso's undoubted appreciation of the ambiguity of human motives and behaviour does not undermine certain moral emphases which remain constant in his work. The values that are stressed in his more explicitly moral parables are also echoed in his historical and satirical plays and even in his lighter comedies.

4. The moral emphases of Tirso's theatre.

Ruth Kennedy's meticulous researches have unearthed many allusions to Olivares, Philip IV and the political situation of the 1620s in Tirso's theatre. There is, particularly in the plays of that period, a sharper satirical tone and a more acute awareness of contemporary realities than was common in Golden Age drama. Nevertheless, Tirso's emphasis was always moral rather than social or political. His portrayals of weak or corrupt monarchs or of proud and ambitious courtiers, who by their abuse of power create poverty and anarchy in the nation, are in no way attacks on the social and political structures. They are attacks on individuals who, by their surrender to selfish passions, endanger the social and political fabric of the nation.

Tirso's attitude to the passions was not fundamentally different from the general assumptions of his time, i.e. that earthly life was a kind of travesty of real values, a prison in which we are chained to self—centred appetites which limit our perspective and stifle our potential for love and charity. It is clear from Tirso's theatre that there is a close relationship between the different passions — eroticism, vanity, lust for wealth and power — in that they share the common denominator of self—gratification and are equally destructive. The same applies to the passions of jealousy and vengeance which stem from the frustration of these desires. The unbridled pursuit of passion, sexual or otherwise, is clearly seen by Tirso as a recipe for destruction for both individual and society. He clearly sees a link between private moral disorder and social chaos, particularly when it affects those who hold the reins of power. In *La república al revés (The State Upside—down)*, Tirso dramatizes the career of Constantine IV in the decadence of the Byzantine empire. Constantino is portrayed as a degenerate character in whom the pursuit of pleasure and the need to satisfy every whim have created an unstable mentality without spiritual or moral harmony. Tirso's purpose is to show the spread of this moral anarchy within Constantino firstly to those around him and ultimately to the society that he governs. Having begun by deposing his mother from the throne and sending her into exile, Constantino's actions breed discontent, rebellion and anarchy which inverts what Tirso saw as the natural hierarchy of authority. Constantino's monstrous villainy is revealed more through action than character analysis and his machinations create a tangled web of plot, counterplot, intrigue, lies and deception which eventually permeates the whole fabric of the society. Natural justice is subverted, the guilty are rewarded and innocent punished. As the situation deteriorates, Constantino loses control over his own deceptions and becomes the victim of the anarchy he has created. Yet Tirso believed in the capacity of human beings to transcend this prison of worldly passions, to recognize truth and achieve love. Many of his plays are parables which relate the triumph of this potential in human nature over circumstances which would normally breed self—indulgence. *Privar contra su gusto (The Reluctant Favourite)* deals with the subtly dehumanizing and corrupting influence of power, even when the person who exercises it is determined to avoid ambition. The central character, appointed against his will as *privado* by a pleasure—seeking king, is by reason of his office compelled to neglect love and friendship and placed in situations in which he cannot speak the truth (III, 1091). The process of corruption is seen to reside not only in those who exercise power, but in the response of those surrounding the *privado* (his servant, his friend and his sister) who are alienated by their own assumptions about him, by the fears, suspicions and jealousy of the privileged position he enjoys. By a combination of practical astuteness and firm principle the hero manages to convince the monarch of his responsibilities, overcome jealousy and ambition in his close associates and withdraw from his post with all his values intact. *El melancólico (The Melancholic)* is a parable of the discovery of love and the overcoming of the worldly forces that oppose it. Rogerio, the protagonist, goes from the extreme of being closed to love to an obsessive passion which sacrifices all rationality. His love is made to pass through several vicissitudes, notably an abrupt change of social status when he is discovered to be the bastard son of a duke, and the temptations of pride of status, intellectual vanity and sexual jealousy which temper and purify it. The same passions are involved in *El mayor desengaño (The Greatest Disillusion)* in which Tirso dramatizes the life of St Bruno who, through a process of disillusionment with erotic adventures, dependence on the favours of unpredictable emperors, worldly triumphs and temporal power, and finally with the vanity of knowledge and learning, comes to the life of devotion to God's service.

Tirso's attitude to human love was different in several ways from that of his contemporaries. He shared a general Renaissance attitude of distrust and censoriousness towards sensuality and sexual desire. The medieval association of sexuality with sin was still very much alive in the seventeenth century and, even when viewed from a more secular perspective, sexuality was regarded as animal, degrading or absurdly irrational, inducing behaviour unworthy of a rational and spiritual being. Yet he did not share the enthusiasm of many of his contemporaries for idealizing philosophies, such as Neoplatonism, which sought to idealize human love as a quest for beauty, reconcile the physical and the spiritual aspects of love and bridge the gap between human and divine love. According to H.W. Sullivan,[17] Tirso is being ironical at the expense of neoplatonic idealism in his play *La celosa de sí misma (Jealous of Herself)*. He is sometimes charged with showing only the physical and sensual aspects of love bereft of any kind of spirituality or idealism. Myron Peyton, for instance, claims that love in Tirso's plays becomes a 'sensual game'[18] and Sullivan that Tirso's feelings on love centre on 'a materialist philosophy with determinisitic undertones'.[19] Yet it would be unjust to conclude that Tirso saw human love purely as an erotic instinct devoid of positive spiritual values. Tirso makes a clear distinction between instinctive desire and 'natural love', and the crucial difference between them is the degree of self—gratification involved. Instinctive or erotic desire was in fact seen as the enemy of natural love, along with all the other passions (ambition, vanity, greed etc.), in so far as they sought mainly to exalt the self. The distinction is well illustrated in the contrasting love relationships of *El vergonzoso en palacio* where the moral basis of the action is the contest between truth and nature on the one hand and egoism, deception and artifice in the service of the passions on the other. Mireno and Madalena are trying to find a way of expressing what they really feel and to reach one another, whereas Antonio and Serafina are two devious rogues who thoroughly deserve one another. Antonio's motives are explicitly erotic — to covertly eye the beauty of the Duke's two daughters — and Serafina is shown as a character contrary to nature in that she has no love for anyone but herself and, like Narcissus, is punished by falling in love with her own image.

This love in conformity with nature was not necessarily a purely asexual, spiritual emotion. In Tirso's lighter comedies there are many none—too spiritual relationships which, with the author's moral approval, are allowed to triumph over worldly greed and social ambition (*Don Gil de las calzas verdes, Marta la piadosa, Por el sótano y el torno (Through the Basement and the Hatch)*). Its essential quality was selflessness rather than an absence of physicality, that it should be a love in which love of the other outweighed the satisfaction of personal appetite. As Alan Paterson suggests, Tirso's ideal comes very close to St Paul's definition of 'charity' in his letter to the Corinthians, a love which is not ambitious and 'seeks not its own'.[20] Paterson claims that this is best illustrated in Rogerio, the protagonist of *El melancólico*, who discovers the demands of a love that transcends any form of self—interest. This control of passion and renunciation of self—interest is seen by Tirso as an important principle underlying both individual moral behaviour and collective living. It is fundamental to love both in its sexual and non—sexual manifestations, such as friendship, paternal or filial love. It is also fundamental to the harmonious relationship between individual and society and consequently to the principle of order, good government and justice.

La prudencia en la mujer (Prudence in Woman) is a fine example of this morality at work in the broader social context. The central conflict is between a queen's philosophy of wise government,

Christian charity and national reconciliation and the self—seeking
ambition and dyed—in—the—wool villainy of the noblemen who
surround her. The queen's 'prudence'[21] is a blend of astuteness,
forbearance and generosity of spirit which consistently refuses to exact
vengeance on the apparently inexhaustible duplicity of her enemies.
Like David's mercy in *La venganza de Tamar*, it may sometimes
appear a naïve philosophy with which to combat cynical self—interest,
but the queen's adherence to Christian principles ultimately
communicates itself to the hearts and minds of her people.

The positive values in Tirso's theatre are closely related to this
idea of disinterested love in the broadest sense — mercy, compassion,
loyalty, generosity of spirit in personal relationships, harmony and
natural justice within the social order. Consistent with these values is
Tirso's rejection of the revenge ethic, which was at the root of
Spain's honour code in the sixteenth and seventeenth centuries. This
is demonstrated in the attitude of the queen in *La prudencia en la
mujer*, in the magnanimity of the Catholic Monarchs towards their
enemies in *Antona García* and in many other works in which
vengance is depicted as a dangerous egocentric passion, on a par with
jealousy, greed or pride, which blinds its possessor to the truth.
These general considerations are naturally relevant to a discussion of
Tirso's moral standpoint in the conflict of passion and emotions of *La
venganza de Tamar*.

5.   Tirso's biblical plays

La venganza de Tamar is one of a group of Old Testament plays
which collectively endorse these moral emphases. The plays are
concerned with critical points in the history of the Jewish people. *La
mejor espigadera (The Best Gleaner)* relates the history of Ruth whose
eventual marriage to Boaz founded a line of succession which led to
the house of David and ultimately to the birth of Christ. *La
venganza de Tamar* focusses on an incident — the incestuous rape of
David's daughter, Tamar, by her half—brother, Amnon — which
contains echoes of David's past and implications for the future of the
kingdom of Israel. *La mujer que manda en casa (The Woman who
Rules the Roost)* is set in the nadir of Israel's decadence, the reign of
Ahab, and traces the licentious career of his queen, Jezabel, and her
conflicts with the prophet Elijah and Naboth, the Jezreelite (1 Kings

xvi—xxii). Finally, *Vida y muerte de Herodes (Life and Death of Herod)*, based largely on Josephus' account of Herod in his *Jewish War*, Book 1, brings us to the slaughter of the Innocents and the birth of the Messiah. It is illuminating to examine some of the repeated patterns of theme and imagery that emerge from this group of plays, before looking at *La venganza de Tamar* in more detail.

The Bible, particularly the Old Testament, was a common source of plots for Golden Age plays. In the eyes of the dramatist, it was a means of presenting familiar material to an audience, but perhaps more importantly, it was a means of implying a divine presence in the affairs of men. Although Tirso makes little direct use of biblical exegesis,[22] his view of the Old Testament was undoubtedly shaped by his knowledge of the exegetical commentaries and his semi—allegorical treatment of the material heightens our awareness of the wider moral conflicts involved and of the divine plan which would culminate in the new order of Christianity.[23] What seems to interest Tirso in these Old Testament stories is the conflict between the forces in human nature which lead to anarchy and destruction and the latent potential in the human soul which the birth of Christianity would later bring to fruition. The forces for evil, as we have seen, are rooted in the human passions: lust, greed, avarice, ambition, vanity, pursuit of sensual pleasure, jealousy, revenge. The Old Testament plays, broadly speaking, are concerned with the clash of these related appetites against the human values that Christianity would later emphasize: charity and compassion (Ruth), loyalty (Naboth) and mercy (David). What ultimately distinguishes Christian values from 'paganism' for Tirso was the capacity to restrain instinctive appetites in the name of a principle beyond self. 'Paganism', the worship of false gods, is associated in Tirso's mind with the surrender to false values: money, power, sex, the gratification of the senses. In *La mujer que manda en casa*, for instance, he establishes a clear correlation between the worship of Baal and the surrender to licentious passion in Jezebel, whose cult of Eros is contrasted with the Christian love of Naboth and his wife, Raquel. Jezebel makes sharing her religion a condition of sharing her bed with Ahab. Naboth describes the cult of Baal as associated with sexual licence, orgies and promiscuity; he evokes a picture of moral anarchy parading as religious ceremony (1, 1589). In *La mejor espigadera* wealth and power are the false gods and avarice the chief passion over which Christian love and charity have to triumph. Tirso makes Ruth a royal princess of the kingdom of Moab, not out of an inherently romantic temperament, but in order to emphasize the worldly values which she must reject when she undergoes her conversion to a new life of poverty and charity in Palestine. She has to release her mind from the assumption that a person's value can only be measured in terms of possessions and status, that 'no tener' (not to have) is equivalent of 'no ser' (not to be). In Ruth's decision to endure poverty and exile with her mother−in−law, Tirso emphasizes not just a change of religious allegiance but the affirmation of a natural quality latent in the human heart.

Tirso also shows an obvious concern for contemporary relevance in his Old Testament plays. Blanca de los Ríos comments on his intention to make these biblical stories accessible to the Spanish *pueblo* in his audience by fusing the biblical Middle East with the atmosphere of rural Castile in the seventeenth century (I, 975). This is achieved through the incorporation of rustic scenes, worksongs, ballads, etc. and through the liberal use of anachronistic detail. Critics have seen allusions to the Spain of Philip IV in the vivid portrayals of the hunger and deprivation of biblical Palestine. The harsh conditions depicted in *La mejor espigadera* and *La mujer que manda en casa* could well have been an allusion to the situation in Tirso's own time in which the common people were starving as a result of the depraved morality of those in power. Yet Tirso could never be accused of idealizing the common people in any way or of allowing his political satire to obscure his real moral emphasis. Poverty and hunger prove no more effective in suppressing selfish human appetites than wealth or power. Famine brings out the brutal instincts of self−preservation at all costs and is equally destructive of the Christian virtue of compassion. In both these plays the rustic subplots do far more than supply conventional 'comic relief'. They echo in a minor key the principal conflicts and relationships and provide a basically serious commentary on the theme of love and the conquest over self−interest. [24]

With the dramatist's instinctive awareness of the difficulties of making virtue interesting, Tirso concentrates mainly on the side of human passion. In *La mujer que manda en casa, Vida y muerte de Herodes* and *La venganza de Tamar*, Tirso stresses the close relationship between the passions and their interdependence in a process of escalating violence and disorder, leading to inevitable self−destruction. The portrait of Ahab reveals within a single character this close association between the different passions. His ambitions for military conquest, sexual desire for Jezabel and greed for Naboth's vineyard are all facets of the same self—centred personality. In Jezabel, sensuality is linked to vanity. The final scene, which takes place after an interval of several years, finds Jezabel at her dressing table contemplating her reflection in a mirror. Significantly, Tirso reminds his audience of the seat of all the passions and appetites: the cult of self which blinds us to all other values. Vanity and the error of trusting in her now fading beauty to save her skin finally prove to be Jezabel's downfall.[25] Herod in *Vida y muerte de Herodes* is portrayed as a monster of egotistical passion in whom lust for sex is naturally associated with lust for blood and power. In his state of pathological insecurity, Herod switches from sexual jealousy to jealousy of the 'King of the Jews' whom he sees as a threat to his temporal power. The criticism that has sometimes been levelled at this play is the apparent disconnection between its various stages. First, Herod's emotional life and his jealousy over Mariamne, then the shift to the broader political stage and Herod's struggle with his brother Faselo over the control of Israel and finally, the shift to the religious stage with the report of Christ's birth and the massacre of the Innocents. The play only makes sense if we appreciate Tirso's understanding of the interdependence between the passions and the natural links he sees between sexual desire, greed for power and self—aggrandisement. As will be seen later, a proper understanding of *La venganza de Tamar* depends on our seeing the relationship between Amnon's lust, Absolom's ambition and Tamar's obsession with vengeance.

Apart from springing from a common root, the passions interact in such a way as to create a common dramatic logic in all three plays mentioned above. This dramatic logic rests on the premise that passion feeds on passion. The action in each case traces a chain reaction in which passion provokes counter—passion in a progressive build—up of unreasoning violence. What we see in *La mujer que manda en casa* is a reversal of the natural order, a world upside—down as the result of passion ruling the head and soul.[26] King Ahab is dominated by his wife because he is the slave of his passions and appetites. She manipulates him because she controls his appetites, in the sense that she holds the key to their satisfaction. This inversion (in the rulers) of the natural master—slave relationship between the soul and the senses causes disruption in the society at large.   Jezabel's disordered appetites sow dissension between Naboth and his wife, through the latter's jealousy, and, on the level of the *pueblo*, we see hunger (created by Jezabel's conduct) undermine the love between Coriolín and Lisarma.   The inverted values of those in power create confusion and conflict in the hearts of their subjects, between doubt and faith as well as between allegiance to king and loyalty to God.   The chain reaction in *Vida y muerte de Herodes* starts with the worldly ambitions of the previous generation, as the two old kings, Antipatro and Hircano, plan marriages of convenience to satisfy their territorial and political ambitions.   This is the direct cause of Herod's jealousy of his brother, Faselo, over the love of Mariamne. Herod then corrupts Mariamne by converting her to his philosophy of love as Eros.   The rejected Faselo is stung to violence and revenge and escalates the conflict by taking political action on a much larger scale.   Arrested on Faselo's orders, Herod is driven to new depths of depravity and orders his wife to be killed if he should die at Faselo's hands.   When he returns to Jerusalem as king, Herod takes his inevitable reprisals on Faselo and kills Mariamne in an attack of jealous rage.   Jealousy and the thirst for vengeance now reach the point of self—destructive madness as they switch to what Herod sees as a threat to his temporal power.   The massacre of the Innocents is an insane act of self—destruction in that Herod commits it against his own people and even includes one of his own children in the slaughter.   It is the culmination of this escalating process of passion against passion[27] and stands in direct antithesis to the new order, symbolized by the birth of Christ, which will break the spiral of violence by mercy, forgiveness and love of others.

Tirso's moral and allegorical emphasis in the Old Testament plays is further revealed in their dramatic presentation.   The settings and decor evoked in the dialogue are for the most part allegorical reinforcements to the moral theme, conceptual landscapes which tell us more about the moral character of the inhabitants than the conditions in which they lived.   Tirso was particularly fond of contrasting scenes in palace gardens with pastoral episodes or scenes in the wilderness. The first Act of *La mejor espigadera* presents an impressive contrast between two kinds of moral anarchy, one springing from famine and starvation in the barren landscape of Palestine, the other from the sensual luxuriance of pagan Moab.   In medieval commentaries on the Bible, the symbolic significance of the garden hovers ambiguously between the 'garden of the soul', a place of innocence and natural harmony, and the 'garden of delights', a place of sensuality and temptation. Tirso generally tends towards the latter presentation. In *La mujer que manda en casa* the royal garden is associated with sensual appetites and pleasures and provides the setting for Jezabel's seduction of Naboth. It is contrasted with Naboth's adjacent vineyard, representing the innocence of his soul, which Ahab tries to annex into the royal pleasure garden. Here, as elsewhere in the biblical plays, the settings are conceptual and the action frankly allegorical. Naboth, in his role as true believer, is subjected first to the temptation of lust in the form of Jezabel and then to that of greed in the form of Ahab attempting to buy the vineyard of his soul.

One of Tirso's most characteristic images of self—indulgence — and one which is extensively developed in *La venganza de Tamar* — is that of the feast or banquet. Allusions to this appear both in the verbal imagery of the plays and in the *apariencias* or static tableaux occasionally revealed in the discovery alcove at the back of the stage. Its most obvious significance is, of course, as a symbol of gluttony and Tirso's parable play, *Tanto es lo de más como lo de menos (Too much is as bad as too little)*[28] contains a tableau scene in which the glutton Nineucio kneels before a table laden with food as if it were an altar (I, 1147). This scene of blasphemous adoration is pitched in a grotesquely comic register reminiscent of Alfred Jarry's Ubu plays, as Nineucio gorges himself amidst the plaintive cries of the starving people of Egypt. Like Dives in the biblical parable, Nineucio is finally condemned to eternal hunger in front of a table on which the dishes give off the flames of Hell. The image is not restricted to the vice of gluttony, however, and may refer to other passions such as ambition and the sexual appetite. The supper table that appears in *La mujer que manda en casa* (I, 601) serves as a general emblem of the inward—looking and self—indulgent lifestyle of the king and queen and the sexual connotation of the image becomes clear in Raquel's dream of Jezabel as a serpent feeding on Naboth's flesh. Since passion feeds on passion and those who live by devouring are occasionally themselves devoured, the feasting metaphor is sometimes used to signify a just and fitting retribution. The fate of Amnon, murdered on top of a banqueting table, is a purely symbolic feast, whereas that of Jezabel is to be literally eaten by dogs.

Another image associated with erotic passion is that of gambling, used by Tamar at the beginning of Act 3 of *La venganza de Tamar* in her condemnation of Amnon's lust. The gaming metaphor is perhaps best explained by reference to an episode in *Vida y muerte de Herodes* in which Herod seduces Mariamne away from his brother and justifies his action in these terms (Act 2, scene vii). Herod converts her to his philosophy in a kind of ritualized debate, after which Mariamne sees love in terms of *mudanza* (mutability) and *coyuntura* (opportunity). Herod describes his success in winning Mariamne as that of the gambler who has bluffed his opponents out of a large pot. After he walks off with his prize, each of the other characters in turn abandon Faselo with the phrase 'There can be no arguments with desire', conceding that love, like a gambler's luck, is a blind irrational force subject to the vagaries of appetite and the exploitation of the opportunist. The gambling image admirably encapsulates the notion of transience and instability, qualities which are antithetical to the concept of divine or eternal values and which Tirso sees as the inevitable corollary of following the dictates of the senses.

6. *La venganza de Tamar*

It is generally thought that *La venganza de Tamar* was written sometime between 1621 and 1624.[29] The source is primarily the Second Book of Samuel, chapter thirteen, and in the main the plot traces the origins of Amnon's love for his half—sister, Tamar, the development of this obsessive passion which leads to the rape of Tamar, and the murder of Amnon by Absolom. David's speech on his return from the siege of Rabbah in Act 2 reveals knowledge of the historical background to David's reign and of his former love affairs and there are one or two variants from the biblical account which suggest that Tirso was familiar with the work of the first—century Jewish historian, Flavius Josephus.[30]

As in his other Old Testament plays, Tirso approaches his material more as a dramatist than as a theologian or historian. He is prepared to enlarge on the emotional human background, modify points of historical detail or shift emphasis in the interest of what he saw as the overall poetic truth of events. For instance, he modifies and enlarges upon his sources in order to clarify the question of motivation. The murder of Amnon is clearly attributed to Absolom's political ambition, whereas both the Bible and Josephus suggest no more than revenge. This links the passion of ambition thematically with that of lust and vengeance and gives relevance to the scenes in

Act 3 of Absolom's rising political aspirations and forthcoming rebellion against his father. Tirso greatly enlarges on Tamar's obsession with revenge. The Bible story is not at all concerned with her motivation and, after the rape, allows her to fade from view. It does, however, supply one detail which Tirso develops in his elaboration of Tamar's feelings and in his moral attitude towards the character: that Amnon's subsequent rejection of her was more wounding than the fact of rape or incest. [31] Tirso's organization of his material also suggests a slight shift of emphasis in the overall moral view behind the events. In 2 Samuel xii, the prophet Nathan predicts the internal dissension and destruction of the house of David as a result of David's abduction of Bathsheba and murder of her husband, Uriah the Hittite. [32] Both the biblical account and Tirso's play suggest the presence of a divine plan behind the worsening internal divisions in David's family. But whereas the Bible makes it clear that Nathan's prophesy alludes to Absolom's rebellion and Absolom's act of sleeping with his father's concubines (2 Samuel xvi 21), Tirso's play hints that David's retribution is the incestuous rape of Tamar and the death of Amnon. In order to make this more plausible, it was necessary to attribute a greater love on David's part for his eldest son, Amnon, than is implied in the Bible story. [33] This, in turn, was necessary in order to focus attention on David's tragic dilemma between justice and mercy in the last Act. The overall structure of the play thus rests on this implied correspondence between David's sins of the flesh and crime of murder, on the one hand, and the violation of Tamar and murder of Amnon, on the other. The sins of the father are reflected in those of the son and the fate of the son serves as retribution for the father.

La venganza de Tamar is not just a play about incest. Even less is it a play which exploits a taboo subject under a cloak of biblical respectability. It is to some degree a play about lust, but it is equally about ambition, vanity and revenge and the relationship between these passions. These other elements place Amnon's passion in perspective and modify our judgement. Although two thirds of the play trace the development of Amnon's obsession with Tamar, it would be a mistake to see it primarily as a character study of Amnon as this would ignore the relevance of Absolom's ambition and the centrality of David to the theme.

As we have already seen, Tirso tended to identify all the passions with the pursuit of worldly self—interest in one form or another.

Hence susceptibility to one passion made one prone to another. Using a time—honoured metaphor, Tirso associates the pursuit of military conquest and glory with the pursuit of erotic love. We see this conjunction of passions in Herod, Ahab and in Absolom. King David in his prime, we are told, was also addicted to both these pursuits. Behind these manifestations Tirso perceives the more fundamental corruption of vanity and incapacity for real love. It is no coincidence that an obsession with self and an incapacity to feel love in Amnon expresses itself in the form of possessive violence and lust.

Besides the moral equation between them, these passions are also locked in a dynamic process in which one passion fuels another. For the first two Acts we are concerned almost entirely with the development of Amnon's desire. Tirso sketches in some of his fundamental characteristics at the beginning. Weary of the war, yet inexperienced in the erotic pursuits of peace time, Amnon appears as a moody individual, difficult to please, isolated in his own imagination and seeking for 'the perfect woman'. His imagination feeds off the conversation with Absolom, who draws comparisons between love and war, taunts Amnon about his lack of sexual interest and finally stimulates his curiosity about his father's concubines. Amnon's curiosity would almost certainly have had a pejorative sense for Tirso. The *Diccionario de Autoridades* defines the word as 'a reckless and irresponsible desire to know things which are not one's concern, which is always a venial sin'. Amnon's hermetic character, prone to unhealthy curiosity and a tendency to live in the imagination, is, in its own way, as egotistic as that of the more obviously vain Absolom. Amnon is equally single—minded in the pursuit of his self—interest and the notion of 'having his way' crops up like a refrain in the dialogue. When the temptation of passion comes, it therefore falls on fertile ground. The sultry heat, darkness and sensual atmosphere of the seraglio garden, the talk of love, sweet music and the sound of female voices work on Amnon's imagination. Both Herod (in *Vida y muerte de Herodes*) and Amnon conceive their passion on the basis of incomplete information. Herod falls in love with a portrait and Amnon with a disembodied voice. Amnon now declares himself to be the slave of passion or, as he puts it, of the 'eyeless' or 'infant' god. Tirso's use of anachronistic classical mythology underlines his moral rather than historical emphasis in the play. His concern is to stress the idea of unreason and Amnon's departure from reality, and the blind god of Roman mythology serves this purpose, as does the symbolic evocation of darkness and the stumbling and groping antics of the characters. The first hint of the destructive power of Amnon's passion is seen at the end of Act 1 in the encounter between Amnon, in disguise, and the object of his love whom he by then knows to be his half—sister, Tamar. The subdued violence of this encounter is contrasted with its setting: the wedding of a couple who are consecrating their 'seasoned love'. Amnon's passionate advance and Tamar's violent response symbolically disrupt the harmony of this occasion.

In the second Act we find Amnon, even further removed from the world of reason and reality, in a profound state of melancholy,[34] interspersing his depression with bouts of manic activity. David accuses him of 'letting his imagination rule his mind'. Amnon indulges in deliberate fantasy as the only means of satisfying his appetite without surrendering to the violence within him. He involves Tamar in role—playing and simulated passion, but is unable to contain his emotions within the fragile mould of play—acting. It only requires the brief intervention of Joab towards the end of Act 2 to provoke jealousy and desire for revenge and to substitute violent action for fantasy. As Tirso builds to the climax of the rape scene, violence comes closer and closer to the surface. In the final act of violation Tirso makes us see, not just the culmination of erotic frenzy, but the expression of revenge, hatred and a satanic assertion of personal appetite over all social and moral constraints.

The responses of other characters who are exposed to Amnon's passion or its effects are equally self—centred. On dimly perceiving that she is the true object of Amnon's love, Tamar shows scant charity for her brother's plight. Faced with the possibility of losing her lover, Joab, she abandons Amnon to his fate. After the rape she develops a passion for vengeance which knows no bounds. Tirso portrays this, not as a natural demand for justice for the violence done to her, but as a deep. brooding obsession which corrupts and destroys all natural feeling in the character. It is significant that Tamar's savage reaction is not so much one of outrage at the violation itself or at the crime of incest. It is provoked mainly by Amnon's rejection and humiliation of her *after* the rape. Tirso thus makes it perfectly clear that Tamar's personal motives of revenge poison her plea for justice.[35] Blanca de los Ríos claims that there is little consistency between the skittish girl of Act 1 and the vengeful harpy of Act 3 (III, 360). The change, however, can be justified both in terms of the character and in terms of Tirso's moral vision. Tamar had already revealed a degree of latent violence and egoism in her reaction to Amnon's advances at the end of the first Act, and it was Tirso's moral purpose to show passion provoking passion. Absolom's ambition had already begun to feed off Amnon's melancholy even before the palace learned the news of Tamar's violation. The precarious state of Amnon's health and the prospect of his death stimulate Absolom's appetite for power. Absolom's earlier appearances in the action had shown him principally as a dandy and a playboy; this new development of his fundamental vanity alerts us to the violence in his nature also. Tamar's appeal for justice and revenge naturally provides him with the ideal pretext to kill Amnon and seize the crown of Israel, to use the Old Testament law of retribution to satisfy private passion.

Even the most casual reader of *La venganza de Tamar* cannot fail to notice Tirso's insistence on food imagery and the abundant references to hunger, dishes, tables, plates, cooking, seasoning, etc. Tirso undoubtedly derived this idea from the Bible story, in which Amnon lures Tamar into his room by feigning illness and loss of appetite and declaring that he would only take food prepared and served by her hand. From this Tirso developed a sustained verbal and visual metaphor which characterizes his attitude to all the passions as forms of instinctive 'appetite' and develops the notion of one passion 'feeding' on another. In the 'acting scene' when Amnon persuades Tamar to play the part of his fictitious Ammonite princess, he compares the object of his love to a feast he can never eat. At the end of Act 2 when, on the literal level, Tamar prepares and serves him the food, she herself becomes, metaphorically speaking, the meal that Amnon eats. In Act 3 Absolom's ambition is drawn into the metaphor when he sees David's crown displayed on a platter before him. By transferring the food imagery to Absolom's appetite for power at this point, Tirso explicitly links it with Amnon's lust, thus incorporating what might have been regarded as an irrelevant subplot into a single thematic purpose. Finally the running metaphor is crystallized in one of the most arresting and dramatic *apariencias* of Golden Age drama: Amnon spreadeagled on a bloodstained banqueting table full of food, with a goblet in his hand and a dagger through his throat. Absolom unveils the 'banquet' and presents it to Tamar, inviting her to taste the flesh and drink the blood. Amnon himself thus becomes the symbolic food that nourishes Tamar's revenge and

Absolom's ambition. If we see the symbolic eating of Christ's body and drinking of his blood in the Eucharist as the communication of his spirit to those who follow Him, we can perhaps see Tirso's use of the feasting metaphor in this and other plays as a kind of worldly travesty of the Eucharist,[36] stressing the process by which selfish and unChristian appetites spread and create their own dynamic of destruction.

But this is not the whole story. In opposition to this frenzy of spiralling violence, Tirso places the quality of mercy embodied in the character of David. His presentation of this quality is both tragic and hopeful. Tragic, because we are made to appreciate the conflicts and contradictions that arise (between justice and mercy, for instance) when this morality is pursued in the real world of self-seeking and opportunist passions. Hopeful, because mercy is a divine quality which would one day be wedded to a different concept of justice in the form of Jesus Christ. David is portrayed as a somewhat weak and fallible individual who, for much of his life, has shared the worldly passions that motivate his sons and, indeed, for whose behaviour he might be held as ultimately responsible. From allusions in Act 1 and his first appearance in Act 2, we learn that he is still addicted to worldly pomp and military glory. However, in his old age he has grown to place greater value on the love of his family. The play depicts the ageing David's tragic efforts to cope with the passions which he himself has engendered in his sons, armed only with the weapons of love and compassion. He is torn between his love as a father and his duties as a king and comes to realize, as Alan Paterson points out, the deep incompatibility betweeen justice as the world understands it and mercy. Although he chooses the latter, David's motives are rather mixed. His forgiveness of Amnon hovers ambiguously between a positive decision and an avoidance of the issue and his blindness to Absolom's true intentions (despite the fact that he has surprised him trying on the royal crown) lays him open to the charge of weakness or gullibility. David's motivation may be flawed and self-deluding, but the principle towards which he strives remains valid and intact: God showed mercy to him, therefore he must do the same to others. The hopeful element in the play is contained in an implicit contrast between Old Testament values and the new Christian ethos, and in the suggestion that, however imperfectly, David's charity could herald a possible end to the long cycle of passion and counterpassion that was the history of the Jewish race. Tirso reminds us of this cycle when, at the end of the play, David compares his own situation with that of Jacob, the one mourning a son killed by vengeance, the other mourning a son killed by envy. The conclusion seems to be that, for the time being, human passion takes its course — Amnon does not profit by his father's mercy and reverts to the vanity of the courtier and dandy in Act 3, Absolom cynically takes advantage of this father's love for him and Tamar obsessively pursues her revenge — but that ultimately Christian love and compassion are the only possible response to the anarchy of passion and to a law which demands an eye for an eye and a tooth for a tooth.

Despite its unquestionably serious and tragic emphasis, *La venganza de Tamar* contains a great deal of humour. This is generally true of Tirso's biblical plays, in which a humorous subplot involving rustic characters echoes the principal theme in a comic register.[37] *La venganza de Tamar* is different in that it has no well—defined subplot and, although there are rustic characters in the play, they do not provide the exclusive, or even principal, source of humour. Amnon's servant, Eliazer, despite one extended anecdote on the medical profession, could not be described as a *gracioso* or conventional funny man. The conventional element of 'comic relief' furnished by the lower orders, so frequently associated with the *comedia*, has little place in *La venganza de Tamar*. In general the humour does not 'relieve' the tension, but contributes to it. For the first two Acts, up to the climax of the rape scene, comedy interacts with madness and violence in varying proportions to produce a new and curiously modern hybrid.[38] Tirso's deft control of register and the balance between the serious and the comic is perhaps one of his greatest dramatic achievements in this play.

This achievement rests largely on Tirso's success in making his audience identify comedy with unreason, which gives the humour a disturbing quality. After presenting the essentials of Amnon's hermetic and introverted character, Tirso immediately places him in a comic role by having him assume the identity of a palace gardener. The audience thus sees this assumed identity, with its rustic accent and ribald humour, against the background of impressions already formed about Amnon's real nature. At this stage the dominant impression would no doubt be a comic one, with the symbolic suggestions of unreason — the darkness and the literal confusion associated with it — kept discreetly in the background. Later, however, this balance changes as increasingly irrational behaviour, abrupt changes of mind and disconnected discourse begin to take on a more sinister meaning. Act 1 culminates on a note of totally serious violence when the masked Amnon snatches a kiss from Tamar's hand and Tamar orders the wedding guests to pursue and kill the intruder. Act 2 follows a similar pattern — farce gradually shading into violence — although at a deeper level of intensity. Amnon's reason is now frankly impaired and the emblematic detail of the hunting hat, inappropriately worn indoors and first thing in the morning, is indicative of his mental state. He makes arbitrary gifts of money, gives contradictory orders, physically ejects the musicians he has ordered to play and attacks the fencing master with a real rapier. The note of authentic violence struck at the end of Act 1 is sustained in the form of slapstick farce with a strong undertone of serious irrationality.

Perhaps surprisingly, in view of the later tragic treatment, even David is subjected to Tirso's comic perspective. The scene of David's triumphant return from the siege of Rabbah is a hollow display of worldly pomp with rhetoric to match. His victory oration with its blatant vanity and impossibly convoluted syntax, deliberately out of character with the general style of the play, has unmistakeably comic overtones which are highlighted by the calculated bathos of the last line: 'How are you?' David's boastful summary of his warlike exploits and none—too—contrite account of his sexual misdemeanours link up with the vanity and sensuality we have seen in his sons. The triumphal nature of the king's return is finally undermined by the contrast between David's verbosity and Amnon's obdurate silence when the whole family tries to make him join in the welcome. Despite the comedy, however, Tirso by no means alienates our sympathy for David in these scenes and strikes a delicate balance between humour and pathos.

The long scene between brother and sister, in which Amnon persuades Tamar to play the part of his lover, builds from a low—key opening to a fully orchestrated expression of Amnon's pent—up emotion. The impact of this scene depends on the dramatic irony of the audience being in possession of knowledge not available to one of the characters. We watch the disturbing progress of Tamar's reactions as she goes from flippant amusement to perplexity, to suspicion and finally to horrified realization of the situation. Yet here too comedy has an important part to play. The play—within—a—play that Tirso has Amnon invent to console his frustrated passion is evidently some kind of burlesque melodrama which demands to be overacted.[39] This sets up a tension between the deliberate 'hamming' of the lines and the genuine feeling behind them, between comic expression and serious content. In this way Tirso reflects what he perceives as an inherent ambivalence in Amnon's situation, in which grotesque farce becomes almost indistinguishable from horror and tragedy. The comic elements are not peripheral to the tragic issue; they arise directly from it. Farce and tragedy are the product of the same situation.

Tirso's skill in controlling the blend of conflicting ingredients has already been observed in general terms. There is, however, one specific theatrical device he uses to highlight the shifting emphases between comedy and violence in the Amnon—Tamar relationship. This is the motif of the hand—kiss. Up to the rape scene this gesture is used seven times in all, three times in Act 1 and four in Act 2. Tirso had used a similar device in *El burlador de Sevilla* when he makes Don Juan ask for the hand of each of his victims in turn in order to give visual impact to Don Juan's treachery and relate that treachery to his retribution at the hands of the statue. In *La venganza de Tamar* the repeated motif of the hand—kiss goes beyond the emblematic depiction of the theme. It serves to mark the progress of the action by punctuating the different stages of Amnon's passion for Tamar and evoking different responses according to Tamar's perception of the action. In the garden scene of Act 1 it is no more than a gesture of erotic curiosity on Amnon's part (since he is unaware of Tamar's identity) and is received with mildly flirtatious annoyance by the latter. The demand for the hand and Tamar's reaction at the end of the Act, however, are given undertones of incest and violence that will accompany this gesture throughout the next Act. The hand—kiss in Act 2 is thus a conventional gesture which has become highly charged with erotic feeling. Tamar's hands become the focus of Amnon's obsession.[40] In the 'acting scene' the dramatist uses it to chart the progressive intensity of Amnon's emotions as he gradually moves out of his role into reality and the growing fear of Tamar as she becomes increasingly aware of the ambiguity of Amnon's gesture. The final occasion on which the hand—kiss is used is between Tamar and Joab. At a point when the audience senses an approaching climax, Tirso skilfully lowers the dramatic temperature by having Joab, who has been eavesdropping on the conversation, make a rather priggish speech of recrimination. This intervention is perhaps more important for the reconciliation that follows after Tamar's explanation. Joab's action in kissing Tamar's hand provides the motivation for a new change of gear in Amnon's passion. Maddened by jealousy, his desire takes on the ugliness of hatred and revenge. It also has the dramatic effect of jolting Amnon out of his make−believe and forcing him to adopt violence in the world of reality.

Although its moral emphases are essentially the same, *La venganza de Tamar* is different from the other biblical plays in that it contains no obviously exemplary characters and, with the possible exception of Absolom, no uniformly blackhearted villains. The passions − even in Absolom's case − are not allegorized to the point of taking over the characters. Tirso's treatment of his characters reflects a degree of complexity, ambiguity and understanding uncommon in Golden Age drama. This does not mean they are fully−drawn portraits with the rich interior texture of Shakespeare's heroes. We are afforded no more than tantalizing glimpses into their inner worlds. Yet they are, for the most part, portrayed as characters who evoke changing responses from the audience as the action develops. For the first two Acts, as Amnon tries to cope with his melancholy and erotic obsession, the audience response to him wavers between distaste and half−sympathetic amusement before plunging to horror and revulsion. Once the violence of the rape is over, our perception of Amnon changes. He is genuinely moved by David's love and refusal to condemn him, rejecting his former notion of love as Eros and acknowledging David's compassion and charity as the 'true God'. The audience, too, is drawn into this mood of compassion as Amnon himself becomes the victim of crude ambition on one side and fanatical revenge on the other. Tirso does not allow this sympathy to develop too far. The next meeting with the veiled Tamar, disguised as a shepherdess, reveals no fundamental change of attitude in Amnon, in whom we see the same arrogant, self−indulgent and potentially violent nature. It is simply that other changes around him have given us a slightly different perspective on his crime. The self−preening vanity of Absolom, faintly ridiculous in the first Act, has grown into cold and murderous ambition and the violence done to Tamar has bred in her a dehumanizing passion for revenge that alienates our sympathy for her as a victim. The death of Amnon is thus a triumph of vengeance and ambition, not of justice. As Paterson observes, Tamar becomes to Amnon what Amnon had been to her.[41] When passion rules, Tirso seems to be saying, we are all victims and oppressors.

But what truly lifts the play above a simple didactic demonstration of this proposition is the depiction of king David in whose character and dilemma lives the authentic stuff of tragedy. He is called upon to resolve a situation to which he himself has contributed by his past sins. He is to some extent reaping the harvest which he has sown by his former devotion to worldly passions. He chooses to follow the divine law of charity, mercy and forgiveness at a time when this is incompatible with the concept of temporal justice and in a context which makes it seem absurdly inadequate. Allied to this are his own inadequacies and suspect motives for pursuing this course. Is his response to Amnon's crime and Absolom's clearly signalled intentions a sincere attempt to follow what he sees as God's law or a demonstration of weakness and gullibility? Tirso does not attempt to answer this question for us. The portrayal of David moves from a register of comic pomposity satirizing the vain worldling to one of tragic pathos as his love for those close to him makes him increasingly vulnerable and the past begins to catch up with him. The play leaves us with the tragic image of David lamenting, in a speech of touching simplicity (in marked contrast to his earlier rhetoric), the death of his eldest son and heir. This final image underlines David's centrality to the theme. It is only through David that we see Amnon's rape of Tamar and retribution at the hands of Absolom as part of a larger historical process which takes us back to David's earlier life and forward to New Testament morality. It is also in David that we see that tension between suffering and hope which is vital to the ennobling effect of tragedy.

7.   A note on staging

La venganza de Tamar was almost certainly intended for performance on the open–air courtyard or *corral* stage of one of Madrid's two public theatres (the Corral del Príncipe or Corral de la Cruz), that is, on an open, uncluttered stage, with two doors at the back, a discovery alcove and a balcony. Enough has been said on Tirso's moral and allegorical emphasis to indicate that historical accuracy or realism were matters of minor importance. He shows little concern for historical authenticity in his references to money and coinage or to musical instruments and the same would almost certainly have been true of costume. The *montera* or hunting hat worn by

Amnon at the beginning of Act 2 was unashamedly an item of seventeenth—century headgear. Costume would generally have been in line with the conventional dress associated with the different classes in Tirso's own day, although the first stage direction does specify that Amnon's servants, Eliazer and Jonadab, wear 'Hebrew' costume, which would probably have been some kind of loose—fitting robe. In general, Golden Age plays, where the action flows uninterruptedly from one location to another, tend to give little sensation of physical place. Such 'atmosphere' as they contain is usually intended to reinforce the moral significance of the action. Tirso's powerful evocation of a dark, hot and airless night in the garden scene of the first Act is more important for its emblematic significance of the senses obscuring the reason than for its realism. The dramatist's use of the banqueting metaphor, the references to sheep—shearing, the royal crown and the distribution of flowers in Act 3 indicate similar priorities.

Audiences were therefore accustomed to collaborating with their imagination. The playwright wrote his plays with the fixtures of the *corral* stage in mind and the audience mentally converted the balcony into a mountain, a tower or the top of a high wall and the discovery alcove into a cave or inner room as required. When Amnon declares he is going to climb the garden wall in Act 1, he would almost certainly climb up some sort of ladder (more or less disguised as ivy) from stage level to the balcony and exit at the upper level. He would then re—appear at stage level after Tamar and Dina had made their entrance. The discovery alcove at the rear centre stage had both practical and symbolic uses and features prominently in *La venganza de Tamar*. It would probably have been used to get Amnon and Tamar off stage at the end of Act 2 when the rape is committed. In the absence of dramatic blackouts or fade—outs, it would have been necessary for Amnon either to pursue or drag Tamar offstage at this point. Since the alcove had just previously been used to denote Amnon's private room and since it usually afforded access to the dressing rooms, it is likely that the director would have used it for this purpose and had Amnon and Tamar emerge from the alcove at the beginning of Act 3. Much more interesting, however, is the use of the alcove to display static images or tableaux, sometimes referred to as *apariencias*. These might involve painted images, stage properties, actors in static poses, or a combination of all three. They were sometimes 'flown in' from the dressing room situated above the alcove or they were simply 'discovered', as in *La venganza de Tamar*, by drawing aside a curtain. The discovery of Amnon in Act 2 in a static 'melancholy' pose, with his hand on his cheek, is not an *apariencia* in the strict sense but it neatly illustrates the use of the alcove as a kind of dramatic shorthand to move characters from one location to another without emptying the stage. It also has the very useful dramatic purpose of focussing the audience's attention on something by 'freezing' the image, in much the same way as the contemporary cinema might use a slow—motion or 'frozen frame' technique. The sudden revelation, centre stage, of a motionless and totally silent Amnon after all the pomp and rhetoric of David's triumphal return would naturally concentrate the audience's mind far more effectively than an entrance. The discovery curtain convention, provided it is sparingly used, enables the dramatist to make a compact visual statement. The royal crown resting temptingly on a platter in front of Absolom's eyes and the impressive *apariencia* of the slaughtered Amnon on the banqueting table convey powerful emblematic images which sum up an important part of the play's moral theme.

34

NOTES TO THE INTRODUCTION

Full details of references quoted in these notes will be found in the Bibliography.

1.	'Le théâtre de Tirso n'est peut-être pas le fruit d'un métier réfléchi, mais il est conçu en fonction d'un ordre préétabli qui assure sa cohérence'. (Serge Maurel, p. 326).
2.	For further details on this question and on Tirso's life, see Margaret Wilson, *Tirso de Molina*.
3.	One of the earliest works that can be approximately dated is *El vergonzoso en palacio (The Shy Man at Court)* which certainly existed in July 1611. The text of the play, though set in the Middle Ages, includes a letter anachronistically dated in that month and year.
4.	See Margaret Wilson, *Spanish Drama of the Golden Age*, chapter 2, for a fuller discussion of this controversy.
5.	The opening salvoes were fired by Ricardo de Turia in his *Apologética de las comedias españolas* (1616), who defended Lope's mixture of tragedy and comedy and Francisco Cascales in his *Tablas poéticas* (1617), who argued in favour of a natural and perennial distinction between the genres. Another attack on Lope's theatre appeared in Cristóbal Suárez de Figueroa's miscellany, *El pasajero*, published in the same year.
6.	In his book *Tirso de Molina and the Drama of the Counter—Reformation*, H.W. Sullivan maintains that, although Catholicism on the whole presented a united front, the material of many *comedias*, particularly those of Tirso, reflected the tensions of the general European schism. Sullivan's argument is that the opposition of the Church stems not only from their objections to the 'secular values' of the *comedia* and the immorality of actors, but to what they saw as a more fundamental threat to established values, even though the plays, broadly speaking, endorsed those values. The plays could, by vulgarizing the debate on certain moral or theological issues, provoke a questioning attitude amongst the populus.
7.	Kennedy, *Studies in Tirso, 1*, pp. 51—8.
8.	Kennedy, *Studies in Tirso, 1*, p. 85 and p. 352.
9.	Kennedy, *Studies in Tirso, 1*, chapter 2.
10.	Ruth Kennedy's arguments for the later intercalation of this speech can be found in *Studies in Tirso, 1*, pp. 169—73.
11.	Tirso de Molina, *Obras dramáticas completas*, ed. Blanca de los Ríos. (Madrid: Aguilar, 1969), vol. 1, pp. 467—8. Future references to this 3—volume collection of Tirso's plays will appear in brackets in the text, listing volume and page number only.
12.	This is Act 1, scene vi, which is discussed by I.L. McClelland in her book *Tirso de Molina: Studies in Dramatic Realism*, pp. 70—71.
13.	Both of these texts have been translated and edited in the present series by Gwynne Edwards and Nicholas Round respectively. For further information on these plays, the reader is referred to the comprehensive Introductions to both these bilingual editions.
14.	Pedro el cruel (Peter the Cruel) succeeded to the throne of Castile in 1350 and was murdered by his illegitimate brother, Enrique de Trastamara, at Montiel in 1369. History paints Pedro as a cruel and tyrannical king, but legend and literature have dealt more leniently with him, balancing his cruelty with a sense of rough justice. He also appears as an important character in Calderón's *El médico de su honra*.
15.	*Romanic Review*, 36 (1945), 43—69.
16.	Karl Vossler, *Lecciones sobre Tirso de Molina*, p. 121.
17.	'Love, Matrimony and Desire in the Theatre of Tirso de Molina', *Bulletin of the Comediantes*, 37 (1985), 83—99.
18.	'Tirso is a skeptic in regard to love. He makes a sensual game of it, because love has lost its validity as a higher sentiment and emotion', (Peyton, *art. cit.* p. 47).
19.	Sullivan, *art. cit.* p. 97.
20.	Introduction to Tirso de Molina, *La venganza de Tamar* (Cambridge, 1969), p. 11.

21.   Tirso sees no moral contradiction between worthy ends and devious means.   Like the hero of *Privar contra su gusto*, the queen is shrewd and calculating in her conduct.   Her *prudencia* consists in her ability to shape the Christian values into practical action, to devise stratagems which allow her Christian principles to work in practical terms.

22.   This is according to Fr. Alonso López, 'La sagrada Biblia en las obras de Tirso', *Revista Estudios* (Madrid), 32 (1949), 381–414.

23.   Consult: S. Maurel, pp. 331–43 and Dawn L. Smith, Introduction to Tirso de Molina, *La mujer que manda en casa*, pp. 48–9.

24.   The rustic subplots are studied in A.A. Heathcote, 'El elemento cómico en las comedias bíblicas de Tirso de Molina' in *Homenaje a William L. Fichter* (Madrid: Castalia, 1971), 269–80.

25.   There is a very similar scene between Constantino's queen, Lidora, and her maid in *La república al revés*, Act 3, scene viii.

26.   See Dawn L. Smith's Introduction to *La mujer que manda en casa*, pp. 22–36.

27.   Serge Maurel (pp. 325–6) points out the conscious symmetry between Herod's blood–curdling account of his military victory at the beginning of the play and the cowardly massacre of the children at the end.

28.   The title of the play spells out Tirso's intention to equate what might otherwise be seen as two opposed passions: prodigality and avarice.   Tirso devises a plot which runs together the parable of Dives and Lazarus (Luke xvi, 19–31) with that of the Prodigal Son in order to show these apparently opposite extremes as united in their egocentricity.   Both the prodigal hedonist and the mean glutton are the expression of self–centred and self–indulgent personalities.   Both are anchored to the present moment in the fulfilment of transient passions.

29.   It was first published in the *Parte tercera* (Third Part) of Tirso's plays in 1634.

30.   Josephus, *Jewish Antiquities*, Book vii, contains the story of David.   I shall be referring throughout to the Loeb Classical Library edition (1934), translated by H. St. J. Thackeray and R. Marcus, volume V.

31.   See 2 Samuel xiii 16 and Josephus, p. 453.

32.   'Thus saith the Lord, Behold, I will raise up evil against thee out of thine own house, and I will take thy wives before thine eyes, and give them unto thy neighbour, and he shall lie with thy wives in the sight of this sun' (2 Samuel xii 11).

33.   The account of Josephus differs on this point: 'Now when her father David learned of this, he was grieved by what had happened, but, as he loved Amnon greatly — for he was his eldest son — he was compelled not to make him suffer' (p. 453).

34.   See note 1 in Act 2.

35.   In the last Act Tirso establishes a clear contrast between the attitude of the country people, who talk of purification by water, and the attitude of Tamar, who thinks only of cleansing honour with blood.

36.   See Dawn L. Smith's Introduction to *La mujer que manda en casa* (pp. 36–8) for a discussion of this image.

37.   See A.A. Heathcote *art. cit.*

38.   Blanca de Los Ríos detects the mixture but sees it as a sign of uncertainty, a wavering between the sublime and the ridiculous (III, 359).

39.   The action of the play–acting scene supposedly takes place in the dark.   Hence the groping gestures of the characters would tend to add to the comedy.

40.   The theme is picked up again in the meeting between Amnon and Tamar in Act 3, 866–72.

41.   'Throughout the play there is a well–defined symmetry between Amón and Tamar.   For part of the action Amón is the aggressor and Tamar the victim; then in the third act, they assume each other's role, calling forth a drastic change in our reactions.   Each, too, exacts claims upon the other: Amón submits his sister to his rule of passion and she in turn imposes on him a crude code of revenge' (Paterson, p. 19).

BIBLIOGRAPHY

This bibliography includes items referred to in the Introduction and Notes as well as books and articles recommended for further reading.

Works of general reference

Correas, Gonzalo de, *Vocabulario de refranes y frases proverbiales* (Madrid, 1924).

Covarrubias Horozco, Sebastián de, *Tesoro de la lengua castellana* (Madrid, 1611).

Josephus, *Jewish Antiquities* (Loeb Classical Library, 1934), vol. V.

Real Academia Española, *Diccionario de la lengua castellana* (Madrid, 1726−39).   This is generally known as the *Diccionario de Autoridades*.

Editions of works by Tirso de Molina

Tirso de Molina, *Los cigarrales de Toledo*. Ed. Víctor Said Armesto (Madrid, 1913).

Tirso de Molina, *La mujer que manda en casa*. Ed. Dawn L. Smith (London: Tamesis, 1984).

Tirso de Molina, *Obras dramáticas completas*.   Ed. Blanca de los Ríos.   3 vols.   (Madrid: Aguilar, 1946, 1952, 1958).

Tirso de Molina, *La venganza de Tamar*. Ed. A.K.G. Paterson (Cambridge, 1969).

Tirso de Molina, *The Trickster of Seville* (bilingual edition).   Ed. and trans. Gwynne Edwards (Warminster: Aris & Phillips, 1986)

Tirso de Molina, *Damned for Despair* (bilingual edition).   Ed. and trans. Nicholas G. Round (Warminster: Aris & Phillips, 1986).

Critical studies on Tirso

Agheana, Ion T. and Sullivan Henry W., *The Situational Drama of Tirso de Molina* (New York, 1972).

Darst, David H., 'Bibliografía general de Tirso de Molina: 1975−1980', *Estudios*, 38 (1982), 63−74.

−−− *The Comic Art of Tirso de Molina* (Estudios de Hispanófila, North Carolina, 1974).

Fornoff, Frederick H., *Tirso's Christmas Tragedy, 'La vida y muerte de Herodes': a Study of Ritual Form in Drama* (Estudios de Hispanófila, Madrid, 1977).

Gijón Zapata, E., *El humor en Tirso de Molina* (Madrid, 1959).

Gilman, Stephen, 'The *comedia* in the light of the New Criticism', *Bulletin of the Comediantes*, 12 (1960), 1−9.

Glaser, Edward, '*La mejor espigadera* de Tirso de Molina', *Lettres Romanes*, 14 (1960), 199−218.

Halkhoree, Premaj, 'Satire and Symbolism in the Structure of Tirso de Molina's *Por el sótano y el torno*', *Forum for Modern Language Studies*, 4 (1968), 374−86.

Halstead, F.G., 'The Attitude of Tirso de Molina towards Astrology', *Hispanic Review*, 9 (1941), 417−39.

Heathcote, A.A., 'El elemento cómico en las comedias bíblicas de Tirso de Molina' in *Homenaje a William L. Fichter* (Madrid: Castalia, 1971), 269−80.

Hesse, Everet W., 'The Incest Motif in Tirso's *La venganza de Tamar*', *Hispania*, 47 (1964), 268−76.

Jones, C.A., 'Tirso de Molina and Country Life', *Philological Quarterly*, 51 (1972), 197−204.

Kennedy, Ruth Lee, *Studies in Tirso, I: The Dramatist and his Competitors 1620−26* (University of North Carolina, Chapel Hill, 1974).

López, Fr. Alonso, 'La sagrada Biblia en las obras de Tirso de Molina', *Revista Estudios* (Madrid), 32 (1949), 381−414.

López, Angel, *El cancionero popular en el teatro de Tirso de Molina* (Madrid, 1958).

MacClelland, Ivy L., *Tirso de Molina: Studies in Dramatic Realism* (Liverpool, 1948).

Maurel, Serge, *L'Univers dramatique de Tirso de Molina* (Poitiers, 1971).

Metford, J.C.J., 'Tirso de Molina's Old Testament Plays', *Bulletin of Hispanic Studies*, 27 (1950), 149−63.

−−− 'The Enemies of the Theatre in the Golden Age', *Bulletin of Hispanic Studies*, 28 (1951), 76−92.

– – – 'Tirso de Molina and the Conde–Duque de Olivares', *Bulletin of Hispanic Studies*, 36 (1959), 15–27.

Moir, Duncan W. (with E.M. Wilson), *A Literary History of Spain: The Golden Age: Drama 1492–1700* (London, 1965), chapter 5.

– – – 'The Classical Tradition in Spanish Dramatic Theory and Practice in the Seventeenth Century' in *Classical Drama and its Influence: Studies Presented to H.D.F. Kitto*. Ed. M.J. Anderson (London, 1965).

Morley, S.G., 'Color Symbolism in Tirso de Molina', *Romanic Review*, 8 (1917), 77–81.

Parker, A.A., 'The Approach to the Spanish Drama of the Golden Age', *Diamante*, 6 (London, 1957).

Peyton, Myron, 'Some Baroque Aspects of Tirso de Molina', *Romanic Review*, 36 (1945), 43–69.

Rank, O., 'The Incest of Amnon and Tamar', *Tulane Drama Review*, 7 (1962), 38–43.

Sloman, A.E., *The Dramatic Craftsmanship of Calderón* (Oxford, 1958). (Chapter 4 contains a comparison of *La venganza de Tamar* and *Los cabellos de Absolón*.)

Sullivan, Henry W., 'Love, Matrimony and Desire in the Theatre of Tirso de Molina', *Bulletin of the Comediantes*, 37 (1985), 83–99.

– – – *Tirso de Molina and the Drama of the Counter–Reformation* (Amsterdam, 1976).

Vossler, Karl, *Lecciones sobre Tirso de Molina* (Madrid: Taurus, 1965).

Wardropper, B.W., 'The Implicit Craft of the Spanish *Comedia*' in *Studies in Spanish Literature of the Golden Age Presented to Edward M. Wilson*. Ed. R.O. Jones (London, 1973).

Williamsen, V.C. and Poesse, W., *An Annotated, Analytical Bibliography of Tirso de Molina Studies 1627–1977* (London, 1979).

Wilson, Margaret, *Spanish Drama of the Golden Age* (Oxford, 1969).

– – – *Tirso de Molina* (New York: Twayne, 1977).

Nathan admonishing David

TAMAR'S REVENGE
La venganza de Tamar

PERSONAS

Amón	David
Eliazer	Micol
Jonadab	Salomón
Absalón	Tirso
Adonías	Braulio
Tamar	Aliso — ganaderos
Dina	Riselo
Abigail, reina	Ardelio
Bersabé	Laureta
Un Criado	Josefo — novios
Un Maestro de Armas	Elisa
Joab	

CHARACTERS

Amnon
Eliazer
Jonadab
Absolom
Tamar
Dina
Abigail, the queen
Bathsheba
A servant
Joab

David
Michal
Solomon
Tirso ⎤
Braulio ⎟
Aliso ⎬ shepherds
Riselo ⎟
Ardelio ⎦
Laureta
Josephus   bridegroom
Elisa   bride

The numbers within the English text refer to the notes on Pp. 220 ff. and the line numbers are those of the Spanish text.

JORNADA PRIMERA

Salen Amón de camino, Eliazer y Jonadab, hebreos.

AMÓN.   Quitadme aquestas espuelas,
y descalzadme estas botas.
ELIAZER.   Ya de ver murallas rotas,
por cuyas escalas vuelas,
debes de venir cansado.   5
AMÓN.   Es mi padre pertinaz;
ni viejo admite la paz,
ni mozo quitó del lado
el acero que desciño.
JONADAB.   De eso, señor, no te espantes;   10
quien descabezó gigantes
y comenzó a vencer niño,
si es otra naturaleza
la poderosa costumbre,
viejo tendrá pesadumbre   15
con la paz.
ELIAZER.   A la grandeza
del reino que le corona
por sus hazañas subió.
AMÓN.   No soy tan soldado yo
cual dél la fama pregona.   20
De los amonitas cerque
David la idólatra corte,
máquinas la industria corte
con que a sus muros se acerque,
que si en eso se halla bien   25
porque sus reinos mejora,
más quiero, Eliazer, una hora
de nuestra Jerusalén,
que cuantas victorias dan
a su nombre eterna fama.   30
ELIAZER.   Si fueras de alguna dama
alambicado galán,
no me espanto que la ausencia
te hiciera la guerra odiosa;

ACT I

Enter Amnon dressed for travelling, with Eliazer and Jonadab in Hebrew costume.[1]

AMNON.   Remove these spurs; take off the boots.
ELIAZER.   You must be weary of the siege,
my lord, seeing ramparts broken
and scaling ladders through the breach.   5
AMNON.   My father's stubborn as a mule.
He can't stand peace, old as he is,
and this sword, which I now remove,
in his youth never left his side.[2]
JONADAB.   Habit's just like second nature,   10
my good lord.   There is no wonder
that one who chopped the heads off giants
and tasted victory as a . boy
should find peace irksome when he's old.   15
ELIAZER.   By the deeds of his hand he rose
to rule the land whose crown he wears.
AMNON.   Well, I'm not such a soldier
as fame would make him out to be.   20
Let David besiege the city
of the idolatrous Ammonite.[3]
Let him devise his war machines[4]
to approach the enemy walls
if that brings him fulfilment   25
and improves his kingdom's lot.
For me, I'd rather have one hour
of our Jerusalem, my friend,
than all the victories that give
eternal honour to his name.   30
ELIAZER.   If you were some moon—struck lover,
I could understand that absence
might make war hateful in your eyes;
a love that rests easy in peace   35

que amor que en la paz reposa   35
pierde armado la paciencia.
Mas, no amando, aborrecer
las armas, que de pesadas
suelen ser desamoradas,
cosa es nueva.
    AMÓN.   Sí, Eliazer,   40
nueva es, por eso la apruebo.
En todo soy singular,
que no es digno de estimar
el que no inventa algo nuevo.

Salen Absalón, Adonías y otros, de camino.

    ABSALÓN.   No gozaremos las treguas   45
que el Rey da al contrario, bien,
no estando en Jerusalén.
    ADONÍAS.   Corrido habemos las leguas
que hay de Rábata hasta aquí
volando.
    ABSALÓN.   ¡Qué bien pensó   50
quien las postas inventó!
    ELIAZER.   No a lo menos para mí.
Doylas a la maldición,
que, batanando jornadas,
me han puesto las dos lunadas   55
como ruedas de salmón.
    ABSALÓN.   ¡O Eliazer! ¿También tú gozas
treguas acá?
    ELIAZER.   ¿Qué querías?
    AMÓN.   ¡O mi Absalón, mi Adonías!
¿Aquí?
    ABSALÓN.   Travesuras mozas   60
nunca, hermano, están de espacio.
Troquemos en nuestra tierra
por las tiendas de la guerra
los salones de palacio.
Diez días que han de durar   65
las treguas que al amonita
David da, el Amor permita

begins to fret once clad in arms.
But not to love yet find the weight
of arms too much to bear: that's new.
    AMNON.   It is indeed, Eliazer.   40
And that's why I approve of it.
In all things I am singular.
Without originality
no man is worthy of esteem.

Enter Absolom, Adonijah and others in travelling costume.

    ABSOLOM.   We would not enjoy this truce   45
the King grants to his enemies,
if we weren't in Jerusalem.
    ADONIJAH.   But we've surely flown the leagues
from Rabbah to here.
    ABSOLOM.   Post horses, [5]   50
friend! Thank God for their inventor!
    ELIAZER.   Not me. I'd damn 'em all to Hell!
with battering day in day out
they've striped my bum like griddled trout. [6]   55
    ABSOLOM.   Eliazer! So you're here too
enjoying David's truce?
    ELIAZER.   Where else?
    AMNON. Dear Absolom! Adonijah!
Here so soon?
    ABSOLOM.   The hot blood of youth   60
has no time to waste, my brother.
So we exchange the tents of war
for palace drawing rooms at home
and, for just ten days of peace   65
that David gives the Ammonite,
we'll breach and scale the walls of Love. [7]
    AMNON.   Walls of Love?
    ABSOLOM.   Why not? You could well
call them so. He who woos by night,   70
does he too not take walls by storm,
climb high windows, patrol the streets?
Does he not give the secret word,

sus murallas escalar.

AMÓN. ¿Murallas de Amor?

ABSALÓN.   Bien puedes
permitirles este nombre;   70
amando de noche un hombre,
¿no asalta también paredes?
¿Ventanas altas no escala?
¿No ronda? ¿El nombre no da?
¿Trazando ardides no está?   75
Luego Amor a Marte iguala.

AMÓN. No te quiero replicar;
ya sé que tiene gran parte
Amor, que es hijo de Marte,
y lo que hay de Marte a amar.   80

ADONÍAS. En ti, Príncipe, infinito,
pues con ser tan gran soldado
nunca fuiste enamorado.

AMÓN. Poco sus llamas permito:
no sé ser tan conversable   85
como tú, hermano Absalón.

ABSALÓN. La hermosura es perfección,
y lo perfecto es amable;
hízome hermoso mi suerte,
y a todas me comunico.   90

AMÓN. Estás de cabellos rico,
y ansí puedes atreverte,
que a guedeja que les des,
las que muertas por las tiendas
te porfían que los vendas,   95
tendrán en ti su interés,
pues si no miente la fama,
tanto tu cabeza vale,
que me afirman que te sale
a cabello cada dama.   100

ELIAZER. Si ansí sus defectos salvas,
¿qué mucho te quieran bien?
pues toda Jerusalén
te llama socorre—calvas.
Y las muchas que compones,   105
debiéndote sus bellezas,

devise his little stratagems? 75
Then all's the same in love and war.
    AMNON. I'll not dispute with you on that.
I know there's much of war in love,
that Eros is the son of Mars. [8]
From Mars to *amare*'s but a step. 80
    ABSOLOM. In your case, Prince, an infinite one.
Splendid soldier though you may be,
you never were a great lover.
    AMNON. Love's flame has little chance with me.
I cannot be as sociable 85
as you, my brother Absolom.
    ABSOLOM. All true beauty is perfection
and what is perfect attracts love;
since fate gave me so much beauty
I share it with all womankind. 90
    AMNON. You can afford to. You're rich enough
in hair. With women clamouring
round your tents for you to sell it, [9] 95
their interest in you will grow
with every lock of hair you give.
For if rumour's to be trusted,
there's such a price upon your head
I'm told it works out at one hair
for every woman in your bed. 100
    ELIAZER. Can you wonder they love you well
when you cover their bald patches?
They call you the hair restorer
in the city of Jerusalem.
So many girls owe you their looks, 105
so many little Absoloms

hacen que haya en las cabezas
infinitos Absalones;
ristros puedes hacer dellas.

ABSALÓN. Eliazer, conceptos bajos   110
dices.

ELIAZER. Fueran ristros de ajos,
si no es por ti, las más bellas.

ABSALÓN. En fin, ¿el Príncipe da
en no querer a ninguna?

AMÓN. Hasta encontrar con alguna   115
perfecta, no me verá
en su minuta el Amor.

ABSALÓN. ¿Elisabet no es hermosa?

AMÓN. De cerca no, que es hoyosa.

ADONÍAS. ¿Y Ester?

AMÓN.   Tiene buen color   120
pero mala dentadura.

ELIAZER. ¿Délbora?

AMÓN   Es grande de boca.

JONADAB. ¿Atalia?

AMÓN.   Esa es muy loca
y pequeña de estatura.

ABSALÓN. No tiene falta María.   125

AMÓN. ¿Ser melindrosa no es falta?

ADONÍAS. ¿Dina?

AMÓN.   Enfádame por alta.

ELIAZER. ¿Ruth?

AMÓN.   Es negra.

JONADAB.   ¿Raquel?

AMÓN.   Fría.

ABSALÓN. ¿Aristóbola?

AMÓN.   Es común;
habla con ciento en un año.   130

ABSALÓN. ¿Judit?

AMÓN.   Tiene mucho paño,
y huele siempre a betún.

ADONÍAS. ¿Marta?

AMÓN.   Encubre muchos granos.

ELIAZER. ¿Alejandra?

AMÓN.   Es algo espesa.

stuck on top of so many heads,
you could string them up like garlic.
    ABSOLOM.   Friend, your conceits are in bad taste.   110
    ELIAZER.   And heads like garlic they would have[10]
— even the best — if it weren't for you.
    ABSOLOM.   But my princely brother here
finds none of them to his liking?
    AMNON.   I'll not feature on Love's menu[11]   115
till I find a perfect woman.
    ABSOLOM.   Elisabeth, is she not fair?
    AMNON.   Not close up. Dimples everywhere.
    ADONIJAH.   And Esther?
    AMNON.   She has good colour,   120
but rotten teeth.
    ELIAZER.   And Deborah?
    AMNON.   Her mouth's too large.
    JONADAB.   Atalia?
    AMNON.   Too short and mad as a hatter.
    ABSOLOM.   Maria has no faults at all.   125
    AMNON.   Priggishness is no small matter.
    ADONIJAH.   Dinah?
    AMNON.   Can't stand her. She's too tall.
    ELIAZER.   Ruth?
    AMNON.   Too dark.
    JONADAB.   Rachel?
    AMNON.   Too cold.
    ABSOLOM.   Aristobola?
    AMNON.   Too easy.
Talks to everyone, young and old.   130
    ABSOLOM.   Judith?
    AMNON.   Blotchy skin. Reeks of fard.
    ADONIJAH. Martha?
    AMNON.   Pimply.
    ELIAZER.   Alexandra?
    AMNON.   Sluttish. Greasy as a lump of lard.[12]

JONADAB. ¿Jezabel?

AMÓN.   Dícenme que ésa   135
trae juanetes en las manos.

ABSALÓN. ¿Zilene?

AMÓN.   Rostro bizarro,
mas flaca, y impertinente.

ELIAZER. Pues no hallas quien te contente,
haz una dama de barro.   140

ABSALÓN. ¡Válgate Dios por Amón,
qué satírico que estás!

AMÓN. No has de verme amar jamás;
tengo mala condición.

ADONÍAS. ¿Luego no querrás mañana   145
en la noche ir a la fiesta
y boda que a Elisa apresta
la mocedad cortesana?

AMÓN. ¿Con quién se casa?

ADONÍAS.   ¿Eso ignoras?
Con Josefo de Isacar.   150

AMÓN. Bella mujer le han de dar.

ABSALÓN. Tú que nunca te enamoras,
no la tendrás por muy bella.
¿Piensas ir allá?

AMÓN.   No sé.

ADONÍAS. Hay rebravo sarao.

AMÓN.   Iré   155
a danzar, pero no a vella.
Mas ha de ser disfrazado,
si es que máscaras se admiten.

ADONÍAS. En los saraos se permiten.

AMÓN. Lástima tengo al casado   160
con una mujer a cuestas.

ELIAZER. Poco en eso te pareces
a tu padre.

AMÓN.   Muchas veces
de ese modo me molestas.
Ya sé que a David mi padre   165
no le han parecido mal,
testigo la de Nabal
y Bersabé, hermosa madre

JONADAB.   Jezabel?

AMNON.   They tell me that she   135
has got bunions on her hands.

ABSOLOM.   Silene?

AMNON.   Handsome of features,
but skinny — and too much to say.

ELIAZER.   Since you can't find one to please you,
you'd better make one out of clay.   140

ABSOLOM.   Goodness me, my dear Amnon!
We are satirical today!

AMNON.   You'll never see me fall in love;
my nature is far too nasty.

ADONIJAH.   You'll not be seen tomorrow night   145
then, at the feast the youth of court
gives for Elisa's wedding day?

AMNON.   Wedding?   With whom?

ADONIJAH.   You don't know that?
With Josephus of Isacar.[13]   150

AMNON.   He's getting a handsome bride.

ABSOLOM.   You surely would not think her so,
you who never fall in love.
Will you attend?

AMNON.   I don't know.

ADONIJAH.   There'll be a right royal reception.

AMNON.   I'll go for the dance, not the bride.   155
But, if face masks be permitted,
I must insist on a disguise.

ADONIJAH.   They may be worn at wedding feasts.

AMNON.   A wife's a burden on your back.   160
I fell sorry for married men.

ELIAZER.   You're not your father's son in that.[14]

AMNON.   You've taunted me like that before.
I know my father's not averse   165
to other men's wives.   Nabal's woman[15]
and the beautiful Bathsheba,
mother of the smiling Solomon,

del risueño Salomón.

ADONÍAS.   Y las muchas concubinas,   170
cuyas bellezas divinas
milagro del mundo son.
Gana he tenido de vellas.

AMÓN.   Guárdalas el Rey de suerte
que aun no ha de poder la muerte   175
hallar por donde vencellas.

ABSALÓN.   El recato de palacio
y poca seguridad
de la femenil beldad
no las deja ver despacio.   180
Mas, por Dios, que ha pocos días
que a una muchacha que vi
entre ellas, Amón, le di
toda el alma.

AMÓN.   Oye, Adonías,
del modo que está Absalón.   185
¿A la mujer de tu padre?

ABSALÓN.   Sólo perdono a mi madre.
Tengo tal inclinación,
que con quien celebra bodas,
envidiando su vejez,   190
me enamoro; y ya habrá vez
en que he de gozallas todas.

AMÓN.   La belleza y la locura
son hermanas; eres bello,
y estás loco.   A tu cabello   195
atribuye tu ventura,
y no digas desatinos.

ADONÍAS.   Ya es de noche.   ¿Qué has de hacer?

ABSALÓN.   Cierta dama he de ir a ver,
en durmiendo sus vecinos.   200

ADONÍAS.   Yo me pierdo por jugar.

AMÓN.   Yo, que ni adoro, ni juego,
leeré versos.

ABSALÓN.   Buen sosiego.

AMÓN.   En esto quiero imitar
a David, pues no le imito   205
en amar, ni en querer tanto.

can bear witness to that taste.

ADONIJAH.   Apart from all the concubines,   170
whose beauty is a miracle
I've always longed to see.

AMNON.   The king
guards them so close that death itself[16]   175.
could not find a way to take them.

ABSOLOM.   The closely guarded palace grounds
and unreliability
of female beauty don't allow
for much detailed inspection.   180
But, by Heaven, some days ago
I saw, Amnon, a girl amongst them
to whom I gave my heart.

AMNON.   Take note,
Adonijah, that Absolom   185
has sunk so low.   You gave your heart
to your father's wife, my brother?

ABSOLOM.   I only spare my natural mother.
It's my temperament.   I fall
in love with every one he weds.
Envy of the old man's luck.   Yet   190
my time will come.   I'll have the lot.[17]

AMNON.   Beauty is akin to madness
and you're as crazy as you're fair.
So don't make absurd predictions.[18]
Your only fortune is your hair.   195

ADONIJAH.   Come along.   It's dark already.
What do you intend to do?

ABSOLOM.   I shall see a certain lady,
once her neighbours are asleep.   200

ADONIJAH.   And I can't wait to join the game.

AMNON.   I, who neither love nor gamble,
shall read poetry.

ABSOLOM.   Most restful.

AMNON.   In this I'll be my father's son,   205
though not in love or in desire.

ABSALÓN. Serás pöeta a lo santo.

ADONÍAS. Los salmos en verso ha escrito,
que es Dios la musa perfeta
que en él influyendo está.   210

ABSALÓN. Misterios escribirá,
que es pöeta, y es profeta.

AMÓN. Divinos estáis los dos.

ABSALÓN. Ya nos vamos a humanar.
¿Quiere nos acompañar?   215

AMÓN. No, hermanos, adiós.

TODOS.   Adiós.

Vanse los dos.

ELIAZER. ¿Qué habemos de hacer agora?

AMÓN. No sé qué se me ha antojado.

ELIAZER. Mas, si estuvieses preñado ...

AMÓN. Tanta mujer que enamora   220
a mi padre ausente y viejo,
¿qué puede hacer encerrada?
Pues es cosa averiguada
que la que es de honor espejo
en la lealtad y opinión,   225
en fin es frágil sujeto,
y un animal imperfeto.

JONADAB. Si toda la privación
es del apetito madre,
deseará su liviandad   230
al hombre, que es su mitad;
y no estando ya tu padre
para fiestas, ya lo ves.

ELIAZER. Iráseles en deseos
todo el tiempo, sin empleos   235
de su gusto.

JONADAB.   Rigor es
digno de mirar despacio.

AMÓN. Bien filosofáis los dos.

ELIAZER. Lástima tengo, por Dios,
a las damas de palacio,   240
encerradas como en hucha.

ABSOLOM. Then you'll be a holy poet.
ADONIJAH. He's written holy psalms in verse,
inspired by God, the perfect muse.   210
ABSOLOM. Then he'll write holy mysteries.
He's a poet and prophet too.
AMNON. I see you're both in holy mood.
ABSOLOM. We're off to humanize ourselves
a little. Will you come with us?   215
AMNON. No, my brothers. Farewell.
BOTH.   Farewell.

Absolom and Adonijah leave.

ELIAZER. What shall we do now?
AMNON.   I don't know ...
Yet I have this curious whim.
ELIAZER. Not pregnant, are you?
AMNON.   These women   220
on whom my aged father dotes
in his absence, what can they do,
cooped up all day? For it's well known
that a woman, who's the mirror
of a man's honour in loyalty   225
and reputation, is in truth
a flawed and imperfect creature,
a fragile vessel.
JONADAB.   If privation
is the mother of appetite,
then she'll want her satisfaction   230
from man, her other half. And since
your father's frolics are all done...
ELIAZER. They'll waste time in wishful thinking,
with no employment to their taste.   235
JONADAB. Bound to. A point on which to dwell.
AMNON. My friends, you reason well.
ELIAZER.   I swear,
I pity the palace women,
locked up like jewels in a case.   240

AMÓN. El tiempo está algo pesado,
y con la noche y nublado
la obscuridad que hace es mucha.
¿Quién duda que en el jardín   245
pedirán limosna al fresco
las damas? Lo que apetezco
he de ejecutar en fin;
curióso tengo hoy de ser.
   ELIAZER. Pues, ¿qué intentas?
   AMÓN.   ¿Qué? Saltar   250
aqueste muro, y entrar
dentro del parque, Eliazer,
por ver qué conversación
a las damas entretiene
de palacio.
   ELIAZER. Si el Rey viene   255
a saberlo, no es razón
que le enojes, pues no ignoras
que al que aquí dentro cogiese,
por más principal que fuese,
viviría pocas horas;   260
que las casas de los Reyes
gozan de la inmunidad
que los templos.
   AMÓN.   Es verdad,
mas no se entienden las leyes
con el Príncipe heredero;   265
Príncipe soy de Israel,
el calor que hace es cruel,
y ansí divertirle quiero.
En dando yo en una cosa
ya sabes que he de salir   270
con ella.
   JONADAB. Empieza a subir;
mas, siendo tan peligrosa
y de tan poco provecho,
no me parece que es justo.
   AMÓN. Provecho es hacer mi gusto.   275
   ELIAZER. ¿Y después que le hayas hecho?
   AMÓN. Esto ha de ser, vive Dios;

AMNON.   It's a close and stifling night,
so overcast, it's inky black.
Who can doubt that our fair ladies   245
will be begging a breath of air?
I'll satisfy my whim.   Why not?
I'm feeling curious today.[19]
    ELIAZER.   What do you mean to do?
    AMNON.   Do? Why,   250
climb this wall, enter the garden,
to see what conversation
entertains the ladies of the court.
    ELIAZER.   Best not risk the anger of the King.   255
If he finds out, you know quite well,
any man caught within these walls
would not survive to tell the tale,
however high his birth might be.   260
The King's palace is sacrosanct,
like the temple of the Lord.
    AMNON.   True,
but laws do not apply to me.
I'm crown prince of Israel.   Besides,   265
it's hellish hot, I need relief.
You know that once my mind's made up,
I'll have my way, no matter what.   270
    JONADAB.   Start climbing then.   But it's not right
to risk so much to so little
purpose.
    AMON.   My purpose is to do   275
my will.[20]
    ELIAZER.   And after you've done it?
    AMNON.   I swear to God, it will be so.

vamos los tres a buscar
por dónde poder entrar.
    ELIAZER.   ¿Entrar?   ¿Quién?
    AMÓN.   Yo, que los dos   280
fuera me esperaréis.
    ELIAZER.   Alto.
    AMÓN.   Hacia allí he visto unas hiedras,
que abrazadas a sus piedras,
aunque el muro está bien alto,
de escala me servirán.   285
    ELIAZER.   Vamos, y a subir empieza;
en dándole en la cabeza
una cosa, no podrán
persuadille a lo contrario
catorce predicadores.   290
    JONADAB.   ¡Qué extraños son los señores!
    ELIAZER.   Y el nuestro, ¡qué temerario! (*Vanse*)

Salen Dina, con guitarra, y Tamar.

    TAMAR.   ¿Viste jamás tal calor?
Aunque tú mejor lo pasas
que yo.
    DINA.   Pues, ¿por qué mejor?   295
    TAMAR.   Porque no juntas las brasas
del tiempo al fuego de amor.
Mas yo, que no puedo más,
y a mi amor junto el bochorno,
¿qué haré?
    DINA.   Donosa estás.   300
    TAMAR.   ¿Qué seré?
    DINA.   Serás un horno
en que a Joab cocerás
pan de tiernos pensamientos
a sustentarle bastantes
contra recelos violentos.   305
    TAMAR.   Sí, que en eso a los amantes
paga Amor sus alimentos.
    DINA.   Notable calma; no mueve
una hoja el viento siquiera.

We'll look for some way in. Let's go.
ELIAZER. Way in? Who?
AMNON.   I'll go in.   You two   280
will wait for me outside.
ELIAZER.   Hold on!
AMNON.   I see some ivy over there
clinging fast to the stones. It's high,
but I'll use it as a ladder. [21]   285
ELIAZER.   Come on then and up you go.
Once things get lodged up in his brain
four dozen preachers could not sway [22]
him to believe the contrary.
JONADAB.   The folly of our lords and masters!   290
ELIAZER.   And ours hell—bent on disaster! (*They leave*)

Enter Dina, with a guitar, and Tamar.

TAMAR.   Did you ever know such heat as this? [23]
Though you feel it less than I do.
DINA.   Less than you, why?   295
TAMAR.   You have no coals
of love to fuel the hot night air.
But I who swelter in love's heat
have no remedy. What shall I do?
DINA.   You are in skittish mood tonight.   300
TAMAR.   Ah, but what will become of me?
DINA.   Then make an oven of yourself
and bake the bread of tender thoughts, [24]
sufficient to sustain Joab
against the hunger of suspicion.   305
TAMAR.   Love repays the hand that feeds it.
DINA.   What a calm! Not a breath of wind.
Not a leaf stirring.

TAMAR. Si aquesta fuente se atreve   310
a aplacar su furia fiera,
que en la taza de oro bebe
de su arena aqueste prado,
denos su margen asiento.

DINA. En cojines de brocado,   315
sus flores de ciento en ciento
te ofrecen su real estrado,
que, en fin, como eres Infanta,
no te contentas con menos.

TAMAR. Pues traes instrumento, canta,   320
que en los jardines amenos
ansí Amor su mal espanta.

DINA. Yo no tengo que espantar,
que no estoy enamorada;
tú al viento puedes llamar,   325
pues siendo tan celebrada
en la música Tamar
como en la belleza, a oírte
correrá el céfiro manso,
alegre por divertirte.   330

TAMAR. ¿Lisonjéasme?

DINA.   Descanso
si amores llego a decirte.

Sale Amón.

AMÓN. La mocedad no repara
en cuanto intenta y procura;
la noche mi gusto ampara;   335
cuanto me entristece obscura
me alegra esta fuente clara.
Como no sé dónde voy,
en cuanto topo tropiezo.

TAMAR. Dina, tristísima estoy.   340

DINA. Cuando yo a cantar empiezo,
treguas a mis penas doy.

TAMAR. Dame, pues, ese instrumento.

AMÓN. Mi deseo se cumplió;
aquí hablar mujeres siento.   345

TAMAR.   Since this stream,   310
which the meadow drinks in the cup
of its golden sands, dares to calm
its frenzied course, let us sit here
upon its bank.
    DINA.   Brocade cushions   315
of its flowers by the thousand
offer you a regal dais.
For you, as princess of the realm,
could never be content with less.
    TAMAR.   You've brought your instrument, so sing.   320
In the beauty of a garden,
singing soothes the pain of love.
    DINA.   I have no pain to soothe, nor need,
since I am not in love.   But you
could conjure up the cooling wind.   325
For such is the reputation
of your beauty and your music,
the gentle Zephyr, keen to please,
would come rushing to hear you play.   330
    TAMAR.   You flatter me that I'm the best?
    DINA.   No, but sweet−talking you like this
might at least give me a rest.

Enter Amnon.
    AMNON.   Youth is too impetuous
to stop and ponder its designs;
black night shields my self−indulgence;   335
though darkness oppresses my heart,
this bright stream restores my spirits.
I don't know where I'm going to.
I stumble over everything. [25]
    TAMAR.   Oh, Dina, I am sick at heart.   340
    DINA.   It gives respite to my sadness
when I start to sing.
    TAMAR.   In that case,
give me your instrument to play.
    AMNON.   My wishes are fulfilled.   I hear
the sound of female conversation. [26]   345

TAMAR.   La música se inventó
en alivio del tormento.
AMÓN.   Cantar quieren; no pudiera
venir a tiempo mejor.
TAMAR.   ¡Ay, si mi amante me oyera!   350
AMÓN.   No hay parte en que no entre Amor;
hasta aquí llegó su esfera.
TAMAR.   *(Canta)* Ligero pensamiento
de amor, pájaro alegre
que viste la esperanza,   355
de plumas y alas verdes,
si fuente de tus gustos
es mi querido ausente,
donde amoroso asistes,
donde sediento bebes,   360
tu vuelta no dilates
cuando a su vista llegues,
que me darán tus dichas
envidia si no vuelves;
pajarito que vas a la fuente,   365
bebe y vente.
Correo de mis quejas
serás cuando le lleves
en pliegos de suspiros
sospechas impacientes   370
con tu amoroso pico.
Si en mi memoria duerme,
del sueño de su olvido
es bien que le despiertes;
castígale descuidos,   375
amores le agradece,
preséntale firmezas,
favores le promete;
pajarito que vas a la fuente,
bebe y vente.   380
AMÓN.   Qué voz tan apacible,
qué quejas tan ardientes,
qué acentos tan süaves.
Ay Dios, ¿qué hechizo es éste?
A su melifluo canto   385

TAMAR. Music was made to soothe our care.
AMNON. They're going to sing for me too.
The timing is impeccable.
TAMAR. If only my love could hear me!   350
AMNON. So Love has found its way in here.
There's nowhere that it does not reach.
TAMAR. *(Sings)* My wanton thoughts of love
like a bird of hope that sings   355
with evergreen plumage[27]
and its evergreen wings.
If my absent lover's heart
is the fount of your pleasure
where you lovingly linger
and drink at your leisure;   360
when you reach his sweet presence
come home without delay;
your joy will make me jealous,
if you prolong your stay;
Bird of hope flying free,   365
drink at my lover's fountain
and come straight back to me.[28]
Be courier to my plaints,
suspicions, impatience, pique.   370
Wrap them up in reams of sighs;
take them in your loving beak.
If his memories of me
should slumber in his keeping,
wake them from forgetfulness
and punish them for sleeping.   375
But if he's true and loving,
give him gratitude and praise;
promise him the favours
of a heart that never strays.
Bird of hope flying free,
drink at my lover's fountain
and come straight back to me.   380
AMNON. How gently, how passionately
she laments! How soft her voice!
Heavens, what bewitchment is this?
The very wind returns again

corrido el viento vuelve,
que en fe que se detuvo
muy bien puede correrse;
y por acompañar
su voz, la hace que temple   390
los tiples de estas hojas,
los bajos de estas fuentes.
Amor, no sé qué os diga,
si vuestro rigor viene
a escuras y de noche   395
porque los ojos cierre.
Como a la voz iguale
la belleza, que suele
ser ángel en acentos
y en rostro ser serpiente,   400
triunfad, niño absoluto,
de un corazón rebelde,
si rústico, ya noble,
si libre, ya obediente.

    DINA.   Vuelve a cantar, señora,   405
si por oírte y verte
el sol, músico ilustre,
que se anticipe quieres.

    AMÓN.   Si por verla y oírla
sus rayos amanecen,   410
¿quién duda que es hermosa?
¿Quién duda que conviene
su cara con su canto?
Ay Dios, quién mereciese
atestiguar de vista   415
lo que de oídas siente.

    TAMAR.   La música, ya sabes, es
que al triste le entristece
como al contento alegra;
pues yo, triste y ausente,   420
¿qué he de cantar si lloro?

    AMÓN.   Entrad, celos crueles,
servid de rudimentos
con que mi amor comience;
¿mujer ausente y firme?   425

shamed by her mellifluous song 385
— and ashamed he might well be
for being becalmed so long.
To serve as her accompaniment
he employs her voice to tune 390
his instruments; high pitched treble
of these leaves, bass of babbling streams.
Oh, Love! How am I to respond?
You exercise your power at night 395
so that my eyes are kept shut tight.
An angel's voice — it's oft the case —
can issue from a serpent's face. [29]
But if her beauty fits the voice, 400
then, infant God, you have triumphed [30]
over this rebellious heart,
if once uncouth, now ennobled,
if wayward, now obedient.
    DINA. Sing again, my lady, if you wish 405
the sun to rise before its time.
He'll surely come to hear and see
another artist such as he. [31]
    AMNON. If dawn itself gets out of bed 410
to see her and hear her playing,
who can doubt that she's beautiful?
Who can doubt that her countenance
and her song are in harmony?
Please God to let my sight confirm 415
what I am feeling with my ears.
    TAMAR. You know quite well that music brings
joy to those already joyful
yet to the sad, more sadness still.
I'm sad and pine for absent love. 420
Why should I sing and weep the more?
    AMNON. So, enter cruel jealousy.
Let that be the primer of my love.
A woman faithful in absence? 425
I present with my jealousy?

¿celoso yo y presente?
¿sin ver, enamorado?
¿hoy libre, y hoy con leyes?
O milagrosa fuerza
de un ciego dios que vence,⁣ 430
sin ojos y con alas,
cuanto desnudo, fuerte.
    DINA. Ansí tu amante goces,
y de sus años cuentes
los lustros a millares, 435
en primavera siempre;
que prosiguiendo alivies
el calor que suspendes,
y oyéndote se amansa.
    TAMAR.   Va, pues que tú lo quieres. 440
(*Canta*) Ay pensamiento mío,
cuánto allá te detienes,
qué leve que te partes,
con qué pereza vuelves;
celosa estoy que goces 445
de mi adorado ausente
la vista, con que aplacas
la ardiente sed de verle.
Si acaso de sus labios
el dulce néctar bebes 450
que labran sus palabras,
y hurtalle algunas puedes,
pajarito que vas a la fuente,
bebe y vente.
    AMÓN. ¿Hay más apacible rato? 455
Espíritus celestiales,
si entre músicas mortales
ver queréis vuestro retrato,
venid conmigo. Acercarme
quiero un poco. Mas caí. *(Cae)* 460
    TAMAR. Ay, cielos, ¿quién está aquí?
    AMÓN. Ya es imposible ocultarme.
aunque la noche es de suerte
que mentir mi nombre puedo,
pues con su obscuridad quedo 465

In love with what I cannot see?
Bound by the force of unseen laws?[32]
And yet today, was I not free?
Oh, the miraculous power   430
of a conquering eyeless God,
who's strongest when most defenceless!
    DINA.   Then may you enjoy your lover
for an eternity of Spring
and the lustrums of his years
be counted in their thousands.   435
Please go on; your music brings relief.
It cools and tames this savage heat.
    TAMAR.   I will, since you would have it so.   440
(Sings) Little love—bird of my thoughts
how long you stray and roam!
How quick you are to leave me,
how slow to come back home!
I'm jealous that you enjoy   445
my absent lover first,
drink in deep his lovely sight
and quench your burning thirst.
If you drink from his sweet mouth   450
the nectar of his voice,
steal the words from off his lips
and make my heart rejoice.
Bird of hope flying free,
drink at my lover's fountain
and come straight back to me.
    AMNON.   Who could conceive a sweeter time?   455
Spirits of Heaven, if you wish
to see your likeness reflected
in the music of mortal men,
then come with me now. I'll approach
a little closer, but I fall ... *(Falls)*   460
    TAMAR.   Great Heavens! Who is here?
    AMNON.   I can no longer hide myself.
Though such is the pitch—black night,
I can conceal my name. No one,   465

seguro que nadie acierte
ni vea el traje en que estoy.
TAMAR.   ¿Qué es esto?
AMÓN.   Deme la mano;
hijo soy del hortelano;
que he caido; al diabro doy   470
la musquiña, que ella hue
ocasión que tropezase
en un tronco y me quebrase
la espinilla.   ¿No me ve?
DINA.   No véis vos por dónde andáis,   475
¿y os hemos de ver nosotras?
AMÓN.   Pardios, damas o quillotras,
lindamente lo cantáis;
oyéraos yo doce días
sin dormir.
TAMAR.   ¿Haos contentado?   480
AMÓN.   Pardios que lo habéis cantado
como un gigante Golías.
Dadme la mano, que peso
un monte.
(Aparte) Tomésela.   (Bésesela)
Beséla, y juro en verdá   485
que a la miel me supo el beso.
TAMAR.   Atrevido sois, villano.
AMÓN.   ¿Qué quiere?   Siempre se vido
ser dichoso el atrevido.
TAMAR.   Al fin, ¿sois el hortelano?   490
AMÓN.   Sí, pardiez, y inficionado
a mosicas.
DINA.   Buen modorro.
AMÓN.   Pardios, vos tenéis buen chorro;
si en la cara os ha ayudado
como en la voz la ventura,   495
con todo os podéis alzar,
aunque no se suele hallar
con buena voz la hermosura.
TAMAR.   Tosco pensamiento es ése.
AMÓN.   ¿No suele, aunque esto os espanta,   500
decirse a la que bien canta,

I'm sure, can see the clothes I wear.
    TAMAR.   Well, what is this?
    AMNON.   Give my your hand,
I'm one of the gardener's sons.
I've fallen down, divil take it, [33]   470
it was the music, so it was,
that made me trip and bark me shin
against a log. Can't you see me
where I am?
    DINA.   How can we see you,   475
if you can't see where you're walking?
    AMNON. Begod, fair ladies or whatever
you be, you sing a pretty tune;
I could listen for days on end
to you, without a wink of sleep.
    TAMAR. It pleased you then?   480
    AMNON.   It did, begod.
The giant Goliath himself
could not have sung it better.
Give us your hand, I weighs a ton.
(Aside) I took her hand. *(Kisses it)* And kissed it too,
I'll vow no honey tasted sweeter.
    TAMAR. You go too far, my man!
    AMNON.   I do?
A man who never went too far,
never got anywhere, I say.
    TAMAR. And so, you are the gardener?   490
    AMNON. I am, begod, yet most partial
to music and fair young ladies. [34]
    DINA. And a regular clown to boot.
    AMNON. You've got a fine voice on you there.
If fortune's been as generous   495
with your features, then you'll run off
with all the prizes. Though fair voice
seldom finds fair face, they do say.
    TAMAR. Then the saying is most uncouth.
    AMNON. Yet to a woman as sings well   500
(no offence, mind) do they not say:
'I would rather hear you at night,
than clap eyes on you by day'?

'quién te oyese, y no te viese'?
TAMAR. Cumpliráos ese deseo
la obscuridad que hace agora.
AMÓN. Antes me aburro, señora,   505
pues ya que os oigo, no os veo.
TAMAR. ¿Pues no me habéis conocido?
AMÓN. Sois tantas las que aquí estáis,
y de día y noche andáis
pisando el jardín florido,   510
que, como no me expliquéis
vueso nombre, no me espanto
que no os conozca en el canto;
porque aunque tal vez lleguéis
a retozarme y me quejo   515
de más de un pellisco u dos
que me dáis, quizá, pardios,
porque el Rey que ya está viejo
os cumple mal de josticia,
tiniendo tanta mujer,   520
soy rudo en el conocer.
TAMAR. ¡Qué villano!
DINA.   ¡Y qué malicia!
TAMAR. ¡Fiad burlas de esta gente!
AMÓN. ¿Quiéreme decir quién es?
y llevaréla después   525
de flor y fruta un presente.
TAMAR. Sois muy hablador.

Quítale el guante de la mano Amón.

AMÓN. *(Aparte)*   El guante
de la mano le quité
cuando a besarla llegué.
TAMAR. Vamos.
AMÓN.   No se vaya, cante,   530
ansí le remoce el cielo
a David, si es su marido.
TAMAR. Un guante se me ha caido.
AMÓN. Debe de estar en el suelo;
halléle; pardios, que gano   535

TAMAR.   Then darkness grants that wish.
AMNON.   No, ma'am.
It irks me that I can hear you,
but not see who you are.
    TAMAR.   Then you
do not recognize who I am?
    AMNON.   There's so many ladies round here,
roaming the garden night and day;   510
how can I tell you by your song,
if you don't tell me who you are?
For you could roll me in the hay   515
and give my bum a pinch or two
— 'cos now the king is getting on
and can't do justice to you all —
and still I wouldn't know the face.   520
I'm bad at recognitions.[35]
    TAMAR.   What a churl!
    DINA.   Too clever by half.
    TAMAR.   Never trade banter with a rogue.
    AMNON.   Will you not tell me who you are?
And then later I will bring you   525
a present of fruit and flowers.[36]
    TAMAR.   You talk too much.

Amnon removes her glove.

    AMNON.   *(Aside)*   I took her glove
when I approached to kiss her hand.[37]
    TAMAR.   Come, let's go.
    AMNON.   Please don't! Stay and sing,
and, if he really is your man,
may God rejuvenate the King.
    TAMAR.   I've dropped my glove.
    AMNON.   Must be on the ground
Here 'tis.   No sooner lost than found.   535

en hallazgos mucho ya.

TAMAR.   ¿Qué es de él?

AMÓN.   Tome.

TAMAR.   Dalde acá.

Le besa la mano Amón.

AMÓN.   Beséla otra vez la mano.

TAMAR.   ¿Quién tanta licencia os dio,
villano?

AMÓN.   Mi dicha sola.   540

TAMAR.   Dadme acá el guante.

AMÓN.   Mamóla.

Vásele a dar, y búrlala.

TAMAR.   Luego ¿no le hallastes?

AMÓN.   No.

TAMAR.   ¿No gustas de lo que pasa?

DINA.   Buen jardinero.

AMÓN.   ¿De amor?
¿Que pensáis todo esto es flor?   545

TAMAR.   Yo haré que os echen de casa.
Vamos.

DINA.   ¿Has de ver mañana
la boda de Elisa?

TAMAR.   Sí.

DINA.   ¿Qué vestido?

TAMAR.   Carmesí.

AMÓN.   Seréis un cıavel de grana.   550
De aquí mis venturas saco.
¿Que sin cantar más, se van?
¿Sus nombres no me dirán?

DINA.   No, que sois muy gran bellaco.

Vanse Tamar y Dina.

AMÓN.   Agora noche, sí que a oscuras quedo,   555
pues un sol hasta aquí tuve delante.
Libre de amor entré, ya salgo amante;

This must be my lucky day.
   TAMAR.   Where is it?
   AMNON.   Take it.
   TAMAR.   Give it here

Amnon kisses her hand.

   AMNON.   Madam, I kissed your hand again.
   TAMAR.   Who gave you leave, you peasant rogue?
   AMNON.   My good fortune.   540
   TAMAR.   Give me the glove!
   AMNON.   *(Is about to give it to her, then takes it back.)*
Fooled you![38]
   TAMAR.   You did not find it?
   AMNON.   No.
   TAMAR.   Don't you find all this amusing?
   DINA.   Some gardener!
   AMNON.   But it's not all
flowers in the garden of love.[39]   545
   TAMAR.   I'll have you dismissed from the house.
Come, Dina.
   DINA.   Will my lady go
tomorrow to Elisa's feast?
   TAMAR.   Yes.
   DINA.   What will you wear?
   TAMAR.   The scarlet dress.
   AMNON. So.   A passion—red carnation   550
which will dictate my fortunes all.
Will you go and sing to me no more?
Then won't you tell me who you are?
   DINA.   You're too impertinent by far.

Tamar and Dina leave.

   AMNON.   And now, sweet night, my true darkness descends,
since till now I had a sun before me.
Free from love I came, now I leave its slave.

reíame antes de él, ya llorar puedo.
Ay amorosa voz, obscuro enredo,
cifrad vuestra ventura en sólo un guante,   560
que si iguala a su música el semblante,
victorioso quedáis, yo os lo concedo.
¡Cuando más descuidado, más rendido!
¡Sin saber a quien quiero, enamorado!
¡Asaltando murallas y vencido!   565
Mas dichoso saldrá vuestro cuidado,
si sacando quién es por el vestido
la suerte echáis, no en blanco, en encarnado. (*Vase*)

Salen Absalón, Adonías, Abigail (reina) y Bersabé.

ABIGAIL.   ¿Quedaba el Rey mi señor
bueno?
ABSALÓN.   Alegre salud goza,   570
que en el bélico furor
parece que se remoza,
y le da sangre el valor.
ABIGAIL.   Quitaréle la memoria
de nosotras el deseo   575
del triunfo de esa victoria.
ADONÍAS.   Amaros es su trofeo,
conversaros es su gloria.
ABSALÓN.   Poca ocasión habrá dado
a que su olvido os espante,   580
pues no sé que se haya hallado
ni en guerra más firme amante,
ni en paz más diestro soldado.
En la más ardua victoria
es vuestro amor buen testigo   585
que tiene, en fe de su gloria,
la espada en el enemigo,
y en vosotras la memoria.
ADONÍAS.   Bien sabe eso Bersabé,
y Abigail no lo ignora.   590
ABIGAIL.   Que estoy triste sin él, sé.
BERSABÉ.   Y yo, que en su ausencia llora
quien vive cuando le ve.

I can but weep at what I used to scorn.
That loving voice, the enigma of the night,
in this one glove their bliss encapsulate.   560
If her face be equal to her music,
then you have triumphed, I concede defeat.
Total surrender, when I felt most sure!
Helpless in love and not to know the cause!
Caught in the ambush, having breached the wall!   565
But all this care will turn to happiness
if, by her dress, to know her I am led
and fate is written, not in black, but red. (*Exit*)⁴⁰

Enter Absolom, Adonijah, Abigail (the queen) and Bathsheba.

ABIGAIL.   I trust my lord the King is well?
ABSOLOM.   He enjoys a rude and boisterous health.   570
The heat of war restores his youth
and the exercise of valour
gives, it seems, new blood to his veins.
ABIGAIL.   Desire for victory in battle   575
has doubtless put us from his mind.
ADONIJAH.   His trophies are his love for you,
his glory, your conversation.
ABSOLOM.   He has given you little cause
to complain that he neglects you.   580
I've never known there to exist
a lover more loyal in war
or a soldier more skilled in peace.
Even in the heat of triumph
his great love for you bears witness   585
that, even as he runs his enemy through,
his thoughts are nonetheless on you.⁴¹
ADONIJAH.   Bathsheba knows this truth full well,
and so do you, dear Abigail.   590
ABIGAIL.   I know that I'm sad without him.
BATHSHEBA.   And that I weep in his absence
and live only for his return.

ABIGAIL.   ¿Pensáis volveros tan presto
al cerco?

ADONÍAS.   Las treguas son   595
tan breves que el Rey ha puesto
que no sufren dilación.

ABSALÓN.   Yo mañana estoy dispuesto
a partirme.

ADONÍAS.   Y yo también.

ABIGAIL.   Escribiré con los dos   600
al Rey, que si quiere bien,
dedique salmos a Dios
seguro en Jerusalén,
y en la guerra no consuma
la plata que peina helada,   605
que aunque en su esfuerzo presuma,
el viejo cuelga la espada,
y esgrime sabio la pluma.

ABSALÓN.   A ambas cosas se acomoda
mi padre.

BERSABÉ.   Galán venís,   610
Absalón.

ABSALÓN.   Soy hoy de boda.

BERSABÉ.   Y vos, Infante, salís
para que la corte toda
se vaya tras vos perdida.

ADONÍAS.   Autorizamos la fiesta,   615
que es la novia conocida.

Salen Amón, muy triste, y Jonadab y Eliazer.

ELIAZER.   ¿Qué novedad será ésta,
señor?

AMÓN.   Es mudar de vida.

JONADAB.   ¿Qué te sucedió que ansí
desde que al jardín entraste   620
ni duermes, ni estás en tí?

ELIAZER.   ¿Qué viste cuando llegaste?

AMÓN.   Triste estoy, porque no vi.
Dejadme, que de opinión
y vida mudar pretendo.   625

ABIGAIL.   You mean to return to the siege
so soon?

ADONIJAH.   The King's truce is so brief,   595
it admits no further delay.

ABSOLOM.   I'm ready to leave tomorrow. [42]

ADONIJAH.   And I.

ABIGAIL.   I'll send word to the King   600
with you that, if he loves me well,
he should compose his psalms to God
safely here in Jerusalem
and not leave his old silver hairs [43]   605
to waste upon the battlefield.
For, though it flatters his manhood,
an old man, if he's wise, hangs up
his sword and brandishes a pen.

ABSOLOM.   My father can encompass both.

BATHSHEBA.   You look most elegant today,   610
Absolom.

ABSOLOM.   For a wedding feast.

BATHSHEBA.   As for you, my lord, where you go
every eye at court will follow.

ADONIJAH.   We honour the festivities   615
since the bride is well known to us.

Enter Amnon (in a state of great depression), Jonadab and Eliazer.

ELIAZER.   What sudden change is this, my lord?

AMON.   A change of life.

JONADAB.   But what happened?
Since you went into the garden,   620
you have not slept nor been yourself.

ELIAZER.   What did you see when you went in?

AMON.   I did not see, that's why I'm sad.
Leave me, for I propose to change [44]   625
my life and my philosophy.
I don't want your conversation.
From now on all converse will be
with my own imagination. [45]

No quiero conversación,
porque ya con quien me entiendo
sola es mi imaginación.
(Aparte) Ay encarnado vestido,
si a verme salieses ya.   630
   ABSALÓN. ¡O Príncipe!
   ABIGAIL.   Amón querido.
   AMÓN. Las treguas que David da
a veros nos han traido.
   ADONÍAS. Y agora el casarse Elisa
nuevas fiestas ocasiona,   635
que dan a las galas prisa.
   AMÓN. Merécelo su persona.
   ABSALÓN. Para vos cosa de risa
son casamientos y amores.
   AMÓN. No sé lo que en eso os diga.   640

Sale un Criado.

   CRIADO. Josefo espera, señores,
que le honréis.
   ADONÍAS.   Y él nos obliga
a que le hagamos favores.
   ABSALÓN. ¿Venís, Príncipe?
   AMÓN.   Después,
que tengo que hacer agora.   645
   ABSALÓN. Adonías, vamos pues.

Vanse si no es Amón.

   AMÓN. Salid ya encarnada aurora,
postraréme a vuestros pies.
Salid celeste armonía,
que en la voz enamoráis.   650
Vea vuestro sol mi día,
y sepa yo si igualáis
la cara a la melodía.
¿Si mudará parecer?
¿Si trocará la color   655
que mi tercera ha de ser?

(Aside) Come, scarlet dress. Let's see you now!   630
   ABSOLOM.   Ah, prince!
   ABIGAIL.   My beloved Amnon!
   AMNON.   The truce that David grants us all
gives us respite to visit you.
   ADONIJAH.   And now Elisa's wedding day
gives new cause for celebration   635
and calls for splendour and display.
   AMNON.   Her quality deserves no less.
   ABSOLOM.   But these things of love and marriage
for you are scarcely worth the fuss.
   AMNON.   I scarcely know how to reply.   640

A servant enters.

   SERVANT.   Noble lords, Josephus awaits
the honour of your company.
   ADONIJAH.   He is deserving of our favour.
   ABSOLOM.   Will you come, my prince?
   AMNON.   Later on,
there is now something I must do.   645
   ABSOLOM.   Then let us go, Adonijah.

They all leave, except Amnon.

   AMNON.   Come, break, my scarlet dawn, and I'll
prostrate my body at your feet.
Break forth, celestial harmony
that kindles love with voice alone,   650
so my reflected day may see
your sun and let me know for sure
if face be peer to melody.
But what if she should change her mind?
What if she should change the colour   655
which is the pander to my love?

¿Si querrá vengarse Amor
de mi libre proceder?
No lo permitáis, dios ciego;
sepa yo, pues que me abraso,   660
quién es la que enciende el fuego.
No hagáis de arrogancias caso,
pues las armas os entrego.
Ya salen acompañando
a los desposados todos.   665

*Música, toda la compañía de dos en dos, muy bizarros, y saca
Tamar un vestido rico de carmesí; y los Novios detrás. Dan una
vuelta y éntranse.*

Dudo alegre, temo amando.
Ay Amor, por qué de modos
almas estáis abrasando.
Quiero, escondido, de aquí
ver sin ser visto si pasa   670
quien me tiraniza ansí.
Ay Dios, ya el fuego me abrasa
de un vestido carmesí.
¿No es ésta de lo encarnado
mi hermana?   ¿No es ésta, cielos,   675
Tamar?   Buena suerte he echado.
Ay imposibles desvelos,
¡de mi hermana enamorado!
Mal haya el jardín, amén,
la noche triste y obscura,   680
mi vuelta a Jerusalén;
mal haya, amén, mi locura,
que para mal de mi bien
libre me obligó a asaltar
los muros de Amor tirano.   685
Alma, morir y callar,
que siendo amante y hermano
lo mejor es olvidar.
Más vale, cielos, que muera
dentro del pecho esta llama,   690
sin que salga el fuego fuera.

And what if Love should seek revenge
for the rashness of my conduct?
That, may the eyeless god forbid.
Since I'm burning, please let me know   660
who it was that lit the fire.
Forgive the arrogance of youth,
I cry surrender and submit!
But here come all the guests in line,
accompanying the bride and groom.   665

*Music.   Enter all the company two by two, splendidly attired, with
bride and groom bringing up the rear.   Tamar is wearing a
sumptuous crimson dress.   They walk round the stage and leave
Amnon alone.*

I doubt my joy and fear my love.
Oh, Love, how many ways you use
to mortify the souls of men!
I'll hide myself and watch unseen
the tyrant of my soul pass by.   670
Oh, God, I feel the burning heat
of a crimson dress. Is that not
my sister in the scarlet gown?
Great Heavens! Is that not Tamar?
The dice of fate have fallen so?[46]   675
To love my sister? There is no
solace or sleep for such despair.
Oh, damn, damn the garden and damn
the gloomy darkness of the night,   680
the journey to Jerusalem,
and damn my madness which withal
prompted me to climb the wall
of tyrant Love against my reason.[47]   685
Be still, my soul, be still and die.
Being brother and her lover too,
best to be silent and forget.
Better by far to kill the flame   690
within my heart and put it out
before the fire spreads outside.
Yet Love's but a passing fancy

Ausente olvida quien ama,
amor es pasión ligera.
Al cerco quiero partirme,
que a los principios se aplaca   695
la pasión que no es tan firme.

Salen Eliazer y Jonadab.

Eliazer.
    ELIAZER.   Gran señor.
    AMÓN.   Saca ...
    ELIAZER.   ¿Qué quieres?
    AMÓN.   Quiero vestirme
de camino y al campo ir;
prevenme botas y espuelas.   700
    JONADAB.   Postas voy a prevenir.
    AMÓN.   Pero ciego y con pigüelas
¿cómo podrá el sacre huir?
Deja eso; dame un baquero
de tela; sácame un rostro,   705
que hallarme en el sarao quiero.

Vanse Eliazer y Jonadab.

De imposibles soy un monstruo,
esperando desespero.
Ame el delfín al cantor,
al plátano el persa adore,   710
a la estatua tenga amor
el otro, el bruto enamore
la asiria de más valor,
que de mi locura vana
el tormento es más atroz   715
y la pasión más tirana,
pues me enamoró una voz,
y adoro a mi misma hermana.

Salen Eliazer y Jonadab con un rostro y baquero.

JONADAB.   Aquí están rostro y disfraz.

and absence makes a man forget.
I'll leave this instant for the siege;
the passion that's not firmly set,   695
at birth is easily appeased.

Enter Eliazer and Jonadab.

Eliazer!
    ELIAZER.   My Lord?
    AMNON.   Prepare ...
    ELIAZER.   What, my good lord?
    AMNON.   I wish to dress
for travel and the battlefield.
Make ready now my boots and spurs.   700
    JONADAB. I'll go and prepare the horses.
    AMNON. But no. How can the falcon flee[48]
when hooded blind and held in chains?
So let that go. Give me a smock,
and get me a mask for disguise.   705
I wish to join the wedding feast.

Eliazer and Jonadab leave.

Of Nature's freaks my love's the worst.
My only hope is desperation.
They talk of the singer and the dolphin,[49]
the plane tree and the Persian King.   710
They talk of one who loved a statue,
the horse and the Assyrian queen,
My torture's a sterile madness,   715
more cruel than any other.
I lost my heart to a woman's voice
and became my sister's lover.

Enter Eliazer and Jonadab with mask and smock.

    JONADAB. Here are your face mask and disguise.

AMÓN. Vísteme, pues; pero quita,   720
que este rigor pertinaz
con la razón precipita
de mi sosiego la paz.
¡Dejadme solo! ¿No os vais?
ELIAZER. ¿Qué le habrá dado a este loco?   725

Vanse Eliazer y Jonadab.

AMÓN. Penas, si esto amor llamáis,
en distancia y tiempo poco
su infierno experimentáis.
No quiera Dios que un deseo
desatinado y cruel   730
venza con amor tan feo
a un Príncipe de Israel.
Morir es noble trofeo;
incurable es mi dolor.
Pues ya soy vuestro vasallo,   735
ciego Dios, dadme favor,
porque adorar y callallo
son imposibles de amor. *(Vase)*

Salen todos los de la boda, y Tamar con ellos, y siéntanse.

TAMAR. Gocéis, Josefo, el estado
con Elisa años prolijos,   740
con la vejez coronado
de nobles y hermosos hijos,
fruto de amor sazonado.
JOSEFO. Si vuestra Alteza nos da
tan felices parabienes,   745
¿quién duda que gozará
nuestra ventura los bienes
que nos prometemos ya?
ELISA. A lo menos desearemos
toda esa dicha, señora,   750
porque con ella paguemos
lo mucho que desde agora
a vuestra Alteza debemos.

AMNON.   Then help me dress; no, stop!   Away!   720
This tyrant passion makes me lose
not just reason, but composure. [50]
Leave me alone!   Why don't you go?
    ELIAZER.   What's got into this madman now?   725

Eliazer and Jonadab leave.

AMNON.   If this misery is called love,
then, in a twinkling, it has turned
its paradise into a hell.
God forbid that a lewd desire,
beyond the pale of reason,
should overcome with lust so foul   730
a royal prince of Israel.
But death has some nobility
and my pain's past all hope of cure.
If I'm to be blind Cupid's slave,   735
then I want something in return.
To adore in silence and unheard
is one thing love can never learn.   *(Amnon leaves)*

Enter all the wedding guests with Tamar amongst them.   They sit
down.

TAMAR.   May the years in plenty bless, Josephus,
your estate of marriage with Elisa   740
and may your union in old age be crowned
with children as fair as they are noble,
the lawful fruit of your seasoned love. [51]
    JOSEPHUS.   If your noble Highness deigns to bestow
such felicitations on our marriage,   745
who can doubt that our fate will keep in store
all the blessings we wish ourselves, and more?
    ELISA.   At least, my lady, we shall both aspire
to all that happiness you desire us.   750
For only in this way can we return
in kind the heavy debt of gratitude
that to your Highness from this day we owe.

Sale un Criado.

CRIADO.   Máscaras quieren danzar.
TAMAR.   Dése principio a la fiesta.   755

Siéntanse. Sale Amón de máscara.

JOSEFO.   El cielo juntó en Tamar
con una hermosura honesta
un donaire singular.

*Danzan y entretanto Amón de máscara hinca la rodilla al lado de
Tamar.*

AMÓN.   ¿De qué sirve entre los dos
mi rebelde resistencia,   760
Amor, si en fuerzas sois dios,
y tiráis con tal violencia
que al fin me lleváis tras vos?
Desocupado está el puesto
de mi imposible tirana;   765
deudor os soy sólo en esto.
Qué de estorbos, cruel hermana,
en mi amor el cielo ha puesto.
(Háblale) Por gozar tal conjuntura
bien me holgara yo, señora,   770
que casara mi ventura
una dama cada hora,
puesto que la noche obscura
también voluntades casa,
hecho tálamo un jardín,   775
donde cuando el tiempo abrasa,
con voces de un serafín
hace cielo vuestra casa.
Yo sé quien antes de veros,
enamorado de oíros,   780
los árboles lisonjeros
movió anoche con suspiros,
y a vos no pudo moveros.

Enter a servant.

SERVANT.   The revellers desire to dance.
TAMAR.   Then let festivities commence.   755

They take their seats.[52]   *Amnon enters wearing a mask.*

JOSEPHUS.   Heaven combined in fair Tamar
the beauty of her innocence
with an uncommon wit and charm.

*They begin to dance and meanwhile the masked Amnon kneels down
beside Tamar.*

AMNON.   What's the use of my resistance?   760
If Love's a god in potency
and draws me on so violently,
at last he'll take me where he will.
Cruel sister, how many walls
have the Heavens built between us![53]
The place beside her is left free.[54]   765
Love, that at least you've done for me.
(Speaks to her)   To relish such a chance as this,
I wish it were my fortune, ma'am,   770
to attend a lady's wedding
every hour of the day.
Though pitch—black night is also apt
to join two wills in sweet accord;
it makes of gardens wedding beds   775
and, in the sultry heat of night,
with just one angel's voice transforms
your house into a paradise.
I know of one who loved your voice
before he saw your face, who moved   780
last night the trees with flattering sighs
and yet could not move you.   I know

Yo sé quien besó una mano
dos veces, fueran dos mil. 785
Yo sé ...
    TAMAR. Fingido hortelano,
para vuestro mal sutil
y para mi honor villano,
ya el engaño he colegido
que en fe de su obscuridad 790
os hizo anoche atrevido.
La sagrada inmunidad
del palacio habéis rompido.
Pero agradeced que intento
no dar a esta fiesta fin 795
que lastime su contento;
que hoy os sirviera el jardín
de castigo y de escarmiento.
    AMÓN. De castigo cosa es clara,
que vuestro gusto cumplió 800
mi fortuna siempre avara,
pero de escarmiento no.
Ojalá que escarmentara
yo en mí mismo; mas no temo
castigos, que el cielo me hizo 805
sin temor con tanto estremo
que yo mismo el fuego atizo
y brasas en que me quemo.
    TAMAR. ¿Quién sois vos que habláis ansí?
    AMÓN. Un compuesto de contrarios, 810
que desde el punto que os vi
me atormentan temerarios,
y todos son contra mí;
una quimera encantada,
una esfinge con quien lucho, 815
un volcán en nieve helada
y, en fin, por ser con vos mucho,
no vengo, Infanta, a ser nada.
    TAMAR. ¿Viose loco semejante?
    AMÓN. Yo sé que anoche perdistes 820
porque yo ganase un guante;
la mano que a un pastor distes

who took your hand and kissed it twice
— I wish it were two thousand times —   785
I know of one ...
    TAMAR.   ... false gardener
who with low and evil cunning
soiled my good name with dirty hands.
I now gather the deception,
underneath that cloak of darkness   790
which last night made you bold and rash.
You have broken the sanctity
of the palace walls. Be thankful
that we are in festive mood
which I do not intend to mar,   795
or this garden would be the scene
of exemplary punishment.
    AMNON. Of punishment, that's clear enough,
since your decree has set the seal   800
on my ever—niggardly fate,
but no deterrent, not for me.
I wish I could learn from myself,
but I fear no retribution.
Heaven gave me such lack of fear   805
that I fan the flames that burn me.
    TAMAR. Who are you that speaks like this to me?
    AMNON. A hybrid of contradictions   810
which, since I saw you, rack my mind
and all of them against myself.
I am a dream within a dream,
a sphynx with whom I pit my wits,   815
a volcano bound in snow.
With you, in short, I'm all in one;
without you, princess, I am none.
    TAMAR. Was there ever such a madman?
    AMNON. I know you lost a glove last night   820
which came into my possession;
the hand you gave a peasant boy,

dalda agora a un noble amante.
TAMAR. Máscara descomedida,
levantáos luego de aquí,   825
que haré quitaros la vida.
AMÓN. Esa anoche la perdí;
tarde vendrá quien la pida.
Mas pues no es bien que a un villano
más favor de noche hagáis   830
que a un ilustre cortesano,
que queráis, o no queráis,
os he de besar la mano.

Bésala, y vase.

TAMAR. Hola, matadme ese hombre,

Levántanse todos, alborotados.

dejad la fiesta, seguilde.   835
JOSEFO. ¿Qué tienes, qué hay que te asombre?
TAMAR. No me repliquéis, herilde,
dalde muerte, o dadme nombre
de desdichada.
ELISA.   Dejemos
el sarao, que hacer es justo   840
lo que manda.
JOSEFO.   Siempre vemos
que del más cumplido gusto
son pesares los estremos.

Fin de la primera jornada

grant it now to a noble's love.

    TAMAR.   Masks make you bold; you go too far.
Get up this instant off your knees   825
or my guards will take your life.

    AMNON.   Then they will come too late to take
what I already lost last night.
It is not just that you should show
more favour to a dolt by night   830
than to a courtier by day.
Whether you'd have it so or not,
I'll kiss your hand and have my way.⁵⁵

He kisses her hand and leaves.

TAMAR.   Guards!   Kill that man!   Kill him, I say!⁵⁶

Everyone gets up in confusion.

The feast is over.   After him!

    JOSEPHUS.   What's the matter?   Why such alarm?   835

    TAMAR.   Don't give me arguments!   Wound him!
Strike him dead or call me debauched!

    ELISA.   We'll abandon the reception.   840
It's right to do as she commands.

    JOSEPHUS.   But even right, we always see,
when pushed too far, can end in grief.

End of Act I

JORNADA SEGUNDA

Sale vistiéndose muy melancólico Amón con ropa, y montera, y
Eliazer, y Jonadab.

JONADAB.　No lo aciertas, gran señor,
en levantarte.
AMÓN.　　　Es la cama
potro para la paciencia.
ELIAZER.　Un discreto la compara
a los celos.
AMÓN.　　　¿De qué modo?　　　　　　5
ELIAZER.　De la suerte que regalan
cuando pocos; si son muchos,
o causan flaqueza, o matan.
AMÓN.　Bien has dicho.　¡Hola!
JONADAB.　　　　　　　　　Señor.
AMÓN.　Dalde cien escudos.
ELIAZER.　　　　　　　Pagas　　　　　10
como príncipe, no sólo
las obras, mas las palabras.

Quiérele dar aguamanos.

AMÓN.　¿Qué es esto?
JONADAB.　　　　　Darte aguamanos.
AMÓN.　Si con fuego me lavara,
pudiera ser que estuviera　　　　　　15
mejor, pues me abrasa el agua.
Dime algo que me entretenga.
¿Qué es la causa de que callas
tanto, Eliazer?
ELIAZER.　　　No sé cómo
darte gusto; ya te enfadas　　　　　　20
con que hablando te diviertan,
ya darte música mandas,
ya a los que te hablan despides,
y riñes a quien te canta.
JONADAB.　Esta tu melancolía　　　　25
tiene, señor, lastimada

ACT II

Enter Amnon, in state of melancholy, being dressed by Eliazer and Jonadab and wearing a montera.[1]

JONADAB. You're wrong to rise so soon, my lord.
AMNON. Bed is like a rack for patience.
ELIAZER. Like jealousy would be more apt
comparison.
AMNON. And how is that?   5
ELIAZER. In moderation it revives,
yet in excess, debilitates
or kills.
AMNON. Well said. Ho, there!
JONADAB.   My lord?
AMNON. Give this man a hundred crowns.[2]
ELIAZER.   You pay   10
with princely generosity
for words as well as services.

He offers him a bowl of water.

AMNON. What's this?
JONADAB.   Water for your hands, my lord.
AMNON. No, water burns me like a fire.
To wash with fire might be better.   15
Tell me something to amuse me.
Why so silent, Eliazer?
ELIAZER. I do not know how to please you.
When we amuse you with our talk   20
you snap at us and throw us out.
You order musicians to play
but if they sing there's hell to pay.
JONADAB. Your melancholia, my lord,   25

a toda Jerusalén.

ELIAZER. No hay caballero ni dama,
que a costa de alguna parte
de su salud no comprara 30
la tuya.

AMÓN. ¿Quiérenme mucho?

JONADAB. Como a su Príncipe.

AMÓN.   Basta,
no me habléis más en mujeres.
Pluguiera a Dios que se hallara
medio con que conservar 35
la naturaleza humana
sin haberlas menester.
¿Vino el médico?

JONADAB.   ¿No mandas
que ninguno te visite?

AMÓN. Si supieran como parlan 40
no estuviera enfermo yo.

ELIAZER. No estudian, señor, palabra;
sangrar y purgar son polos
de su ciencia.

AMÓN.   ¿Y su ganancia?

JONADAB. Todo es seda, ámbar y mulas. 45
Si dos de ellos enviara
a Egipto o Siria David,
con solas plumas mataran
más que su ejército todo.

ELIAZER. Juntáronse ayer en casa 50
de Délbora seis doctores,
que ha días que está muy mala,
para consultar entre ellos
la enfermedad, y aplicarla
algún remedio eficaz. 55
Apartáronse a una sala,
echando la gente de ella;
diole gana a una criada
(que bastaba ser mujer),
de escuchar lo que trataban, 60
y cuando tuvo por cierto
que del mal filos faran

gives all Jerusalem concern.

ELIAZER.   There's not a man or woman here
who would not trade his health for yours.   30

AMNON.   They really love me?

JONADAB.   As their prince.

AMNON.   Stop talking to me like women!
I wish to God there was some way
to procreate the human race   35
without them.   Has the doctor come?

JONADAB.   You ordered no one to come near.

AMNON.   If their minds could grasp what their tongues
can speak, then I would not be ill.

ELIAZER.   They don't study a word, my lord.
Bleeding and purging are the limits
of their science.

AMNON.   Not their income?

JONADAB.   No.   That's all silks, mules and amber. ³   45
If David sent just two of them
to Egypt or to Syria,
they'd kill more men with quills alone
than his whole army with their swords. ⁴

ELIAZER.   There were six of them yesterday   50
together in Deborah's house —
she's been ill for several days —
discussing her illness, trying
to find some treatment between them.   55
They retired to a private room,
throwing out those who were inside.
Now a serving wench decided
— she is a woman after all —
to listen to the conversation   60
— when she was positive, that is,
that they were talking of the case,

de la enferma, y experiencias
acerca de él relataran,
oyó preguntar al uno: 65
'Señor doctor, ¿qué ganancia
sacará vuesa merced
una con otra semana?'
Respondió: 'Cincuenta escudos,
con que he comprado una granja,   70
veinte alanzadas de viñas,
y un soto en que tengo vacas.
Pero no me descontenta
el buen gusto de las casas
que tuvo vuesa merced.'   75
Dijo otro: 'Son celebradas.
No sé qué hacer del dinero
que gano. Cosa extremada
es ver que, sin ser verdugos,
porque matamos nos pagan.'   80
'Dejad eso,' replicó
otro, 'y decid de qué traza
os fue en el juego de anoche.'
'Perdí, son suertes voltarias
las de los dados. ¿Mas vos   85
jugáis?' 'Con una muchacha,'
respondió, 'de catorce años.
Fuila a ver una mañana,
enferma de opilaciones;
halléla sola en la cama,   90
tentéla el pulso y los pechos,
y esto del tacto arrebata
los apetitos tras sí.
Díjela ciertas palabras,
que luego puse por obra,   95
y, al fin, ya está gorda y sana.
Hale parecido bien
mi olor, talle, gusto y habla,
y de mi amor está enferma.'
'¿Gozáisla?' 'No, sino el alba.   100
Estremado es nuestro oficio;
no hay para él puerta cerrada,

comparing notes on the disease —
she hears one ask another one: 65
"My good sir, what is your income
taking one week with another?"
"Some fifty crowns", the other says,
"with which I've bought a good—sized farm, 70
twenty or so acres of vineyard
and a meadow for grazing cows.
But I must say, I don't dislike
the villas you've bought. First class taste." 75
"Very nice too", another says.
"I simply don't know what to do
with all the money that I make.
Quite remarkable. They pay us,
like full—time executioners, 5
for slaughtering the populace!" 80
"Never mind that", another says.
"Tell us. How was the game last night?"
"I lost. The dice are fickle friends.
Are you a gambling man yourself?" 85
"I do my gambolling in bed", 6
the other says, "Nice little thing,
fourteen years old. Went to see her
one morning. Touch of the vapours. 7
Found her all alone in bed. 90
I felt her pulse, then felt her breast
and, since touching stirs the appetites,
I whispered my prescription
into her ear and then forthwith 95
proceeded to the treatment.
Now she's fat and in the pink.
She must have liked my figure well,
my taste, my voice and even smell,
so now she's sick with love of me." 100
"Did you enjoy her?" "It was not
the Holy Ghost for sure. Ours is
a remarkable profession.
There's no door closed; none affords

ni más segura ocasión.
La mujer más recatada
que da a quien muere por ella   105
adarme y medio de cara
tras un año de servicios,
por un manto alambicada
nos abre al primer achaque
puerta al apetito franca,   110
haciendo brindis al gusto
moza y desnuda en la cama.
Aquí no entra el refrán,
pues en nuestro oficio se halla
juntamente honra y provecho.'   115
'Yo, a lo menos, si reinara,'
dijo otro, 'no consintiera
sino que eunucos curaran,
o mujeres a mujeres
y hombres a hombres.'   'Dejara   120
yo el oficio,' respondió
el otro, 'que no hay ganancia
igual a tener derecho
a doncellas y casadas.'
'¿Pero tenéis muchos libros?'   125
'Doscientos cuerpos no bastan
con cuatro dedos de polvo,
que ni ellos hablan palabra,
ni yo las que encierran miro.
Ostentación y ignorancia   130
nos han dado de comer.
Más ha de cuatro semanas
que no hojeo sino son
pechugas de pavos blancas,
lomos de gazapos tiernos,   135
y con pimienta y naranja,
perdiz, pichón y vaquita;
ansí a la ternera llaman
los hipócritas al uso.
Pero lo parlado basta;   140
vamos a ver nuestra enferma,
que estará muy confiada

a safer opportunity.
The coyest prude who gives a man,
after years of steadfast courtship,   105
the glimpse of half an eye distilled
through a blanket as sole reward,
at the first indisposition
will open up all doors to lust,   110
offering herself to pleasure
virginal and naked in her bed.
The adage simply isn't true:
we get respect and profit too."[8]   115
"If I had power", said a voice,
"I would have none but eunuchs treat
the sick, or women for women
and men for men".   "I'd leave the job,"   120
replied the former.   "No amount
of cash is worth the right to have
one's wicked way with maidenheads
or married women in their beds."
"You have plenty of books, I trust?"   125
"Two hundred tomes, but not enough
to do much else but gather dust.
They do not speak a word to me
and I don't open them to see
those they contain.   Ostentation   130
and ignorance give us our meat.
All I've opened for several weeks
is the snow—white breast of turkeys,
tender rabbits' thighs and, smothered   135
in orange and black pepper sauce,
partridge, pigeon and *côtes de veau*[9]
(that's the French for veal you know).
But enough said, let us return   140
to see our patient who awaits
— so trustingly — the outcome

en nuestra consulta.' Fueron,
y dijo el de mayor barba:
'Lo que se saca de aquí   145
es que al momento se haga
una fricación de piernas,
y por todas las espaldas
le echen catorce ventosas,
las tres o cuatro sajadas.   150
Pónganle en el corazón
un socrocio y fomentada
con manteca de azahar.
Tenga en el cielo esperanza,
que la consulta de hoy   155
la ha de dar tan presto sana
que a estos señores doctores
tenga después que dar gracias.'
Diéronles doscientos reales,
y volviéronse a sus casas,   160
tan medrados de la junta
como te he contado.
   AMÓN.   Calla,
relator impertinente,
que me atormentas y cansas;
¿es posible que hables tanto?   165
   ELIAZER.   Tú, señor, ¿no me lo mandas?
Si callo te doy pesar,
en hablando me amenazas.
Dios te dé sosiego y gusto.
   AMÓN.   ¿Qué es aquello?   Hola, ¿quién canta?   170
   JONADAB.   Músicos que recebistes,
para que sus consonancias
tu melancólico humor
alivien.
   AMÓN.   Industria vana.

Cantan de dentro.

Pajaricos que hacéis al alba   175
con lisonjas alegre salva,
cantalde a Amón,

of our consultation." Then said
the doctor with the longest beard:
"This much is clear and must be done   145
forthwith: massage of the legs,
then fourteen cups upon her back[10]
with three or four incisions made.   150
Embrocation over the heart
and orange blossom poultices.
In heaven let her place her trust,
for today's deliberations   155
will put her on her feet so fast
she'll thank God for our profession."
Two hundred reals they collected[11]
as their fat remuneration   160
and went back home to taste the spoils
of fruitful cooperation.
    AMNON. Be silent! I'm sick to death
of your tedious anecdotes.
How can you find so much to say?[12]   165
    ELIAZER. But didn't you command it, Lord?
If I keep silent you're upset,
if I talk you utter threats.
God give you peace and contentment.
    AMNON. What's that noise? Ho, there! Who's singing?
    JONADAB. The musicians that you summoned,
my good lord, to alleviate
with their harmonies the blackness
of your melancholy humour.
    AMNON. Well tell them they're wasting their breath.

Singing is heard within.

Little birds that welcome[13]   175
the dawn with joyful song
lest he die of sadness
sing to my Prince Amnon,

que tristezas le quitan la vida,
y no sabe si son de amor,
y no sabe si de amor son.   180
AMÓN.   Hola, Eliazer, Jonadab,
echaldos por las ventanas,
daldos muerte, sepultaldos,
haciendo ataúd las tablas
de sus necios instrumentos;   185
tendrán sepultura honrada
como gusanos de seda
en sus capullos.
JONADAB.   ¡Qué extraña
pasión de melancolía!
AMÓN.   ¿No imitan en una casa   190
a su señor los criados?
¿Yo llorando, y ellos cantan?
¿Mi enfermedad los alegra?

Sale un Maestro de Armas.

ELIAZER.   Aquí está el maestro de armas
que viene a darte lición.   195
AMÓN.   Dadme pues la negra espada;
aunque, pues se queda en blanco
mi nunca verde esperanza,
mejor que la espada negra
pudiera jugar la blanca.   200
MAESTRO.   Vuelva el cielo, gran señor,
los colores a tu cara,
que la tristeza marchita,
con la salud que te falta.
AMÓN.   Retórico impertinente,   205
el que es diestro jamás habla.
Jugad las armas callando,
o no os preciéis de las armas.
MAESTRO.   Perdóneme vuestra Alteza.
Dije en la lición pasada   210
que con estas dos posturas
al enemigo se ganan
medio pie de tierra.

who does not know if he sighs,
who does not know if he dies
for love.   180
    AMNON.   Come Eliazer, Jonadab.
Throw these clowns out of the window!
Run them through, coffin their bodies
in their own stupid instruments!   185
They shall have a decent burial
like silkworms in their own cocoons.
    JONADAB.   A strange case of melancholy!
    AMNON.   What! Do the servants of the house
no longer imitate their master?
Shall I weep and they sing for joy?
Does my malady amuse them?

Enter the fencing master.

    ELIAZER.   The fencing master's here to give
your lesson.   195
    AMNON.   Give me the black foil.[14]
And yet my prospects are so bleak,
I might as well play it for real
and use the rapier of steel.   200
    FENCING MASTER.   May heaven restore, my noble lord,
the hue to your sadness — withered
cheeks, with the health that you desire.
    AMNON.   Spare me your idle rhetoric;   205
a swordsman never wastes his breath.
Ply your blade in silence, sir,
or never presume to wear a sword.
    FENCING M.   I beg you Highness's pardon.
As I said in my last lesson,   210
by adopting these two postures
you gain half a foot's advantage
on your opponent.

AMÓN.   Siete,
que son los que a un cuerpo bastan,
cuando os haya muerto a vos   215
darán quietud a mis ansias. (*Da tras él*)
 MAESTRO. ¿Qué es lo que hace vuestra Alteza?
 AMÓN. Castigar vuestra arrogancia.
Necios, el mal que me aflige,
siendo de amor, no se saca   220
con bélicos instrumentos.
Morid todos, pues me matan
invisibles enemigos. (*Tras de todos*)
 MAESTRO. Huyamos mientras se amansa
el frenesí de su furia. (*Huyen todos*) 225
 AMÓN. Si hubiera armas que mataran
la memoria que me aflige,
¡qué buenas fueran las armas!
Hola, Eliazer, Jonadab,
Josefo, Abiatar, Sisara,   230
¿no hay quien venga a dar alivio
al tormento que me abrasa?

 Salen Eliazer y Jonadab.

 JONADAB. Gran señor, sosiégate.
 AMÓN. ¿Cómo, si es quimera mi alma,
de contradicciones hecha,   235
de imposibles sustentada?
¿No estaba en la cama yo?
¿Quién me ha cubierto de galas?
¡Desnudadme presto, presto!
 ELIAZER. Tú te vistes y levantas 240
contra la opinión de todos.
 AMÓN. Mentís.
 JONADAB.   Desnúdale y calla.
 AMÓN. ¿Yo sedas en vez de luto?
Ay libertad mal lograda,
¿muerta vos y yo de fiestas?   245
Sayal negro, jerga basta
os tienen de hacer desde hoy
las obsequias lastimadas.

AMNON.   Seven feet!
I'll not be satisfied with less.
That's all the ground your corpse will need   215
when I have laid you down to rest. (*Goes after him*)
    FENCING M.   But what is your Highness doing?
    AMNON.   I'm punishing your arrogance.
Love's canker cannot be excised,   220
you fools, with instruments of war.
I am dying at the hands
of enemies I cannot see.
So you die too, because of me. (*Pursues them*)
    FENCING M.   Let us retreat from hence till time
abates the fury of his wrath.   (*They all flee*)
    AMNON.   If only there were swords to kill
this memory that haunts my mind,
how wonderful a sword would be!
Come back Eliazer, Jonadab,
Josephus, Abiathar, Sisara!   230
Will no one come to rid my soul
of torment?

Enter Eliazer and Jonadab.

JONADAB.   Calm yourself, my lord.
    AMNON.   How, pray, if my soul's an insane
fantasy of contradictions   235
nourished on impossible dreams?
But was I not in bed just now?
Who decked me in this finery?
Off with the lot at once, I say!
    ELIAZER.   You rose and dressed yourself, my lord,   240
against our best advice.
    AMNON.   That's lies.
    JONADAB.   Just undress him and keep quiet.
    AMNON.   What? Silks! Shouldn't I wear mourning
for my late—lamented freedom?[15]
All this pomp when freedom lies dead?   245
No, from this day onward, I'll pay
my painful last respects to her
in black sackcloth and coarse homespun.

Suenan cajas dentro.

¿Qué es esto?
 JONADAB. Gran señor, viene
tu padre, rey y monarca   250
de las doce ilustres tribus,
entre clarines y cajas
triunfando a Jerusalén,
después que por tierra iguala
del idólatra amonita   255
las ciudades rebeladas.
Sálenle con bendiciones,
músicas, himnos y danzas
a recebir a sus puertas,
cubiertas de cedro y palma,   260
los cortesanos alegres,
y la victoria le cantan
con que triunfó de Golías
sus agradecidas damas.
Sal a darle el parabién,   265
y con su célebre entrada
suspenderás tu tristeza.
 AMÓN. Al melancólico agravan
el mal contentos ajenos.
Idos todos de mi casa,   270
dejadme a solas en ella
mientras veis que me acompañan
desesperación, tristeza,
locura, imposibles, rabia;
pues cuando mi padre triunfe,   275
muerte me darán mis ansias. (*Vase*)
 JONADAB. Lastimoso frenesí.
 ELIAZER. Que no se sepa la causa
de tanto mal.
 JONADAB. ¿Si es de amor?
 ELIAZER. A sello, ¿quién rehusara 280
a quien hereda este reino?
 JONADAB. No sé, por Dios; mas pues calla
la ocasión de su tristeza,

Sound of drums within.

What is that?
    JONADAB.   Your father, my lord,
our noble king and sovereign   250
of Israel's twelve illustrious tribes,[16]
who comes amidst drums and fanfares
in triumph to Jerusalem,
after levelling the cities
of the idolatrous Ammonite.   255
The courtiers are rushing out
joyfully to welcome his return,
calling down blessings on his head,
playing music, singing anthems,
dancing in the streets.   Their portals
are decked with palm leaves and cedar.   260
In gratitude the women sing
the victory song that celebrates
the fall of great Goliath.   Go on![17]
Give him your congratulations.   265
You will drown your melancholy
in the triumph of his entry.
    AMNON.   The sight of others' happiness
aggravates the melancholic.
All leave my house! Leave me alone!   270
You can see I have my sadness
for company, my rage, despair,
madness and unquenchable thirst.
If I saw my father's triumph,   275
my craving heart would surely burst. *(Exit)*
    JONADAB.   A most pitiable derangement!
    ELIAZER.   The cause of which were best not known.
    JONADAB.   If it were love?
    ELIAZER.   If that were so,   280
Who'd refuse the heir to the throne?
    JONADAB.   I couldn't say, I swear to God.
But since he's loth to name the cause,

o Amón está loco, o ama. (*Vanse*)

*Salen marchando con mucha música por una puerta Joab, Absalón,
Adonías, y tras ellos David, viejo coronado; por otra Abigail, Tamar,
Bersabé, Micol, y Salomón; dan vuelta y dice David.*

DAVID. Si para el triunfo es lícito adquirido   285
después de guerras, levantar trofeos,
premio, si muchas veces repetido,
aliento de mis bélicos deseos;
si tras desenterrar del viejo olvido
de asirios, madianitas, filisteos,   290
de Get y de Canaan victorias tantas,
inexhausta materia a plumas santas;
si después que los brazos guedejudos
del líbico león, fuerzas bizarras
hipérboles venciendo, hicieron mudos   295
elogios que el laurel convierte en parras,
y en juvenil edad, miembros desnudos
galas haciendo las robustas garras
del oso informe, entre el crespado vello,
como joyas sus brazos me eché al cuello;   300
en fin, si tras hazañas adquiridas
en la robusta edad que amor dilata,
grabada su memoria en las heridas,
ejecutoria de quien honras trata,
agora a ésta pequeña reducidas   305
cuando a mi edad el tiempo paga en plata
el oro que le dio juventud leda,
que pues se trueca y pasa ya es moneda,
por sola una corona que he quitado
al amonita rey de los cabellos,   310
cuatro coronas mi valor premiado
en vuestros ocho brazos gano bellos;
quisiera, con sus círculos honrado,
que brotaran de aquéste otros tres cuellos,
y hecha Jerusalén de amor teatro,   315
viera un amante con coronas cuatro.
Ya Rábata, que corte incircuncisa
del amonita fue, rüinas solas

Amnon is mad or he's in love.   *(They all leave)*

Enter to the accompaniment of great fanfares through one door
Joab, Absolom, Adonijah and behind them the old king David
wearing his crown; through the other, Abigail, Tamar, Bathsheba,
Michal and Solomon. They process round the stage, after which
David speaks. [18]

DAVID.   If, after wars, it is legitimate to display
the trophies of our achievement which are both
the reward, albeit an oft—repeated one,
and the stimulus of my warlike spirit,
If, after rescuing from the arms of old oblivion
so many victories over Assyrians, Midianites, Philistines, [19]
over Gath and Canaan, inexhaustible material for our holy chroniclers,
If, after the shaggy paws of the Libyan lion [20]
had been raised in silent hommage
to my prodigious strength passing all hyperbole
and covered with the victor's laurel
soon to be transformed into the vineleaves of celebration,
If, after I had in my tender years cloaked my back
in the matted skin and decked my naked limbs
with the robust claws of the shapeless bear [21]
and draped its paws like a necklace round my neck,
If, in short, the many deeds of valour accumulated in my prime,
the souvenirs of which are engraved in the wounds
which are the letters patent of one who deals in honour,
are now reduced to this one small trifle,   305
now that time pays back to age in silver
what carefree youth loaned to it in gold [22]
(for time, like money, passes and is changed),
and if for this one small crown that I have wrenched
from the head of the Ammonite king,   310
my valour is rewarded with no fewer than four
in your eight lovely arms encircling my brow,
then I wish that I could grow — to reciprocate the honour —
three other heads, and that all Jerusalem,
transformed into a theatre of love, not war,
should see their lover—king quadrupally crowned with its victory.
Now, Rabbah, which was once the proud court

ofrece al tiempo que caduco pisa
montes altivos y cerúleas olas.   320
Ya la tristeza transformada en risa,
muerta Belona, cuatro laureolas
lisonjean mi gozo en sus lazos,
reduciendo mi cuello a vuestros brazos.
Micol querida, que por tantos años   325
a indigno posëedor distes trofeos,
a envidia venganza, a amor engaños,
al tiempo qué contar, y a mí deseos,
dadme entre esos abrazos desengaños,
como yo a vuestras aras filisteos   330
sus prepucios al rey incircuncisos,
plumas al sabio y a la fama avisos.
Discreta Abigäil, a quien el cielo
gracias de aplacar cóleras ha dado,
del bárbaro pastor en el Carmelo   335
premio no merecido ni estimado,
en esos brazos, polos del consuelo,
en quien vive mi amor depositado,
descanse mi vejez, que pues los goza,
si largos años cuenta, ya está moza.   340
Hermosa Bersabé, ninfa del baño,
que sirviéndoos de espejo en fuentes frías,
brillando el sol en ellas, de un engaño
dieron causa a un pequé lágrimas mías,
ya se restaura en vos el mortal daño   345
del mal logrado por leal Urías,
pues dais quien edifique templo al Arca,
paz a los tiempos y a Isräel monarca.
Y vos, mi Salomón, noble sujeto
en quien Dios ciencia infusa deposite,   350
de la fábrica çélebre arquiteto
que la gloria de Dios en niebla imite,
el líbano de Hirán, grato y discreto,
cedros os corta donde eterna habite
la incorrupción que el tiempo no maltrata;   355
con oro os sirve Ofir, Tarsis con plata.
Bellísima Tamar, hija querida,

of the uncircumcized Ammonites, offers only ruins
to the weary feet of time which grinds down
the proudest hills and dries the cerulean waves.   320
Now, with Bellona, the war goddess, dead[23]
and sorrow turned to laughter, the four laurel leaves
of your arms bow my neck and set the seal upon my happiness.
Dearest Michal, who for so many years[24]   325
paid hommage to an unworthy possessor,
gave envy scope for revenge, repaid love with deception,
gave to history tales of scandal and to me aching desires,
disabuse me of suspicion in your embrace,
just as I gave Philistines to your sacrificial altars,   330
sent their uncircumcized foreskins to your King,
gave wings of inspiration to historians and lessons to posterity.
Abigail the wise, on whom Heaven bestowed the gift of turning away
anger, the one—time undeserved and unappreciated prize
of that boorish peasant from Mount Carmel;[25]
let those arms, like twin poles of consolation   335
which attract my love, be the resting place of my old age
which, since it enjoys their embrace,
though it be rich in years, now regains its youth.   340
Beautiful Bathsheba, the bathing nymph,[26]
mirrored in the cold waters of a limpid spring
on which the sun's reflections gave rise to my delusion
— though my tears gave rise to a contrite psalm.
In you we see the restoration of the mortal hurt   345
committed against the unfortunate Uriah,
whose only sin was loyalty, since you provide us with
the prince who will build the temple for the Ark of the Covenant,[27]
who will bring peace to our times
and who shall rule over the kingdom of Israel.
And you, my Solomon, the noble vessel
in whom the Lord deposits his gift of wisdom,   350
architect of the celebrated temple,
sanctified by the glory of God in the form of a cloud;[28]
that temple for which Ophir sends you its gold
and Tharshish its silver,[29]
for which the Lebanese subjects of the wise and affable Hiram[30]
cut down the cedars that will eternally contain
the purity of our law, proof against the corruption of time. 355

cárcel del sol en vuestras hebras preso,
dichosa mi victoria reducida
al triunfo que con veros intereso,   360
¿cómo estáis?
    TAMAR.   Dando albricias a la vida
que, vos ausente, en contingencia al seso,
gran señor, puso.
    ABIGAIL.   Y yo a mi deseo
pagando costas, pues que sano os veo.
    DAVID.   ¿Estáis, mi Abigail, buena?
    ABIGAIL.   A serviros   365
dispuesta, gran señor, eternamente.
    DAVID.   ¿Vos, hermosa Micol?
    MICOL.   Tristes suspiros
en gozo trueco pues os veo presente.
    DAVID.   ¿Y vos, mi Bersabé?
    BERSABÉ.   De ver veniros
tierno en amores si en valor valiente,   370
rindiéndoos toda el alma por despojos
que a gozaros se asoma por los ojos.
    DAVID.   Esta corona, peso de un talento,
o veinte mil ducados, rica y bella,
lo fue del amonita que os presento,   373
alegre en ver que sois las piedras della.
Mi general Joab, merecimiento
de la fama que envidias atropella,
de mi victoria la ocasión ha sido,
valiente capitán, si comedido.   380
A Rábata redujo a tanto aprieto
que, cifrando su sed, asoló un pozo;
dejó su asalto de llegar a efeto
y ser ejecución de su destrozo
por avisarme, a la lealtad sujeto,   385
que a mis victorias aplicase el gozo.
De esta conquista que su fe publica,
las veces que Isräel me la dedica,
dalde las gracias de ella.
    JOAB.   En esas plantas
puesta la boca, quedaré premiado,   390
pues a mayores glorias me levantas

Fairest Tamar, my beloved daughter ...
The very sun shines out from you,
captive in your golden hair ...
I count my victory most fortunate
since it brings the triumph that I feel on seeing you.
How are you all?   360
    TAMAR.   We render grateful thanks to life for your return, my
lord.   Anxiety for your absence drove us close to madness.
    ABIGAIL.   To see you sound and well
repays all my hours of longing.
    DAVID.   And are you well, my Abigail?
    ABIGAIL.   Well enough to serve you
all your days, my lord.   365
    DAVID.   And you, my fair Michal?
    MICHAL.   Sighs of sadness
turn to joy now that you are with us.
    DAVID.   And you, my Bathsheba?
    BATHSHEBA.   Seeing you return,   370
not just full of manly valour but tender in your love for us,
I surrender as the spoils of war all my heart
which lights a welcome in my eyes.
    DAVID.   This fine rich crown — over a talent in weight [31]
and twenty thousand ducats in value — which I now present to you,
once adorned the head of the Ammonite king.
I rejoice to see that you are now the jewels that adorn the crown.
To my commander—in—chief Joab, a brave captain and a gentleman
whose merits silence the envious tongues
that carp at his reputation,
to him alone I owe my victory.
Attacking the enemy's water supply, he destroyed a well [32]   380
and reduced the city of Rabbah to a desperate plight.
His own attack failed to reach its completion
since, bound by loyalty, he sent word to me   385
that I should come and enjoy the fruits of victory.
This conquest is a tribute to his faith in me
and whenever Israel gives me credit for it,
the thanks are due to him.
    JOAB.   My mouth pressed against your feet
is reward enough for me.
Your majesty raises me to greater glory   390

con sólo el nombre, o Rey, de tu soldado.
Cuelga ante el Arca con tus armas santas
trofeos que a la envidia den cuidado,
y al arpa dulce, de tu gusto abismo,   395
cántate las victorias a ti mismo.
DAVID. Hablad a mí, Absalón, a mí, Adonías,
diestros en guerra, si en la paz galanes.
ABSALÓN. A tu lado señor, ¿qué valentías
podrán dar luz a ilustres capitanes?   400
SALOMÓN. Dadnos los brazos.
ABIGAIL.   ¿Vieron nuestros días,
al tremolar hebreos tafetanes,
juntar en dos sujetos la ventura
el esfuerzo abrazado a la hermosura?
DAVID. Mi Amón, mi mayorazgo, el primer fruto   405
de mi amor, ¿cómo está?
ABIGAIL.   Dando a tu corte
tristeza en verle, a su pesar tributo,
prisa a la muerte que sus años corte,
llanto a sus ojos y a nosotras luto,
pues callando su mal no hay quien reporte   410
la pálida tristeza que enfadosa
gualdas siembra en su cara y hurta rosa.
SALOMÓN. No hay médico tan célebre que acierte
la causa de tan gran melancolía,
ni con música, o juegos se divierte,   415
ni va a cazar, ni admite compañía.
BERSABÉ. A los umbrales llama de la muerte
para dar a tu reino un triste día.
ABIGAIL. Háblale, y el dolor que le molesta
aliviarás. Su cuadra es, señor, ésta.   420

*Corren una cortina, y descubren a Amón asentado en una silla muy
triste, la mano en la mejilla.*

DAVID. ¿Qué es esto, amado heredero?
Cuando tu padre dilata
reinos que ganarte trata,
por ser tú el hijo primero,
dejándote consumir   425

simply by calling me your soldier.
Hang your holy weapons and all your battle trophies before the Ark
and let envy do its worst.
Take your harp and sing; immerse your soul   395
in the celebration of your victories.
    DAVID. Speak to me, Absolom; to me, Adonijah: my sons,
whose prowess in war is equalled only by their skill in the peaceful
art of seduction.
    ABSOLOM. What other deeds besides your own, my lord,
could possibly inspire your ·illustrious captains?   400
    SOLOMON. Give me your arms, my lord.³³
    ABIGAIL. Our times are privileged to see
two such men in whom destiny has joined comeliness
with valour marching under the Hebrew flag.
    DAVID. And where is Amnon, my eldest son, the first fruit 405
of my love. How is he?
    ABIGAIL. Your court is sad
to see him as he is now. He feeds on melancholy
and is moping himself into an early grave.
He is constantly in tears and causing us consternation.
Since he will not speak of the cause, no one can shake him free 410
from the pale dejection that robs colour
from his cheeks and jaundices his life.
    SOLOMON. Not even the most distinguished physicians
can diagnose the cause of this great melancholy.
He tolerates no company, refuses to join the hunt   415
and finds no pleasure in either sport or music.
    BATHSHEBA. He is hammering on death's door
as if resolved to bring a day of sorrow to your kingdom.
    ABIGAIL. You speak to him, my lord, it will ease
the pain he feels. This is his chamber.   420

*A curtain is drawn aside and Amnon is discovered sitting dejectedly
in a chair resting his cheek on his hand.*

    DAVID. What's this? You are my son, my heir.
Here am I, your father, trying
to extend by conquest the kingdoms
that will, as eldest son, be yours
and you cast this pall of sadness   425

de tus imaginaciones,
¿luto al triunfo alegre pones
que me sale a recebir?
Diviértante los despojos
que toda tu corte ha visto.   430
Todo un reino te conquisto;
alza a mirarme los ojos,
llega a enlazar a mi cuello
los brazos, tu gusto admita
esta corona, que imita   435
el oro de tus cabellos.
Hijo, ¿no quieres hablarme?
Alza la triste cabeza,
si ya con esa tristeza
no pretendes acabarme.   440
    ABSALÓN. Hermano, la cortesía
¿cuándo no tuvo lugar
en vuestro pecho, a pesar
de cualquier melancolía?
Mirad que el Rey, mi señor,   445
y padre hablándoos está.
    ADONÍAS. Si Adonías causa da
a conservar el amor
que en vos mostró la experiencia
por él os ruego que habléis   450
a un monarca que tenéis
llorando en vuestra presencia.
    SALOMÓN. No agüéis tan alegre día.
    TODOS. Ah, Príncipe, volvé en vos.
    DAVID. ¡Amón!
    AMÓN.   ¡Oh, válgame Dios,   455

Alza la cabeza muy triste.

qué impertinente porfía!
    DAVID. ¿Qué tienes, caro traslado
de este triste original?
que en alivio de tu mal,
de todo el hebrëo estado   460
la mitad darte prometo.

over my welcome home?   You let
imagination rule your mind?
Feast your eyes on these spoils of war.
The whole court has seen them.   So look!   430
I lay a kingdom at your feet
so raise your eyes to look at me.
Come, put your arms around my neck!
Take pleasure in this crown I bring;
it matches with your golden hair.
Why won't you speak to me, my son?
Lift your head.   Hear me when I cry;
unless this melancholia
is resolved to see me die.³⁴   440
    ABSOLOM.   And when did courtesy not find
a place in your heart, my brother,
melancholy notwithstanding?
I remind you this is the king,   445
my father, who's addressing you.
    ADONIJAH.   If Adonijah can give cause
for you to manifest that love
experience has shown in you,
then I beseech you in its name,   450
speak to a king who stands and weeps
before you!
    SOLOMON.   Don't mar this day's joy!
    ALL.   Come, my lord, be yourself once more!
    DAVID.   Amnon!
    AMNON.   For God's sake, what a bore!   455

Sadly raising his head.

How tiresome you are!
    DAVID.   My son,
You are the first precious casting
from this poor original mould.
So tell me what your troubles are.   460
I'd promise you half my kingdom
if I thought that it would help you.

Gózale, y no estés ansí,
pon esos ojos en mí,
de todo mi gusto objeto.
No se obscurezca el Apolo   465
de tu cara; el mal despide.
¿Qué quieres? Háblame, pide.
　AMÓN.　Que os vais, y me dejéis solo.
　DAVID.　Si en eso tu gusto estriba,
no te quiero dar pesar;   470
tu tristeza ha de causar
que yo sin consuelo viva.
Aguado has el regocijo
con que Israel se señala;
¿pero qué contento iguala   475
al dolor que causa un hijo?
¿Que no mereciera yo,
aunque fingiéndolo fuera,
una palabra siquiera
de amor? Dirásme que no.   480
Príncipe, ¿un mirarme sólo?
Cruel con mis canas eres.
¿Qué has? ¿Qué sientes? ¿Qué quieres?
　AMÓN.　Que os vais, y me dejéis solo.
　ABSALÓN.　El dejarle es lo más cuerdo,   485
pues persuadirle es en vano.
　DAVID.　¿Qué vale el reino que gano,
hijos, si al Príncipe pierdo?

Vanse, y al entrarse Tamar llámala Amón, y levántase de la silla.

　AMÓN.　¡Tamar! ¡Ah Tamar! ¡Señora!
¡Ah hermana!
　TAMAR.　¿Príncipe mío?   490
　AMÓN.　Oye de mi desvarío
la causa que el rey ignora.
¿Quieres tú darme salud?
　TAMAR.　A estar su aumento en mi mano,
sabe Dios, gallardo hermano,   495
con cuánta solicitud
hierbas y piedras buscara,

It's yours. Take it. Enjoy it now.
Only turn your eyes towards me.
You are the sun, the source of life   465
to me. Don't let the clouds obscure
your face. Drive this sorrow away.
Tell me what you want of me. Speak!
    AMNON. Go away and leave me alone.
    DAVID. If that's your pleasure, I shall not
distress you. This sorrow of yours   470
will leave me past consolation.
You have crushed the jubilation
with which Israel marks this day.
For what elation can withstand   475
the pain of a son's rejection?
Am I not worth one loving word,
even one not from the heart?
No, I suppose not. Not even,   480
Prince, a glance in my direction?
You show no thought for these grey hairs,
no charity. What troubles you?
Tell me what you feel, what you want.
    AMNON. I want you to leave me alone!
    ABSOLOM. It would be wise to leave him, sire,   485
since he cannot be persuaded.
    DAVID. Tell me, children, what have I won?
I've gained a kingdom and lost a son.

*As they are leaving, Amnon calls Tamar back and rises from his
chair.*

    AMNON. My lady! Tamar! Sister, alas!
    TAMAR. What is it, Prince?   490
    AMNON.   I will tell you
the cause I could not tell the king.
You'd like to see my health restored?
    TAMAR. If restoration of your health
were in my hands, God knows, brother,   495
I'd climb the wildest hills and scour

experiencias aprendiera,
montes ásperos subiera,
filósofos consultara   500
para volver a Isräel
un príncipe que la muerte
quitalle pretende.
    AMÓN.   Advierte,
que no siendo tú crüel,
sin piedras, drogas, ni hierbas,   505
metales, montes o llanos,
está mi vida en tus manos,
y que en ellas la conservas.
Toma este pulso, en él pon (*Tómale*)
los dedos como instrumento,   510
a cuyo encendido acento
conceptos del corazón
entiendas.
    TAMAR. Desasosiego
muestra.
    AMÓN. Cáusanle mis penas.
Sangre encierran otras venas;   515
en las mías todo es fuego.
Ay manos que el alma toca, (*Tómalas y bésalas*)
pagando en besos agravios,
quien se hiciera todo labios
para gloria de esta boca.   520
    TAMAR. Por ser tu hermana consiento
los favores que me haces.
    AMÓN. Y porque ansí satisfaces
la pena de mi tormento.
    TAMAR. Dime ya tu mal. ¡Acaba!   525
    AMÓN. Ay hermana, que no puedo;
es freno del alma el miedo.
Darte parte de él pensaba,
pero vete, que es mejor
morir mudo. ¿No te vas?   530
    TAMAR. Si determinado estás
en eso, sigo tu humor.
Voyme, adiós.
    AMÓN.   Crueldad extraña.

the earth for herbs and stones, study
remedies and consult with men   500
of learning to bring Israel back
its prince from the jaws of death.
    AMNON.   No need for drugs or herbs or stones,   505
or minerals from hills or plains.
All I need's a little kindness.
Nonetheless, you do hold my life
in your hands. Take my pulse. Just there.

   Tamar feels his pulse.

Decypher with your fingers   510
from this intense and fevered beat
the secret message of the heart.
    TAMAR.   The beat's a shade irregular.
    AMNON.   That's the beat of an aching heart.
Other veins have blood, mine have fire.   515
Oh, hands whose cruelty my heart
repays with the touch of kisses!

   He takes her hands and kisses them.

I wish I had a thousand lips   520
to taste this glory in my mouth.
    TAMAR.   I could not admit these favours,
sir, if I were not your sister.
    AMNON.   Nor if they did not alleviate
a brother's torment.
    TAMAR.   What torment?
Well, tell me!   525
    AMNON.   Oh, my dear sister,
I can't. I fear to trust my heart.
I was about to tell you all,
but no. Please go. Better to die
than speak of it. Will you not go?   530
    TAMAR.   Oh, well, if you've made up your mind.
Your whim is my command. I'll go.
Goodbye.
    AMNON.   No, it's too cruel! Come back

¡Oye!

TAMAR. Vuelvo.

AMÓN.   Pero vete.

TAMAR. Alto.

AMÓN.   Vuelve y contaréte   535
el fiero mal que me engaña.

TAMAR. Si de una hermana no fías
tu secreto, ¿qué he de hacer?

AMÓN. (*Aparte*) De ser mi hermana y mujer
nacen mis melancolías.   540
¿Posible es que no has sacado
por el pulso mi dolor?

TAMAR. No sé yo que haya doctor
que tal gracia haya alcanzado.
Si hablando no me lo enseñas,   545
mal tu enfermedad sabré.

AMÓN. Pues yo del pulso bien sé,
que es lengua, que habla por señas.
Pero pues no conociste
por el tacto desvarío,   550
en tu nombre y en el mío,
hermana, mi mal consiste.
¿No te llamas tú Tamar?

TAMAR. Este apellido heredé.

AMÓN. Quítale al Tamar la T,   555
¿y dirá Tamar?

TAMAR.   Amar.

AMÓN. Ese es mi mal. Yo me llamo
Amón; quítale la N.

TAMAR. Serás amo.

AMÓN.   Porque pene
mi mal es amar; yo amo.   560
Si esto adviertes, ¿qué preguntas?
Ay bellísima Tamar,
amo, y es mi mal amar,
si a mi nombre el tuyo juntas.

and listen.
    TAMAR. I'm back.
    AMNON.   Better go.
    TAMAR. Enough! I'm off!
    AMNON.   No, please! Come back!   535
I'll tell you the cruel passion
that deludes my brain.
    TAMAR.   If you can't
trust a sister with your secret,
what can a sister do to help?
    AMNON. *(Aside)* You're a woman and my sister.
That's my secret and my torment.   540
Did you not detect my trouble
when you felt my pulse?
    TAMAR.   No doctor
that I know has that kind of skill.
If I don't hear it from your lips,   545
I'll never know what ails you.
    AMNON. I know the pulse is a signal
that speaks as loud as words. But since
you could not diagnose by touch   550
the fever that consumes my mind,
I'll tell you. The trouble lies hid
in your name, dear sister, and mine.
Yours is Tamar.
    TAMAR.   So they tell me.
    AMNON. Take away 'T' and add an 'e'.   555
What would Tamar in Latin be?[35]
    TAMAR. *Amare.*
    AMNON.   To love: my secret.
And now we take my name, Amnon.
Take off one 'n', then another.
What becomes of elder brother?
    TAMAR. *Amo?*
    AMNON..   *Amo* I love. For my sins
it is my misfortune to love.   560
Knowing that, what more do you need
to know? My beautiful Tamar,
take my name with yours and you'll see.
Love is my cruel destiny.

TAMAR. Si, como hay similitud   565
entre los nombres, le hubiera
en las personas, yo hiciera
milagros en tu salud.
    AMÓN. ¿Amor no es correspondencia?
    TAMAR. Ansí le suelen llamar.   570
    AMÓN. Pues si entre Amón y Tamar
hay tan poca diferencia,
que dos letras solamente
nos distinguen, ¿porqué callo
mi mal cuando medios hallo   575
que aplaquen mi fuego ardiente?
Yo, mi Tamar, cuando fui
contra el amonita fiero,
y en el combate primero
del Rey mi padre seguí   580
las banderas y el valor,
vi sobre el muro una tarde
un sol bello, haciendo alarde
de sus hazañas amor.
Quedé ciego en la conquista   585
de sus ojos soberanos,
y sin llegar a las manos
me venció sola su vista.
Desde entonces me alistó
Amor entre sus soldados;   590
supe lo que eran cuidados,
que hasta aquel instante no.
Tiré sueldo de desvelos,
sospechas me acompañaron,
imposibles me animaron,   595
quilataron mi amor celos.
Y procurando saber
quién era la causa hermosa
de la pasión amorosa
en que me siento encender,   600
supe que era la princesa,
hija del bárbaro rey,
contraria en sangre y en ley,
si una sola amor profesa.

TAMAR.   If our natures were as alike   565
as our names, I could do wonders
for your health.
AMNON.   But they say that love
is only love when matched with like.
TAMAR.   So they say.   570
AMNON.   If there's so little
difference between you and me
— what are two letters more or less? —
then why do I not dare to speak,
now that I find the means to quench   575
this burning thirst within my soul?
Dear Tamar, when I marched against
the fierce Ammonite, following
the standard and brave example
of the king, our father, I saw   580
in our very first encounter,
a blinding sun upon the wall,
a brave vision of love which shone
and put our warlike deeds to shame.
I was dazzled by the onslaught   585
of her captivating eyes
and, though she did not strike a blow,
I was defeated by her sight.
From that time on I was a conscript
in Love's army.   Such suffering[36]   590
I endured as I had never known.
My wages were of sleepless nights,
distrust my constant company.
Wild impossible dreams excite   595
my fantasy and jealousy
tests the quality of my love.
On attempting to discover
whose beauty had set me aflame,
I learnt it was the fair princess,   600
daughter to the barbarian king
and alien in her blood and creed,
though love professes only one.

Y como imposibilita   605
la nuestra el mezclarse, hermana,
sangre idólatra y pagana
con la nuestra isräelita,
viendo mi amor imposible,
a la ausencia remití   610
mi salud, porque crëí
que de su rostro apacible
huyendo, el seso perdido,
a pesar de tal violencia
ejecutara la ausencia   615
los milagros del olvido.
Volvíme a Jerusalén,
dejé bélicos despojos,
quise divertir los ojos
que siempre en su daño ven,   620
pero ni conversaciones,
juegos, cazas o ejercicios
fueron remedios ni indicios
de aplacarse mis pasiones.
Creció mi mal de día en día   625
con la ausencia, que quien ama
espuelas de amor la llama,
y en fin mi melancolía
ha llegado a tal estremo
que aborrezco lo que pido,   630
lo que me da gusto olvido
y me anima lo que temo.
Aguardé a mi padre el Rey
para que cuando volviese
por esposa me la diese,   635
que aunque de contraria ley,
la nuestra, hermana, dispensa
del Deuteronomio santo,
con que cuando amare tanto
como yo, y casarse piensa   640
con mujer incircuncisa,
ganada en lícita guerra,
la traiga a su casa y tierra,
donde en paz sus campos pisa,

But since our law forbids us blend,   605
my sister, our Israelite blood
with pagans and idolaters, [37]
I saw my love could never be.
Absence was the only remedy.   610
I thought: despite the brutal wrench,
despite my distraught mind, I'd flee
and put her gentle face behind me
and let time work the miracle   615
of my heart's oblivion.
I returned to Jerusalem.
I relinquished the spoils of war.
I tried to cheat my heart but saw
her face no matter where I looked.   620
Good conversation, hunting, sport,
these pastimes gave no cure nor sign
of placating my desires.
Day by day the pain grew stronger,   625
for absence is love's spur, they say,
and at last my melancholy
has now brought me to such a state
that I reject what I myself   630
have commanded, that I forget
what used to give me pleasure
and I pursue what I most dread.
I waited for the king's return
to ask her hand in marriage.   635
I know she has an alien law
but holy Deuteronomy, [38]
our law, sister, makes exemption
for one who loves as much as I
and who is bent on marriage   640
with a woman — though uncircumcised —
won as the legal spoils of war.
If he brings her to his homeland
where she may roam his fields in peace,

le quite el gentil vestido,   645
y la adorne de otros bellos;
le corte uñas y cabellos,
y pueda ser su marido.
Esta esperanza en sosiego
hasta agora conservé,   650
pero ya, Infanta, que sé
que mi padre a sangre y fuego
la ciudad de quien adoro
destruyó, quedando en ella
muerta mi idólatra bella,   655
sangre por lágrimas lloro.
Este es mi mal, imposible
de sanar, ésta mi historia;
consérvala mi memoria
para hacerla más terrible.   660
Ten piedad, hermana bella,
de mí.
    TAMAR.   Dios, hermano, sabe
si cuanto es tu mal más grave
me aflige más tu querella.
Mas yo, ¿cómo puedo, Amón,   665
remediarte?
    AMÓN.   Bien pudieras,
si tú, mi Tamar, quisieras.
    TAMAR.   Ya espero la conclusión.
    AMÓN.   Mira, hermana de mi vida;
aunque es mi pasión extraña,   670
como es niño Amor se engaña
con cualquier cosa fingida.
Llora un niño, y a su ama
pide leche, y dale el pecho
tal vez otra sin provecho,   675
donde creyendo que mama
solamente se entretiene.
¿No has visto fingidas flores
que en apariencia y colores
la vista a engañarse viene?   680
Juega con la espada negra
en paz quien la guerra estima,

if he removes her gentile dress   645
and cloaks her in more pleasing garb,
if he pares her nails, cuts her hair,
then he may be her husband.
This hope I nurtured till just now.   650
But now, my princess, now I know
my father has put her city
to the fire and sword and she,
my beautiful idolatress,   655
lies dead among the ruins.
The tears I weep are tears of blood.
That's my story; that's what ails me.
The memory aggravates my grief
and there is no possible cure.   660
Please take pity, my fair sister;
take pity on me.
    TAMAR.   Dear brother,
Heaven knows your lamentations
touch my heart when yours is grieved.
But how can I help you?   665
    AMNON.   You could,
sweet Tamar, if only you would ...
    TAMAR. Well? I wait for your conclusion.
    AMNON. Well then look, my dearest sister.
It may be strange this whim of mine,   670
but Love's a child and is beguiled
by any crude deception.
A baby cries and asks its nurse
for milk, yet may suck contented
at some other's dried up breast,   675
believing fondly that it feeds.
Have you not seen those false flowers
whose shape and colour dupe the eye?   680
One who hankers after battle
takes to fencing in time of peace
and deludes his warlike taste

engañando con la esgrima
las armas con que se alegra.
Hambriento he yo conocido 685
que de partir y trinchar
suele más harto quedar
que los otros que han comido.
Pues mi amor, en fin, rapaz,
si a engañarle, hermana, llegas, 690
si amorosas tretas juegas,
si tocas cajas en paz,
si le das fingidas flores,
si el pecho toma a un engaño,
si esgrime seguro el daño, 695
si de aparentes favores
trincha el gusto que interesa,
podrá ser, bella Tamar,
que sin que llegue al manjar,
le satisfaga la mesa. 700
Mi princesa mal lograda
fue imagen de tu hermosura;
suspender mi mal procura,
en su nombre transformada.
Sé tú mi dama fingida, 705
consiente que te enamore,
que te ronde, escriba, llore,
cele, obligue, alabe, pida,
que el ser mi hermana asegura
a la malicia sospechas, 710
y mis llamas satisfechas
al plato de tu hermosura
mientras el tiempo las borre,
serás fuente artificial,
que alivia al enfermo el mal, 715
sin beber mientras que corre.
TAMAR. Si en eso estriba, no más,
caro hermano, tu sosiego,
tu gusto ejecuta luego,
que en mí tu dama hallarás, 720
quizá más correspondiente
que la que ansí te abrasó.

for arms with the harmless foil.
I've even heard of hungry men[39]   685
for whom to cleave and carve the meat
gives them greater satisfaction
than others who sit down to eat.
Well, my love's just a callow boy.
If you, sister, would deceive it,   690
if you would play at games of love,
beat battle drums in time of peace,
give it artificial flowers,
and if it sucked the empty breast,
fenced with death without the danger,   695
if it would be content to carve
a dish of counterfeit favours,
then my love might just be able
to satisfy its hunger,
yet not approach the table.   700
My poor unfortunate princess
was the image of your beauty.
So try to bring my heart relief,
assuming her identity.
Be my sweet lover's substitute.   705
Let me court you, woo your love,
write you letters, weep tears for you,
be jealous, compel your favours,
praise you, beg. You are my sister.
That is proof against suspicion.   710
Yet your beauty is the only dish
to satisfy this hungry flame,
till time at last can cool the fire.
You'll be the artificial spring   715
that slakes my thirst, yet flows on by
and will not let me drink.
    TAMAR.   Brother,
dear Brother, if your peace of mind
depends on this, then do your will.
In me you will find your princess,   720
perhaps more giving than the one
who burnt your heart to ashes.

Ya no soy tu hermana yo,
preténdeme diligente,
que con industrioso engaño   725
mientras tu hermana no soy,
para que sanes te doy
de término todo este año.
    AMÓN. O lengua medicinal,
o manos de mi ventura,   *(Bésalas)*   730
o cielo de la hermosura,
o remedio de mi mal.
Ya vivo, ya puedo dar
salud a mi mortal llama.
    TAMAR. ¿Dícesme eso como a dama,   735
o sólo como a Tamar?
    AMÓN. Como a Tamar hasta agora,
mas desde aquí como a espejo
de mi amor.
    TAMAR. ¿Luego ya dejo
de ser Tamar?
    AMÓN.   Sí, señora.   740
    TAMAR. ¿Princesa soy amonita?
    AMÓN. Finge que en tu patria estoy,
y que a hablar contigo voy
al alcázar donde habita
tu padre el rey, que cercado   745
por el mío está afligido,
y yo, en tu amor encendido,
después de haberte avisado
que esta noche te he de ver,
entro atrevido y seguro   750
por un portillo del muro;
y tú, por corresponder
con mi amor, a recebirme
sales.
    TAMAR. Donosa aventura,
comienzo a hacer mi figura;   755
no haré poco en no reírme.

*Apártanse cada uno por su parte, y luego sale Amón, como que sale
de noche.*

I'm not your sister any more,
so you can woo for all you're worth.
Use what seductive guile you please.   725
You have one year to recover
while you've got me as your lover!

AMNON.   The medicine falls from your sweet lips!
My fate is in these healing hands!   (*Kisses her hands*)
Oh, beauty, Heaven—sent to soothe
my suffering heart!   Now I live
in hope to cure this mortal fire!

TAMAR.   Was that said to me as lover,   735
or only as Tamar?

AMNON.   Till now,
Tamar.   From now I speak to you
as to the mirror of my love.

TAMAR.   So now I cease to be Tamar?

AMNON.   Yes.   740

TAMAR.   I'm an Ammonite princess?

AMNON.   Imagine I'm in your country.
You father's palace endures
the siege of my father's army.   745
I have sent you a message
that I must see you tonight
and, burning with desire, have come
to speak with you.   With confident[40]
and courageous heart I enter —   750
a secret doorway in the wall.
You, to reciprocate my love,
come down to meet me.

TAMAR.   Sounds great fun.
I will compose my tragic face,[41]   755
though it'll be hard to keep it straight.

They go off into the wings.   Amnon enters as if groping in the dark.

AMÓN.　Entro, pues.　Arboles bellos
de este jardín, cuyas hojas
son ojos, que mis congojas
llora amor por todos ellos, 760
¿habéis visto a quien adoro?
Pero sí, visto la habéis,
pues el ámbar que vertéis,
condensado en gotas de oro,
de su vista le heredáis. 765
TAMAR.　¿Si habrá el Príncipe venido?
¿Sois vos mi bien?
AMÓN.　　　¿Que he adquirido
el blasón con que me honráis?
Dichoso mi amor mil veces.
TAMAR.　¿Venís solo?
AMÓN.　　　　No es discreto 770
el amor que no es secreto.
¿Cómo, amores, no me ofreces
esos brazos amorosos
que con mis suspiros merco,
pues que con los míos os cerco, 775
cielos de amor luminosos?
Zona soy que se corona
con los signos de oro bellos
de esos hermosos cabellos.
Estrellas son de esa zona 780
esos ojos; esas manos,
que al cristal envidia dan,
la vía láctea serán
de mis gustos soberanos.
Ay mis manos, que me abraso, (*Bésalas*) 785
si a los labios no os arrimo,
con que sus llamas reprimo.
Remediadme.
TAMAR.　Paso, paso,
que no os doy tanta licencia.
AMÓN.　¿Dícesme eso como a hermano, 790
o como a amante, que ufano
estoy loco en tu presencia?

AMNON.   So I make my entrance.   Oh, trees
of this fair garden, whose leaves
are like a thousand weeping eyes   760
that shed the tears of my despair!
Have you seen the one I love?
Ah, I see you have.   This amber
which falls like drops of golden rain
could only come from her sweet sight.   765
     TAMAR.   Is that my prince who comes this night?
Is it you, my love?
     AMNON.   My love?
Have I deserved this honour?
My love is fortunate indeed.
     TAMAR.   You've come alone?
     AMNON.   A secret love   770
demands discretion.   How is it
love offers me no loving arms
that I have paid for with my sighs?
Yet mine encircle you with love   775
like the shining spheres of Heaven.
My Heaven is crowned with the sign[42]
of your glorious golden hair,
that Heaven where your eyes are stars   780
and your hands, more pure than crystals,
are constellations that dictate
my sovereign desires ... These hands ...
I'll burn to death if I don't put
you to my lips and quench the flame. (*Kisses them*)
Oh, for God's sake, help me!
     TAMAR.   Gently,
gently, my lord!   I cannot give
you licence for such conduct.
     AMNON.   Was that   790
to me as brother or as suitor
for being beside myself with joy
at being beside you?

TAMAR.　Como a hermano y a galán,
que si de veras te abrasas,
las leyes de hermano pasas;　　　　　　795
y si favores te dan
ocasión de que así estés
la primera vez que vienes
a ver tu dama, no tienes
de medrar por descortés.　　　　　　800
Basta por agora esto.
¿Cómo te sientes?
AMÓN.　　　　　Mejor.
TAMAR.　Donosas burlas.
AMÓN.　　　　　　　De amor.
TAMAR.　Ya es sospechoso este puesto.
Vete.
AMÓN.　¿No eres tú mi hermana?　　　805
TAMAR.　El serlo recato pide.
AMÓN.　Como a galán me despide.
TAMAR.　Vaya, pues esto te sana.
AMÓN.　Adiós, dulce prenda.
TAMAR.　　　　　　　Adiós.
AMÓN.　¿Queréisme mucho?
TAMAR.　　　　　　　Infinito.　　810
AMÓN.　¿Y admitís mi amor?
TAMAR.　　　　　　Sí, admito.
AMÓN.　¿Quién es vuestro esposo?
TAMAR.　　　　　　　Vos.
AMÓN.　¿Vendré esta noche?
TAMAR.　　　　　　A las once.
AMÓN.　¿Olvidaréisme?
TAMAR.　　　　En mi vida.
AMÓN.　¿Quedáis triste?
TAMAR.　　　　　Enternecida.　　815
AMÓN.　¿Mudaréisos?
TAMAR.　　　　Seré bronce.
AMÓN.　¿Dormiréis?
TAMAR.　　　　Soñando en vos.
AMÓN.　¡Qué dicha!
TAMAR.　　　　¡Qué dulce sueño!
AMÓN.　Ay mi bien.

TAMAR.   To you both.
For if this passion is not feigned,
it goes beyond a brother's love.   795
And if a lady's favours make
you so discourteous a boor
when you first come to see her,
she'll send you packing through the door.   800
Enough for now.   How do you feel?
    AMNON.   A great deal better than before.
    TAMAR.   What a circus!
    AMNON.   And I'm love's clown!
    TAMAR.   You look suspicious kneeling down.[43]
Better go.
    AMNON.   Aren't you my sister?   805
    TAMAR.   We must be prudent even so.
    AMNON.   Say goodbye as a lover would.
    TAMAR.   Very well, if it does you good.
    AMNON.   Farewell, my precious jewel![44]
    TAMAR.   Farewell!
    AMNON.   Will you always love me?
    TAMAR.   I will!   810
    AMNON.   And let me adore you?
    TAMAR.   Oh, do!
    AMNON.   Who will be your betrothed?
    TAMAR.   Why, you!
    AMNON.   When shall I come?
    TAMAR.   Eleven tonight.
    AMNON.   Never forget me!
    TAMAR.   Never, my life.
    AMNON.   Sad to see me go?
    TAMAR.   Moved to tears.   815
    AMNON.   Will you be constant?
    TAMAR.   Through the years.
    AMNON.   Will you sleep?
    TAMAR.   But dreaming of you.
    AMNON.   What rapture!
    TAMAR.   Sweet dreams for me too.
    AMNON.   Ah, my sweet love!

TAMAR.   Ay caro dueño.
AMÓN.   Adiós, mis ojos.
TAMAR.   Adiós. (*Vase Amón*)   820

Ha estado escuchando esto Joab, y sale.

JOAB. Escuchando de aquí he estado,
aunque a mi pesar, finezas,
requiebros, gustos, ternezas
de un amor desatinado.
¿Usanse entre los hermanos,   825
aun de la gente perdida,
esto de mi bien, mi vida,
ceñir cuellos, besar manos?
¿Ay mi esposa, ay caro dueño?
¿Mudaráste? ¿Seré bronce?   830
¿Vendré esta noche? ¿A las once?
¿Soñaré en tí, dulce sueño?
No sé yo que haya señales
de una hermanada afición
como éstas, si ya no son,   835
Tamar, de hermanos carnales.
En pago de mis hazañas
pedirte al Rey pretendí;
por esta causa emprendí
dificultades extrañas.   840
El primero que asaltó,
a vista del campo hebreo,
con muerte del jebusëo,
muros en Sión fui yo.
Su capitán general   845
el Rey Profeta me hizo,
con que en parte satisfizo
mi pecho noble y leal.
En muestras de este deseo,
siempre que a la guerra fui,   850
partí, llegué, vi y vencí;
y agora llego, entro y veo
amores abominables,
ofensas de Dios, del Rey,

TAMAR.   Ah, my dear lord!
AMNON.   Farewell, light of my eyes!
TAMAR.   Goodbye. (*Amnon leaves*)

Enter Joab, who has been eavesdropping on this dialogue.

JOAB.   I could not help but overhear
your amorous conversation,
wooing, cooing, turtle−doving
like two perverted lovers.
Even in the lower classes,   825
do a sister and a brother
behave like that?   'My life', 'my love',
with fond embraces, kissing hands?
With 'my betrothed' and 'my dear lord'?
With 'I'll be constant through the years',   830
'see you at eleven tonight',
'dreaming of you with such sweet dreams'?
No brotherly love that I know
would manifest itself like this,   835
though there were no blood relation.
As recompense for services
to the king, I aspired to your hand.
For that same reason I undertook
some extraordinary exploits.   840
In full view of the Hebrew camp,
it was I who led the assault
on Zion's walls − the Jebusites⁴⁵
know this to their cost − after which   845
the Prophet king gave me command
of all his troops, which satisfied,
in part, my loyal and noble heart.
As a token of this great love,
every time I went to war,   850
I came and saw and conquered all
and now I come and what I see
are these perversions, an offence
to God, to your king, to your blood   855

de tu sangre, de tu ley,   855
y con efectos mudables,
olvidados mis servicios,
menospreciado mi amor,
mal pagado mi valor,
y de tu deshonra indicios.   860
Mas gracias a Dios que ha sido
en tiempo que queda en pie
mi honra. Desde hoy haré
altares al cuerdo olvido.
Al Rey diré lo que pasa,   865
como testigo de vista,
pues cuando extraños conquista,
afrentáis propios su casa.
Y mientras hace el olvido
en mi pecho habitación,   870
en el incestuoso Amón
tendrás hermano y marido.

Vase a ir, y tiénele Tamar.

TAMAR.   Oye, espera, Joab valiente,
ansí alargue Dios tus años,
que escuches los desengaños   875
de un amor sólo aparente.
Si a un loco que con furor
rey se finge, el que es discreto,
por librarse de un aprieto,
le va siguiendo el humor,   880
le intitula majestad,
cual vasallo se le humilla,
le habla hincada la rodilla,
y teme su autoridad;
con que su furia sosiega.   885
A que adviertas te provoco
que está Amón de amores loco,
y que de esta pasión ciega
ha de morir brevemente,
con que a mi padre ha de dar,   890
si no le mata el pesar,

and to your religion. I see
all my services forgotten,
with fickle change my love despised,
my gallantry ill recompensed
and your name stained with dishonour. 860
But, thank God, it has come in time
while mine is still intact. From today
I'll raise altars to common sense
and oblivion. I'll tell the king 865
the events that I have witnessed,
for while he conquers foreign soil
his kith and kin defile his house.
And while oblivion must seek
in my wounded heart for cover, 870
you can look for a husband
in your incestuous brother.

He tries to leave but is prevented by Tamar.

TAMAR. Wait! Listen! My brave Joab!
God give you patience and long life
to hear me out. The love you saw 875
was love only in appearance.
If a madman thinks he's a king,
the wise man, to save his skin, may
humour him, call him majesty, 880
humble himself like a vassal,
address him on his bended knee
and tremble at his power,
and with that placate his frenzy. 885
Now, I urge you to believe me,
Prince Amnon is mad. With love.
A love that will lead him blindfold
to an early grave and my father 890
to a bleak and sad old age, that is

vejez triste y inclemente.
Quiso a una dama amonita
que con los demás murió
cuando a Rábata asaltó   895
la venganza israëlita.
Tiénela en el alma impresa,
y la ama sin esperanza;
dice soy su semejanza,
y que si del mal me pesa   900
que le abrasa, finja ser
la que adora, y cuando venga
con amores le entretenga.
Es mi hermano; sé el poder
del ciego amor que le quema,   905
y para que poco a poco
aplaque el tiempo este loco,
sigo, como ves, su tema.
Mas pues resulta en tu daño
y en riesgo de mi opinión,   910
muérase mi hermano Amón,
y cese desde hoy tu engaño.
Si él ama, yo amo también
las partes de un capitán,
el más valiente y galán   915
que ha visto Jerusalén.
Pídeme a mi padre luego,
que otras hijas ha casado
con vasallos que no han dado
las muestras que en ti a ver llego.   920
Y no ofenda esta maraña
el valor de mi firmeza,
ni un amor en la corteza
que a un enfermo amante engaña.
¿Estás ya desenojado?   925
    JOAB.   Y juntamente corrido
de haber hoy tan necio sido
que tal de ti haya pensado.
Conozco tu discreción,
y tus virtudes no ignoro;   930
tu honesta hermosura adoro,

if sorrow does not kill him first.
He loved an Ammonite princess.
When Israel's vengeance struck Rabbah,   895
she died along with all the rest.
Her memory is branded on his soul
and he still loves it hopelessly.
He tells me I'm her double, that,
if I took pity on his plight,   900
I should pretend to be the one
he loves and, when he comes, I should
entertain him with lover's talk.
Well, he is my brother and I know
the hold of blind and stubborn love.   905
So, till time can calm the fever,
I humour him, as you have seen.
But if that harms you or risks
my reputation, then this game,   910
and your delusion, stops forthwith.
If Amnon dies, then he must die.
If he's in love, then so am I
with my bold captain, the bravest   915
man in all Jerusalem.See my father; request my hand.
He's married other daughters off
to commoners with less than half
the qualities I see in you.   920
But do not let this comedy,
this skin—deep passion which can fool
none but a madman sick with love,
do not, I pray, let it debase
the value of my loyalty.
There. Are you still angry with me?   925
    JOAB.   No, just ashamed that I thought this
of you. It was foolish of me.
I know your great discretion.
I am aware of your virtues.   930
I worship your chaste beauty

y celebro tu opinión.
No haya más celos ni enojos;
perdone a Joab Tamar,
que desde hoy jura no dar   935
crédito ni fe a sus ojos,
si ser tu esposo intereso.
    TAMAR. Será premio de mi amor.
    JOAB. En fe de aquese favor,
la mano hermosa te beso. (*Vase*)   940

Sale Amón cuando le besa la mano.

    AMÓN. Besar la mano donde el labio ha puesto
su Príncipe un vasallo es hecho aleve,
que el vaso se reserva donde bebe,
el caballo, el vestido, y el real puesto.
Como hermano es mi agravio manifiesto,   945
como amante a furor mi pecho mueve.
Idolo de mi amor, hermana leve,
¿tan presto atormentar, celos tan presto?
Como amante ofendido y como hermano,
a locura y venganza me provocas;   950
daré la muerte a tu Joab villano.
Y cuando niegues tus mudanzas locas,
desmentiráte tu besada mano,
pues por tener con qué, buscó dos bocas.
    TAMAR. Ya sea, Amón, tu hermana, ya tu dama,   955
aquélla verdadera, ésta fingida,
quimeras deja, tu pasión olvida,
que enferma porque tú sanes mi fama.
Si una difunta en mí busca tu llama,
diré que estoy para tu amor sin vida.   960
Si siendo hermana soy de tí oprimida,
razón es que aborrezca a quien me infama.
No me hables más palabras disfrazadas,
ni con engaños tu afición reboces
cuando Joab honesto amor pretenda.   965
Que andamos yo y tu dama muy pegadas,
y no sé yo cómo tu intento goces
sin que la una de las dos se ofenda. (*Vase*)

and your spotless reputation.
No more jealousy or anger.
I ask you to forgive your Joab
who swears he will not trust his eyes   935
from this day forth, if he would be
your husband.
    TAMAR.   That will be reward
enough for the love I bear you.
    JOAB.   For this favour I kiss your hand.   940

He kisses her hand and leaves.[46]   *Enter Amnon.*

    AMNON.   To kiss the hand his Prince's lips have touched
is an act of treason.   A prince's horse,
a prince's robes, the cup from which he drinks,
his royal place, are kept for him alone.
The insult to me as your brother is plain;   945
as lover, it stings my heart to fury.
Oh, fickle sister, idol of my love!
Teasing so soon?   And I so soon jealous?
Both as brother and offended lover,
you're driving me to madness and revenge.   950
I will kill that low—born slave, your Joab!
And please do not deny your fickle heart;
your twice—kissed hand will give the lie to that.[47]
    TAMAR.   Amnon, whether you see me as I am,   955
your sister, or as your imagined love,
this fantasy must stop, this passion end.
My good name lies sick just to make you well.
In me you seek a love that's dead and I
have no life to give you. If you offend   960
me as your sister, then I must hate you
as offender.   The love that Joab seeks
is true, so no more of your dissembling words,[48]
no more flirtations wrapped up in deceit.   965
Your mistress and I are too close allied.
I simply cannot see how you can have
your way with her without offence to me. (*Tamar leaves*)

AMÓN.   ¿Ansí te vas, homicida,
con palabras tan resueltas?   970
¿La venda a la herida sueltas
para que pierda la vida?
Pues yo te daré venganza,
cruel, mudable Tamar,
que en fin acabas en mar   975
por ser mar en la mudanza.
Que me abraso, ingratos cielos,
que me da muerte un rigor.

Sale Jonadab.

JONADAB.   ¿Qué es aquesto, gran señor?
AMÓN.   Mal de corazón, de celos.   980
JONADAB.   ¿Celos?   ¿No sabré yo acaso
de quién?
AMÓN. Sí, que pues me muero
no puedo callar, ni quiero.
Por Tamar de amor me abraso.
JONADAB.   ¿Qué dices?
AMÓN.   No me aconsejes,   985
dame muerte, que es mejor.
JONADAB.   Desatinado es tu amor;
mas para que no te quejes
de mi lealtad conocida,
tu pasión quiero aliviar.   990
Pierda su honra Tamar,
y no pierdas tú la vida.
Fíngete malo en la cama.
AMÓN.   No es mi tormento ficción.
JONADAB.   Disimula tu afición,   995
y al Rey que te adora llama.
Pídele que venga a darte
Tamar tu hermana a comer,
y cuando esté en tu poder,
no tengo que aconsejarte.   1000
Discreto eres, la ocasión
lo que has de hacer te dirá.

AMNON. She leaves me, just like that, for dead?
And with such unyielding words.   9 7 0
She unbinds the wound she has dressed
and cruelly lets me bleed to death?
Well, cruel, inconstant — as — the — sea [4 9]
Tamar, I will give you vengeance!   9 7 5
Cruel Heavens, my heart is on fire
and yet I feel the chill of death.

Enter Jonadab.

JONADAB. What's this, my lord?
AMNON.   An aching heart,
jealousy.   9 8 0
JONADAB. Jealousy? For whom
might I perhaps enquire?
AMNON.   You might.
When death stares him in the face,
a man does not disguise the truth.
My jealousy is for Tamar.
JONADAB. What, my lord?
AMNON.   Don't give me advice.   9 8 5
Give me death. It's preferable.
JONADAB. This love's sheer lunacy, of course.
But you'll have no cause for complaint
about my proven loyalty.
I shall alleviate your pain.   9 9 0
It's better that Tamar should lose
her honour than Amnon his life.
Pretend that you are ill in bed.
AMNON. This torture's real; it's no pretence.
JONADAB. But you must disguise your feelings.   9 9 5
The king loves you well, dotes on you.
So ask him as a special favour
to send Tamar to serve your food,
and once she's in your power ... well,
my advice need go no further.   1 0 0 0
You are an intelligent man;
the situation must dictate
your actions.

AMÓN.   En ese remedio está
mi vida o mi perdición.
Ve por mi padre.   ¿Qué aguardas?   1005
    JONADAB.   Como andas a tiento Amor,
no distingues de color,
ni a hermanos respeto guardas.   (*Vase*)
    AMÓN.   Si amor consiste sólo en semejanza
y tanto los hermanos se parecen   1010
que en sangre, en miembros y en valor merecen
igual correspondencia y alabanza,
¿qué ley impide lo que amor alcanza?
De Adán los mayorazgos nos ofrecen,
siendo hermanos, ejemplos que apetecen   1015
lo mismo que apetece mi esperanza.
Perdone, pues, la ley que mi amor priva,
vedando que entre hermanos se conserve,
que la ley natural en contra alego.
Amor, que es semejanza, venza y viva,   1020
que si la sangre, en fin, sin fuego hierve,
¿qué hará sangre que tiene tanto fuego?

Salen David, Jonadab y Eliazer.

    DAVID.   De que envíes a llamarme,
hijo, arrimo de mi vida,
ya mi tristeza se olvida,   1025
ya vuelves a consolarme.
Habla; no repares; pide.
    AMÓN.   Padre, mi flaqueza es tanta
que la muerte se adelanta
si tu favor no lo impide.   1030
No puedo comer bocado,
ni hay manjar tan exquisito
que alentando el apetito
mi salud vuelva a su estado.
Como el mal todo es antojos   1035
paréceme, padre, a mí,
que a venir Tamar aquí,
con sólo poner los ojos
y las manos en un pisto,

AMNON.   In that remedy
lies my ruin or salvation.
Fetch my father.   Why do you wait?   1005
    JONADAB.   They say love's blind and gropes its way
with no sense of shade or colour.
It can't even tell the difference
between a sister and a lover.   (*Exit*)
    AMNON.   If love consists in like attracting like [50]
and between a brother and a sister   1010
no distinction can be made, being in blood,
appearance and in merit equally
deserving of each other's devotion,
what law can prevent what love has decreed?
Adam's children offer us examples [51]   1015
of this same need that I am feeling now.
The law by which my passion stands condemned
must yield.   I hold to the law of Nature.
The love of like for like shall have its head.   1020
If blood, without the aid of fire, can boil,
veins so full of fire must not go unbled.

Enter David, Jonadab and Eliazer.

    DAVID.   That you have asked me to return,
my son, gives me consolation
and makes me forget my sadness.   1025
My life needs your love to lean on.
Speak without fear.   Ask what you will.
    AMNON.   Father, I feel so very weak
that I shall die before my time
if your love does not prevent it.   1030
There is nothing I can eat.   No dish
so exquisite that it can tempt
the appetite and restore my health.
I know this thing is in my mind,   1035
father, and yet I have this whim
that if Tamar would come to me,
merely by placing hand or eye

una sustancia o bebida, 1040
términos diera a la vida,
que ya de camino has visto.
¿Quiere, señor, vuestra Alteza,
concederme este favor?
    DAVID.   Poco pides a mi amor. 1045
Si ansí alivias tu tristeza,
Tamar vendrá diligente.
    AMÓN.   Beso tus pies.
    DAVID.   Eso es justo.
    AMÓN.   Guisa Tamar a mi gusto,
y entiéndelo solamente. 1050
    DAVID.   No le quiero dilatar,
voy a llamar a la Infanta. (*Vase*)
    AMÓN.   Eliazer, dime algo, canta,
si alivia a Amor el cantar.
    ELIAZER.   (*Canta*)
Cuando el bien que adoro 1055
los campos pisa,
madrugando el alba,
llora de risa.
Cuando los pies bellos
de mi niña hermosa 1060
pisan juncia y rosa,
ámbar cogen dellos;
va el campo a prendellos
con grillos de flores,
y muerta de amores, 1065
si el sol la avisa,
madrugando el alba,
llora de risa.

Sale Tamar con una toalla al hombro, y una escudilla de plata entre dos platos de lo mismo.

    TAMAR.   Mandóme el Rey mi señor
que a vuestra Alteza trujese 1070
de mi mano que comiese
porque conozco su humor.

on any sustenance or drink,   1040
or even on the humblest broth,
she would halt this fatal journey
that my life has undertaken.
Would Your Highness grant this favour?
    DAVID.   You ask but little of my love.   1045
If this can relieve your sadness,
Tamar shall come immediately.
    AMNON.   I kiss your feet.
    DAVID.   Then all is well.
    AMNON.   Only Tamar can cook to my taste.
Only she knows how.   1050
    DAVID.   Then I'll call
the princess without more delay. (*Exit*)
    AMNON.   Say something, Eliazer. Sing then.
Singing is supposed to soothe me.[52]
    ELIAZER.   *(Sings)* In the fields of early morning   1055
when my true love appears,
the dawn will rise to see her come
and smile with happy tears.

When my sweet girl steps lightly   1060
through the flowers with dainty toes,
she gives amber to the rushes
and perfume to the rose.

The daisies of the meadow
try to catch her in their chains
and, if the sun wakes up the dawn   1065
when my true love appears,
then it will rise to see her come
and smile with happy tears.

Enter Tamar with a towel over her shoulder and carrying a silver
bowl between two silver plates.

    TAMAR.   My lord the king commanded me
to bring food to Your Royal Highness,   1070
that you may eat from my own hand.
Yet since I know your humour, Prince,[53]

Ya no tendrá buen sabor
si de gusto no ha mudado,
porque aunque yo lo he guisado,   1075
si llaman gracia a la sal,
yo vendré, Príncipe, tal
que no estará sazonado.
    AMÓN.   Jonadab, salte allá afuera;
cierra la puerta, Eliazer,   (*Vanse éstos*)   1080
que a solas quiero comer
manjares que el alma espera.
    TAMAR.   Lo que haces considera.
    AMÓN.   No hay ya que considerar.
Tú sola has de ser manjar   1085
del alma a quien avarienta
tanto ha que tienes hambrienta,
pudiéndola sustentar.
    TAMAR.   Caro hermano, que harto caro
me saldrás si eres cruel,   1090
príncipe eres de Isräel;
todos están en tu amparo.
Mi honra es espejo claro
donde me remiro y precio;
no sufrirá su desprecio   1095
si le procuras quebrar,
ni tú otro nombre ganar
que de amante torpe y necio.
Tu sangre soy.
    AMÓN.   Ansí te amo.
    TAMAR.   Sosiega.
    AMÓN.   No hay sosegar.   1100
    TAMAR.   ¿Qué quieres?
    AMÓN.   Tamar, amar.
    TAMAR.   Detente.
    AMÓN.   Soy Amón, amo.
    TAMAR.   ¿Si llamo al Rey?
    AMÓN.   A Amor llamo.
    TAMAR.   ¿A tu hermana?
    AMÓN.   Amores gusto.
    TAMAR.   Traidor.
    AMÓN.   No hay amor injusto.   1105

this dish, though cooked by my own hand,
cannot have much salt or savour   1075
for you, unless your tastes have changed.
And I, Prince, am in no humour
to provide the seasoning. 54
    AMNON. Outside, my friends, and close the door.   1080

Jonadab and Eliazer leave.

I feel a hunger in my soul.
I wish to eat this meal alone.
    TAMAR.   Consider what you are doing.
    AMNON.   There is no more to consider.
You have denied my soul too long.
You are the food and you alone   1085
can serve it.
    TAMAR.   Dearest brother, stop!
If you don't, that name will surely   1090
cost me dear. You are Israel's prince.
All are under your protection.
My honour is the untarnished
mirror of my self—respect.
It will not bear this infamy   1095
if you try to break it and all
you will gain is degradation.
I am your blood. 55
    AMNON.   I want you so.
    TAMAR. My lord, be calm.
    AMNON.   There is no calm.   1100
    TAMAR. What do you want?
    AMNON.   To love Tamar.
    TAMAR. Amnon, please stop!
    AMNON.   Love cannot stop.
    TAMAR. I'll call the king!
    AMNON.   And I on Love!
    TAMAR. For your sister's sake!
    AMNON.   For Love's sake!
    TAMAR. Traitor!
    AMNON.   Love knows no treachery!   1105

TAMAR.	¿Tu ley?	
AMÓN.		Para amor no hay ley.
TAMAR.	¿Tu Rey?	
AMÓN.		Amor es mi Rey.
TAMAR.	¿Tu honor?	
AMÓN.		Mi honor es mi gusto.

Fin de la segunda jornada

Nathan admonishing David

TAMAR.   To Israel's law!
AMNON.   Love has no law!
TAMAR.   To your king!
AMNON.   Love is my king!
TAMAR.   Your honour!
AMNON.   My honour is a whore!

End of Act II

Amnon and Tamar

JORNADA TERCERA

Sale Amón echando a empellones a Tamar, y Eliazer y Jonadab.

AMÓN. Vete de aquí, salte fuera,
veneno en taza dorada,
sepulcro hermoso de fuera,
arpía que en rostro agrada,
siendo una asquerosa fiera.   5
Al basilisco retratas,
ponzoña mirando arrojas;
no me mires que me matas,
vete, monstruo, que me aojas,
y mi juventud maltratas.   1 0
¿Que yo te quise es posible?
¿Que yo te tuve afición?
Fruta de Sodoma horrible,
en la médula carbón
si en la corteza apacible,   1 5
sal fuera, que eres horror
de mi vida y su escarmiento.
Vete, que me das temor.
Más es mi aborrecimiento
que fue mi primero amor.   2 0
Hola, echádmela de aquí.
TAMAR. Mayor ofensa y injuria
es la que haces contra mí,
que fue la amorosa furia
de tu torpe frenesí.   2 5
Tirano de aquese talle,
doblar mi agravio procura,
hasta que pueda vengalle.
Mujer gozada es basura.
Haz que me echen en la calle,   3 0
ya que ansí me has deshonrado;
lama el plato en que has comido
un perro al suelo arrojado;
di que se ponga el vestido
que has roto ya algún criado;   3 5
honra con tales despojos,

ACT III

*Enter Amnon violently ejecting Tamar from his room.   Eliazer and
Jonadab follow.*

AMNON.   Get out of here!   Out I said!   Out!
You poison in a golden cup!
So beautiful on the outside,
yet putrid as the grave within!
You vile and loathesome animal,   5
you harpy with an angel's face!
Don't look at me, you basilisk![1]
There's venom in your eyes and death.
Their evil gaze has maimed my life.
Away!   How could I have loved you!   1 0
Felt desire?   Vile fruit of Sodom,[2]
silky on the surface and ashes
at the core!   Get away from me!
Out!   You fill me with revulsion!   1 5
I'll never look on you again!
I dread your eyes upon me!   Go!
My hatred's stronger than my love
ever was.   Servants, throw her out!   2 0
TAMAR.   With this you do me greater wrong[3]
than brutish lust could ever do.
You are the tyrant of this body,   2 5
so go on, pile on the insults,
till my time comes and I avenge them!
A woman who's been used is dross,
so have them throw me in the street.   3 0
You've dishonoured me, so why not?
Fling me to the ground and let dogs
lick the plate from which you have fed!
This dress that you have torn, give it[4]
to some servant and honour him   3 5
with the spoils of your victory,

a quien se empleó en servirte,
y a mí dame más enojos.
    AMÓN. ¡Quién por no verte ni oírte
sordo naciera y sin ojos!   40
¿No te quieres ir, mujer?
    TAMAR. ¿Dónde iré sin honra, ingrato,
ni quién me querrá acoger,
siendo mercader sin trato
deshonrada una mujer?   45
Haz de tu hermana más cuenta,
ya que de ti no la has dado.
No añadas afrenta a afrenta,
que en cadenas del pecado
perece quien las aumenta.   50
Tahur de mi honor has sido,
ganado has por falso modo
joyas que en vano te pido.
Quítame la vida y todo,
pues yo lo más he perdido.   55
No te levantes tan presto,
pues es mi pérdida tanta
que aunque el que pierde es molesto,
el noble no se levanta
mientras en la mesa hay resto.   60
Resto hay de la vida, ingrato,
pero es vida sin honor,
y ansí de perderla trato.
Acaba el juego, traidor;
dame la muerte en barato.   65
    AMÓN. Infierno ya no de fuego,
pues helando me atormentas,
sierpe, monstruo, vete luego.
    TAMAR. El que pierde sufre afrentas
porque le mantengan juego;   70
mantenme juego, tirano,
hasta acabar de perder
lo que queda. Alza, villano,
la mano, quítame el ser,
y ganarás por la mano.   75
    AMÓN. ¿Vióse tormento como éste?

in payment for his services!
But just give me more anger!
   AMNON. Oh, that I'd been born blind and deaf
so as not to see or hear you!   40
Will you not go!
   TAMAR.   Oh, treachery!
And where shall I go dishonoured?
A woman without her honour   45
is a merchant without barter.
So who will take me in exchange?
Listen to your sister, since you
have failed to listen to yourself.
Do not heap insult on contempt.
With every sin you add a chain   50
and you will die in bondage.
You have gambled with my honour.[5]
You've played me false, robbed a jewel
which, though I beg, you can't restore.
So take my life; I've lost the rest.   55
No. Don't get up from the table!
Losers can be a bore, I know,
but stay; I've lost so much, why not?
An honest gambler does not leave
while there's still money in the pot!   60
I still have my life, you traitor,
but since it's life with no honour,
I'm throwing it away. Finish
the game, traitor! Let my death be
your winner's generosity![6]   65
   AMNON. So, fire and brimstone turn to ice.
Now you're the serpent that torments.[7]
Fiend, get out of here!
   TAMAR.   A loser
takes all the insults just to stay   70
in the game. Keep me in the game
till I've lost all that I have left.
Raise your hand, butcher. Strike me dead.
Get your blow in and stay ahead.   75
   AMNON. Was there ever a rack like this?

Hola, ¿no hay ninguno ahí?
¡Que esto un desatino cueste!

Salen Eliazer y Jonadab.

    ELIAZER.   ¿Llamas?
    AMÓN.   Echadme de aquí
esta víbora, esta peste.   80
    ELIAZER.   ¿Víbora?   ¿Peste?   ¿Qué es de ella?
    AMÓN.   Llevadme aquesta mujer;
cerrad la puerta tras ella.
    JONADAB.   Carta Tamar viene a ser;
leyóla, y quiere rompella.   85
    AMÓN.   Echalda en la calle.
    TAMAR.   Ansí
estará bien, que es razón,
ya que el delito fue aquí,
que por ellas dé un pregón
mi deshonra contra tí.   90
    AMÓN.   Voyme por no te escuchar.   *(Vase)*
    JONADAB.   Extraño caso, Eliazer,
¿tal odio tras tanto amar?
    TAMAR.   Presto, villano, has de ver
la venganza de Tamar.   *(Vanse)*   95

Salen Absalón y Adonías.

    ABSALÓN.   Si no fueras mi hermano, o no estuvieras
en palacio, ambicioso, brevemente
hoy con la vida, bárbaro, perdieras
el deseo atrevido y imprudente.
    ADONÍAS.   Si en tus venas la sangre no tuvieras   100
con que te honró mi padre indignamente,
yo hiciera que quedándose vacías,
de púrpura calzaran a Adonías.
    ABSALÓN.   ¿Tú pretendes reinar, loco, villano?
¿Tú, muerto Amón del mal que le consume,   105
subir al trono aspiras soberano
que en doce tribus su valor resume?
¿Que soy, no sabes, tu mayor hermano?

Ho, there!   Are there no servants here?
To think that madness costs so dear!

Enter Eliazer and Jonadab.

ELIAZER.   You called?
AMNON.   Throw out this pestilence!
This viper!   80
ELIAZER.   Viper?   Pestilence?
What's she done?
AMNON.   Remove this woman
and lock the door behind her!
JONADAB.   Tamar came just like a letter.
He's read her, now he tears her up.   85
AMNON.   Throw her in the gutter!
TAMAR.   That's fine!
The deed was done here in private,
but from the gutter I'll proclaim
my dishonour and your shame!   90
AMNON.   I will not hear another word!   *(Exit)*
JONADAB.   It's most strange.   After so much love,
who'd think that hate could go so far?
TAMAR.   You may not hear, but soon your eyes
will see the vengeance of Tamar.   *(Exit)*   95

Enter Absolom and Adonijah.

ABSOLOM.   If you were not my brother and we were
not here in the palace, you would soon lose
that bold and brash ambition, my proud friend,
together with your life.
ADONIJAH.   And if your veins   100
did not run with blood unworthily bequeathed
by my father, then I would drain them dry.
My feet would stand in pools of purple dye. 8
ABSOLOM.   You presume to rule?   A madman?   Peasant?
You think, if Amnon dies, you can ascend 9   105
the sovereign throne that shields a dozen tribes?
I am your elder.   Or don't you know that?

¿Quién competir con Absalón presume,
a cuyos pies ha puesto la ventura   110
el valor, la riqueza y la hermosura?
   ADONÍAS. Si el reino isräelita se heredara
por el más delicado, tierno y bello,
(aunque no soy yo monstruo en cuerpo y cara),
a tu yugo humillara el reino el cuello;   115
cada tribu hechizado se enhilara
en el oro de Ofir de tu cabello,
y convirtiendo hazañas en deleites,
te pecharan en cintas y en afeites.
Redujeras a damas tu consejo,   120
a trenzas tu corona, y a un estrado
el solio de tu ilustre padre viejo,
las armas a la holanda y al brocado.
Por escudo tomaras un espejo,
y de tu misma vista enamorado,   125
en lugar de la espada a que me aplico,
esgrimieras tal vez el abanico.
Mayorazgo te dio naturaleza
con que los ojos de Isräel suspendes.
El cielo ha puesto renta en tu cabeza,   130
pues sus madejas a las damas vendes,
cada año haciendo esquilmos tu belleza
cuando aliviarla de su peso entiendes;
repartiendo por tiendas su tesoro,
se compran en doscientos siclos de oro.   135
De tu belleza ser el rey procura;
déjame a mí a Isräel, que haces agravio
a tu delicadeza, a tu blandura.
   ABSALÓN. Cierra, villano, el atrevido labio.
Que el reino se debía a la hermosura,   140
a pesar de tu envidia, dijo un sabio,
señal que es noble el alma que está en ella,
que el huésped bello habita en casa bella.
Cuando mi padre al enemigo asalta,
no me quedo en la corte dando al ocio   145
lascivos años, ni el valor les falta
que con mis hechos quilatar negocio.
Mi acero incircuncisa sangre esmalta;

You think you can compete with Absolom?
My feet tread paths of destiny which gave   110
me valour, wealth and beauty.
    ADONIJAH.   If the throne
of Israel passed to the weakest in line,
to the softest skin and prettiest face
(though I'm not one of Nature's freaks myself),
the whole kingdom would bow its neck to you.   115
All the tribes would be united with magic
threads from your golden hair and, exchanging[10]
deeds of war for frivolities of peace,
would send you tithes of ribbons and cosmetics.
Your council would be a clutch of women,   120
your crown a ring of plaited hair and your
illustrious father's throne a boudoir.
For armour, you'd wear linen and brocade.
For a shield, you would grasp your looking glass
and fall in love with your own reflection   125
and, whereas I prefer to use a sword,
you would no doubt repel me with your fan!
Mother Nature's given you a birthright
on which all Israelites gaze in wonder.
Heaven has placed a fortune on your head   130
which, to ease the weight, you harvest every year
and hawk your treasure round the ladies' tents.
Two hundred gold shekels a skein, I'm told!   135
You concentrate on being a beauty queen
and leave me to be Israel's king instead.
A monarch's crown might bruise that dainty head![11]
    ABSOLOM. Hold your impudent tongue, you peasant dog!
Despite your envy, a wise man once said   140
that beauty was the soul of government.
A noble form denotes a noble heart
and beauty does not dwell in ugliness.[12]
When my father attacks his enemies,
I do not idle at the court, debauch   145
my youth away. My record of courage,
my actions, are there to back my claim.
My blade is bright with uncircumcised blood.

la guerra que jubila al sacerdocio
en mis hazañas enseñar procura   1 5 0
cuán bien dice el valor con la hermosura.
¿Mas, para qué lo que es tan cierto he puesto
en duda con razones? Haga alarde
la espada contra quien te has descompuesto
si, porque soy hermoso, soy cobarde.   1 5 5
    ADONÍAS. Por adorno, no más, te la habrás puesto.
No la saques, ansí el amor te guarde,
que te desmayarás si la ves fuera.
    ABSALÓN. Si no saliera el Rey ...
    ADONÍAS.   Si no saliera ...

Salen el Rey David, y Salomón.

    DAVID. Bersabé, vuestra madre, me ha pedido   1 6 0
por vos, mi Salomón. Creced, sed hombre,
que si amado de Dios sois y querido,
conforme significa vuestro nombre,
yo espero en el que al trono real subido
futuros siglos vuestra fama asombre.   1 6 5
    SALOMÓN. Vendráme, gran señor, esa alabanza
por ser de vos retrato y semejanza.
    DAVID. ¿Príncipes?
    ABSALÓN.   ¿Gran señor?
    DAVID.   ¿En qué se entiende?
    ADONÍAS. La paz ocupa el tiempo en novedades;
galas la mocedad al gusto vende,   1 7 0
si el desengaño a la vejez verdades.
    ABSALÓN. La caza que del ocio nos defiende
nos convida a correr sus soledades.
Esta trazamos, y tras ella fiestas.
    DAVID. Válgame Dios, ¿qué voces serán éstas?   1 7 5

Sale Tamar descabellada y de luto.

    TAMAR. Gran Monarca de Isräel,
descendiente del león,
que para vengar injurias
dio a Judá el viejo Jacob,

Though battlefields are no place for preachers,
my exploits are like sermons in action,   150
living proof that beautiful can be brave.
But why discredit truth with arguments?
You've shown me your temper, now show me your sword.
We'll see if beauty has a chicken's heart!   155
    ADONIJAH. The Good Lord save us, don't take out your sword!
You only wear it for decoration,
the sight of naked steel might make you faint!
    ABSOLOM. Here comes the king. If not ...
    ADONIJAH.   If not, then what?

Enter King David and Solomon.

    DAVID. Your mother, Bathsheba, has made requests   160
on your behalf, Solomon, my boy.
Grow to your manhood and, if God loves you,
as your name implies, it shall be written[13]
on Israel's throne, and centuries to come[14]
shall marvel at your glory.   165
    SOLOMON.   Such praise, sire,
can only be my due as one fashioned
in your image.
    DAVID.   Princes?
    ABSOLOM.   Sire?
    DAVID.   What's afoot?
    ADONIJAH. Oh, frivolous pursuits of peacetime, sire.
Youth squanders its wealth on life and pleasure;   170
and old age repays the debt at leisure.
    ABSOLOM. A hunt is what we were planning, my lord.
A fast gallop through the wilds of nature
keeps idleness at bay. And then a feast.
    DAVID. Heaven preserve us! What's all this shouting? 175

Enter Tamar with dishevelled hair and dressed in mourning.[15]

    TAMAR. Great king of Israel, descendant
of the lion that Jacob gave[16]
to Judah to avenge its wrongs,   180

si lágrimas, si suspiros,   180
si mi compasiva voz,
si lutos, si menosprecios
te mueven a compasión,
y cuando aquesto no baste,
si el ser hija tuya yo,   185
a que castigues te incita
al que tu sangre afrentó,
por los ojos vierto el alma,
luto traigo por mi honor,
suspiros al cielo envío   190
de inocencias vengador.
Cubierta está mi cabeza
de ceniza, que un amor
desatinado, si es fuego,
sólo deja en galardón   195
cenizas que lleva el aire.
Mas aunque cenizas son,
no quitarán mancha de honra,
sangre sí, que es buen jabón.
La mortal enfermedad   200
del torpe Príncipe Amón
peste de la honra fue;
pegóme su contagión.
Que le guisase mandaste
alguna cosa a sabor   205
de su postrado apetito.
Ponzoña fuera mejor.
Sazonéle una sustancia,
mas las sustancias no son
de provecho si se oponen   210
accidentes de afición.
Estaba el hambre en el alma,
y en mi desdicha guisó
su desvergüenza mi agravio.
Sazonóle la ocasión,   215
y sin advertir mis quejas
ni el proponelle que soy
tu hija, Rey, y su hermana,
su estado, su ley, su Dios,

if my tears, sighs, lamentations,
if my grief and humiliation
can stir the pity in your heart
or, if that were not enough,
the fact that I am your daughter,   185
punish one who has stained your blood.
I'm in mourning for my honour,
I shed my soul through weeping eyes.   190
As avenger of the innocent,
to Heaven I direct my sighs.
My head is covered with ashes[17]
— that's all lust leaves as its reward —   195
burnt—out ash that blows in the wind.
But ashes cannot wash the stain
on honour. Blood is the only soap.
Vile Prince Amnon's mortal illness   200
was a plague that ravaged honour
and I have been infected.
You ordered me to cook him food
to tempt his jaded appetite.   205
I wish I'd given him poison!
I made, with all its seasoning,
a bowl of good, substantial broth.[18]
But what's the use of wholesome food   210
when it's the palate that is sick?
His was a hunger of the mind.
It was he who did the cooking,
fried my honour and self—respect
on the fire of his lechery!
Chance gave edge to his appetite   215
and, heedless of my cries, heedless
of his status, his law, his God,

echando la gente fuera
a puerta cerrada entró
en el templo de la fama
y sagrado del honor.
Aborrecióme ofendida;
no me espanto, que al fin son
enemigas declaradas
la esperanza y posesión.
Echóme injuriosamente
de su casa el violador,
oprobios por gustos dando,
paga, en fin, de tal señor.
Deshonrada por sus calles
tu corte mi llanto oyó;
sus piedras se compadecen,
cubre sus rayos el sol
entre nubes por no ver
caso tan fiero y atroz.
Todos te piden justicia;
justicia, invicto señor.
Dirás que es Amón tu sangre;
el vicio la corrumpió.
Sángrate de ella si quieres
dejar vivo tu valor.
Hijos tienes herederos,
semejanza tuya son
en el esfuerzo y virtudes.
No dejes por sucesor
quien deshonrando a su hermana
menoscabe tu opinión,
pues mejor afrentará
los que sus vasallos son.
Ea, sangre generosa
de Abrahán, si su valor
contra el inocente hijo
el cuchillo levantó,
uno tuvo, muchos tienes,
inocente fue, Amón no.
A Dios sirvió ansí Abrahán,
ansí servirás a Dios;

220

225

230

235

240

245

250

255

of the fact that I'm your daughter
and his sister, he sent his men   220
out of the room, he locked the door
and defiled the inner sanctum
of honour and reputation.
Once he'd had his way, he loathed me.
Should that surprise me? After all,   225
possession is the enemy
of desire. So he threw me out,
with insults. The violator
repays his pleasure with contempt.   230
A man like that can give no more.
I dragged my shame through city streets[19]
and people heard my cries. The stones
took pity on me and the sun
covered up its eyes with clouds   235
so as not to see. Demanding
justice, all of them, justice, sire.
You may say Amnon's blood is yours,   240
but blood that's rank with infamy
must be let, if not your glory
will surely die. Your sons and heirs,
in courage as in rectitude,
should be fashioned in your image.   245
Do not leave as your successor[20]
one who soils his sister's honour
and tarnishes his father's name,
for how much more would such a man   250
abuse those who are his vassals.
Show that noble blood of Abraham!
He raised his knife against his child.[21]   255
You have many, he only one;
his was innocent, not Amnon.
That's how Abraham served his God
and that's how you will serve him too.

véncete Rey a ti mismo,   260
la justicia a la pasión
se anteponga, que es más gloria
que hacer piezas al león.
Hermanos, pedid conmigo
justicia; bello Absalón,   265
un padre nos ha engendrado,
una madre nos parió.
A los demás no les cabe
de mi deshonra y baldón
sino sola la mitad;   270
mis medios hermanos son,
vos lo sois de padre y madre;
entera satisfacción
tomad, o en eterna afrenta
vivid sin fama desde hoy.   275
Padre, hermanos, israelitas,
calles, puertas, cielos, sol,
brutos, peces, aves, plantas,
elementos, campos, Dios,
justicia os pido a todos de un traidor,   280
de su ley y su hermana violador.
    DAVID.   Alzad, Infanta, del suelo.
Llamadme al Príncipe Amón.
¿Esto es, cielos, tener hijos?
Mudo me deja el dolor;   285
hablad, ojos, si podéis,
sentid mi mal, lenguas sois;
lágrimas serán palabras
que expliquen al corazón.
Rey me llama la justicia,   290
padre me llama el amor,
uno obliga y otro impele;
¿cuál vencerá de los dos?
    ABSALÓN.   Hermana, nunca lo fueras.
Da lugar a la razón;   295
pues no le halla la venganza,
freno a tus lágrimas pon.
Amón es tu hermano y sangre,
a sí mismo se afrentó.

You must supress your feelings, sire.   260
Justice must outweigh affection.
There is more true glory in that
than tearing lions limb from limb.²²
Brothers, cry with me for justice!
Fair Absolom, the same father   265
gave us life and the same mother²³
bore us in her womb.   All the rest,
half—brothers, share but half my shame.   270
You, my blood brother, take it all.
So take your full revenge or live
with dishonour from this day forth.   275
I call on you: father, brothers,
men of Israel, the streets and gates
of this city, beasts of its fields,
fish of the sea and birds of the air,
flowers of the earth, the sun, the sky
and all the elements, God Himself,
to give me justice on a traitor,   280
this violator of his law
and his sister's name.
   DAVID.   Rise, my child.
Let Prince Amnon be called at once.
Is it for this we raise children?
I cannot speak the pain I feel.   285
These eyes must speak and be the tongues,
my tears must be the feeling words
that give expression to my heart.
Justice calls me, as I'm your king.   290
As his father, love compels me.
Between love and obligation,
which one should prevail?
   ABSOLOM.   My sister,
though I wish to God you were not,
it's your reason that must prevail.   295
Vengeance is no way.   Dry your eyes.
Amnon is your brother.   Your flesh
and blood are also his and so
he offended against himself.

Puertas adentro se quede   300
mi agravio y tu deshonor.
Mi hacienda está en Efraín,
granjas tengo en Bahalasor;
casas fueron de placer,
ya son casas de dolor.   305
Vivirás conmigo en ellas,
que mujer sin opinión
no es bien que en cortes habite,
muerta su reputación.
Vamos a ver si los tiempos   310
tan sabios médicos son,
que con remedios de olvido
dan alivio a tu dolor.
   TAMAR.   Bien dices; viva entre fieras
quien entre hombres se perdió,   315
que a estar con ellas yo sé
que no muriera mi honor. (*Vase*)
   ABSALÓN. (*Aparte*) Incestüoso tirano,
presto cobrará Absalón,
quitándote vida y reino,   320
debida satisfacción. (*Vase*)
   ADONÍAS. A tan portentoso caso
no hay palabras, no hay razón
que aconsejen y consuelen.
Triste y confuso me voy. (*Vase*)   325
   SALOMÓN. La Infanta es hermana mía,
del Príncipe hermano soy;
la afrenta de Tamar siento;
temo el peligro de Amón.
El Rey es santo y prudente;   330
el suceso causa horror.
Más vale dar con el tiempo
lugar a la admiración. (*Vase*)

Sale temeroso Amón, y David esté llorando.

   AMÓN. El Rey mi señor me llama.
¿Iré ante el Rey mi señor?   335
¿Su cara osaré mirar

The affront to me and your disgrace 300
must not transgress beyond these walls.
I have an estate in the land
of Ephraim, farms in Baal—hazor;
places meant for recreation
will be for suffering and tears. 305
You will come and live there with me.
A woman without reputation
cannot live at court. We shall see
if time, like a shrewd physician, 310
can heal the wound with remedies
of obscurity.
    TAMAR.   You are right.
One whom the world of men destroyed 315
had better live with beasts. With them,
I know, honour would have survived. *(Exit)*
    ABSOLOM. *(Aside)* ·From you, my incestuous Prince,
soon Absolom will get his due,
by taking from you Israel's crown [24] 320
after first removing you. *(Exit)*
    ADONIJAH. For such a monstruous crime as this
there are no words, no rational
advice to counsel or console.
Sad and distraught, I take my leave. *(Exit)*
    SOLOMON. As brother to the princess, [25]
I feel the wrong that has been done.
As brother to the Prince I fear
for Amnon's life. The crime fills me
with the utmost horror and yet
the king's a prudent, holy man. 330
Better to stand aside in awe
and leave the judgement to time's law. *(Exit)*

Fearfully Amnon enters. David is weeping.

    AMNON. *(Aside)* My lord the king has summoned me.
Shall I dare to go before him? 335
How shall I look into his eyes

sin vergüenza ni temor?
Temblando estoy a la nieve
de aquellas canas, que son
los pecados frías cenizas   340
del fuego que encendió amor.
¡Qué animoso antes del vicio
anda siempre el pecador!
¡Cometido, qué cobarde!
    DAVID. ¿Príncipe?
    AMÓN.   A tus pies estoy.   345

De rodillas, lejos.

    DAVID. (*Aparte*) ¿No ha de poder la justicia
aquí más que la afición?
Soy padre; también soy Rey.
Es mi hijo; fue agresor.
Piedad sus ojos me piden,   350
la Infanta satisfacción.
Prenderéle en escarmiento
de este insulto. Pero no;
levántase de la cama;
de su pálido color   355
sus temores conjeturo.
¿Pero qué es de mi valor?
¿Qué dirá de mí Isräel
con tan necia remisión?
Viva la justicia y muera   360
el Príncipe violador.
¿Amón?
    AMÓN. Amoroso padre.
    DAVID. El alma me traspasó;
padre amoroso me llama,
socorro pide a mi amor.   365
Pero muera. ¿Cómo estás?

Vuelve a él furioso, y en viéndole se enternece.

    AMÓN. Piadoso padre, mejor.
    DAVID. En mirándole es de cera

without fear or shame? I tremble
at the sight of those grey hairs.
Our sins are like the cold ashes   340
of the fires lit by passion.
How full of lusty energy
is the sinner before the sin!
Once done, how full of craven fear!
    DAVID. Amnon?
    AMNON.   Sire, I kneel at your feet.   345

He kneels some distance away.

    DAVID. *(Aside)* And should not justice overrule
my love in this? I am a king
before I am a father. My son,
but guilty of violation.
His eyes beg for mercy, but hers   350
demanded justice and redress.
I'll arrest him for this outrage
as a warning and example.
But no. The boy's scarcely risen
from his bed. In his pallid cheeks   355
I see the fear that's in his heart.
And my own brave heart? What of that?
What would Israel say of me
if I showed such foolish weakness?
So let right prevail. The rapist   360
must die. Amnon!
    AMNON.   Loving father ...
    DAVID. Loving father he calls me.
That word pierces me to the heart.
He seeks refuge in my love. Yet   365
he must die.

He turns angrily towards him, but is moved on seeing him.[26]

         How are you, my son?
    AMNON. Better, most merciful father.
    DAVID. His face is like a sun that turns
all my wrath to wax. The just Lord

mi enojo, y su cara es sol.
El adulterio homicida   370
con ser Rey me perdonó
el justo Juez, porque dije
un pequé de corazón.
Venció en él a la justicia
la piedad. Su imagen soy.   375
El castigo es mano izquierda,
mano es derecha el perdón.
Pues ser izquierdo es defeto.
Mirad, Príncipe, por vos;
cuidad de vuestro regalo,   380
¡Ay prenda del corazón!   (*Vase*)

Levántase Amón.

AMÓN.   Oh poderosas hazañas
del amor, único Dios,
que hoy a David ha vencido,
siendo Rey y vencedor.   385
Que mirase por mí dijo;
blandamente me avisó.
El castigo del prudente
es la tácita objeción;
temió darme pesadumbre.   390
Por entendido me doy;
yo pagaré amor tan grande
con no ofendelle desde hoy.   (*Vase*)

Sale Absalón solo.

ABSALÓN.   ¿Que una razón no le dijo
en señal de sus enojos?   395
¿Ni un severo mirar de ojos?
Hija es Tamar, si él es hijo.
Mas no importa, que ya elijo
la justa satisfacción
que a mi padre la pasión   400
de amor ciega, pues no ve.
Con su muerte cumpliré

forgave me, though I was a king,
for adultery and murder[27]   370
because I said with all my heart
'Father I have sinned'. In Him[28]
mercy triumphed over justice
and I, who am His image,   375
must do the same. I hold the scales:
retribution in my left hand,
forgiveness in my right, but since[29]
left is sinister, defective,
let the right outweigh. Look, my prince,
to yourself; guard your privilege.   380
Ah, my dear boy, my dearest heart! (*Exit*)

Amnon rises.

AMNON. Oh, the marvellous power of love[30]
— true love that is the only God —
that has today subdued the power
of David, the all—conquering king!   385
'Look to yourself, my son', he said.
It was a gentle warning,
an unspoken rebuke which is
the wise man's punishment, and yet
he feared to leave me with remorse.   390
Well I understand his meaning
and that great love I shall repay
and sin no more against him
from this day. (*Exit*)

Enter Absolom alone.

ABSOLOM. Not a word of anger? Not one
harsh look of censure in his eyes?   395
Tamar is as much a daughter
as he is son; but no matter.
I choose the path of just redress
which my fond father cannot see,
blinded as he is by passion.   400
With Amnon's death I shall fulfil

su justicia y mi ambición.
No es bien que reine en el mundo
quien no reina en su apetito.   405
En mi dicha y su delito
todo mi derecho fundo.
Hijo soy del Rey segundo;
ya por sus culpas primero.
Hablar a mi padre quiero   410
y del sueño despertalle
con que ha podido hechizalle
amor siempre lisonjero.
Aquí está, ¿pero qué es esto?

Tira una cortina, y descubre un bufete, y sobre él una fuente,
y en ella una corona de oro de rey.

¿La corona en una fuente   415
con que ciñe la real frente
mi padre grave y compuesto?
La mesa el plato me ha puesto
que ha tanto que he deseado.
Debo de ser convidado;   420
si el reinar es tan sabroso,
como afirma el ambicioso,
no es de perder tal bocado.
Amón no os ha de gozar,
cerco en quien mi dicha encierro,   425
que sois vos de oro, y fue yerro
el que deshonró a Tamar.
Mi cabeza quiero honrar
con vuestro círculo bello.
Mas rehusaréis el hacello,   430
pues aunque en ella os encumbre,
temblaréis de que os deslumbre
el oro de mi cabello. (*Corónase*)
Bien me estáis; vendréisme ansí
nacida, y no digo mal,   435
pues nací de sangre real,

his justice and my ambition.
No man should control a kingdom
who can't control his appetite.   405
His transgression gives me the right
and it falls to my advantage.
Though I am David's second son,
now, by Amnon's crime, I am the first.
I'll speak with the king my father   410
and wake him from the spell of sleep
that love — always the sorceress —
has used to stultify his brain.
Here is his chamber. But what's this?[31]

He pulls a curtain aside revealing a desk on which there is a
platter with a golden crown.

The royal crown on a platter?   415
The crown that rings my father's brow
with such regal solemnity?
This table serves me up a dish[32]
for which I've craved so long. Surely
this must be an invitation.   420
If, as ambition claims, the taste
of power is so succulent,
this morsel should not be despised.
Oh, little ring that circumscribes   425
my joy! Amnon shall not have you!
You are made of gold, but he who
sinned against his sister deserves
a baser metal. I'll adorn[33]
my head with your lovely circle.
An honour you may well decline,   430
if you are frightened that your gold
will lose its lustre next to mine.[34]

He places the crown on his head.

There. You suit me well. You will come
to me as to the manner born   435
and that's no lie I'm telling you,

y vos nacéis para mí.
¿Sabréos yo merecer?   Sí.
¿Y conservaros?   También.
¿Quién hay en Jerusalén   440
que lo estorbe?   ¿Amón?   Matalle.
¿Mi padre que ha de vengalle?
Matar a mi padre.
  DAVID.   ¿A quién?

Saca la espada, sale al encuentro David, y hállale coronado.

  ABSALÓN. ¡Ay cielos! A quien no es
vasallo de vuestra Alteza.   (*De rodillas*)   445
  DAVID. Coronada tu cabeza,
no dices bien a mis pies.
  ABSALÓN. Pienso heredarte después,
que anda el Príncipe indispuesto.
  DAVID. Hástela puesto muy presto.   450
No serás sucesor suyo,
que de esa corona arguyo,
que como llega a valer
un talento, ha menester
mayor talento que el tuyo.   455
En fin, ¿me quieres matar?
  ABSALÓN. ¿Yo?
  DAVID.   ¿No acabas de decillo?
  ABSALÓN. Si llegaras bien a oíllo,
mi fe habías de premiar.
Si vengo, dije, a reinar,   460
vivo tú en Jerusalén,
mi enojo probará quien
fama por traidor adquiere,
y por ser tirano quiere
matar a mi padre.
  DAVID.   Bien.   465
¿Pues quién hay a quien le cuadre
tal título?
  ABSALÓN. No sé yo.

since I was born of royal blood
and you were born for me alone.
Shall I be worthy of you? Yes.
Can I keep you safe? Ay, that too.
Who is there in Jerusalem   440
to stop me? Amnon? Him I'll kill.
My father who will avenge him?
Then kill him too.
    DAVID. *(Entering)* Kill who?

*David draws his sword and, advancing towards Absolom, finds him
with the crown on his head.*

    ABSOLOM.   My God!
Why, any man who will not bend
his knee to you, your Majesty! *(He kneels)* [35]
    DAVID. Your humble posture at my feet
ill becomes the crown on your head.
    ABSOLOM. In due time I may succeed you.
The Prince is somewhat indisposed.
    DAVID. And you are somewhat premature.   450
His successor will not be you.
That crown, I calculate, is worth
a good talent, and that is more [36]
than you can offer. So, my son,   455
you wish to kill me?
    ABSOLOM.   I, my lord?
    DAVID. Did you not just say so?
    ABSOLOM.   My lord,
If you had heard me correctly,
you would reward my loyalty.
I said that, if I came to rule,   460
(you living in Jerusalem)
that any man who earned a name
as a traitor and a tyrant,
any man who'd kill my father,
would taste my displeasure.
    DAVID.   I see.   465
Who fits in with this description?
    ABSOLOM. I do not know, but any man

Quien a su hermana forzó
también matará a su padre.

    DAVID. Por ser los dos de una madre   470
contra Amón te has indignado.
Pues ten por averiguado
que quien fuere su enemigo,
no ha de tener paz conmigo.

    ABSALÓN. Sin razón te has enojado.   475
¿Sólo yo te hallo crüel?

    DAVID.   ¿Qué mucho, si tú lo estás
con Amón?

    ABSALÓN. No le ama más
que yo nadie en Israel.
Antes, gran señor, con él   480
y los príncipes quisiera
que vuestra Alteza viniera
al esquilmo que ha empezado
en Balhasor mi ganado,
y que esta merced me hiciera.   485
Tan lejos de desatinos
y venanzas necias vengo,
que allí banquetes prevengo,
de tales personas dignos.
Honre nuestros vellocinos   490
vuestra presencia, señor,
y divierta allí el dolor
que le causa este suceso.
Conocerá que intereso
granjear sólo su amor.   495

    DAVID. Tú fueras el fénix de él
si estas cosas olvidaras
y al Príncipe perdonaras,
no vil Caín, sino Abel.

    ABSALÓN. Si hiciere venganza en él,   500
plegue a Dios que me haga guerra
cuanto el sol dora y encierra,
y contra ti rebelado,
de mis cabellos colgado,
muera entre el cielo y la tierra.   505

    DAVID. Si eso cumples, mi Absalón,

who could violate his sister
could also kill his father.

    DAVID.   Tamar's mother is also yours,   470
hence your anger against Amnon. [37]
But you may be assured of this:
that any enemy of his
can never be a friend of mine.

    ABSOLOM.   You have reproached me without cause.   475
Why are you so cruel to me?

    DAVID.   And why are you so cruel to him?

    ABSOLOM.   There's not a man in Israel, lord,
who loves him more than I do.
On the contrary, sire, I wish   480
that Your Highness would come with him
and all the princes to my farm
in Baal—hazor where the shearing
of sheep has just begun.   Indeed,
I beg you, grant me this favour.   485
Far from plotting pointless vengeance,
you'll see that I'm preparing feasts
worthy of such honoured guests.
Grace our fleeces with your presence,   490
my lord, and there forget this thing
that gives you so much grief and pain.
My only purpose, as you'll see,
is to regain your love for me.   495

    DAVID.   If you could forgive Amnon,
if you could forget these things,
you'd be the Phoenix of his life,
not the monstrous Cain, but Abel.

    ABSOLOM.   If I take my revenge, please God   500
that every land beneath the sun
should turn its arms against me,
and, if I rebel, may I die,
suspended by my golden hair,
between the earth and sky. [38]   505

    DAVID.   If you,

mocedades te perdono.
Con los brazos te corono
si mejor corona son.

ABSALÓN.   En mis labios los pies pon,   510
y añade a tantas mercedes
porque satisfecho quedes,
señor, el venir a honrar
mi esquilmo, pues da lugar
la paz, y alegrarte puedes.   515

DAVID.   Harémoste mucho gasto.
No, hijo, goza tu hacienda.
Al reino pide que atienda
la vejez que en canas gasto.

ABSALÓN.   Pues a obligarte no basto   520
a esta merced, da licencia
que supliendo tu presencia
Adonías, Salomón,
hagan, yendo con Amón,
de mi amor noble experiencia.   525

DAVID.   ¿Amón?   Eso no, hijo mío.

ABSALÓN.   Si melancólico está,
sus penas divertirá
el ganado, el campo, el río.

DAVID.   Temo que algún desvarío   530
dé nueva causa a mi llanto.

ABSALÓN.   De la poca fe me espanto
que tiene mi amor contigo.

DAVID.   La experiencia en esto sigo,
que cuando con el disfraz   535
viene el agravio de paz,
es el mayor enemigo.

ABSALÓN.   Antes el gusto y regalo
que he de hacelle ha de abonarme.
En esto pienso esmerarme.   540

DAVID.   Nunca el recelar fue malo.

ABSALÓN.   Plegue al cielo que sea un palo
alguacil que me suspenda
cuando yo al Príncipe ofenda.
No me alzaré de tus pies,   545
padre, hasta que a Amón me des.

my Absolom, fulfil this vow,
I forgive your youthful follies,
If my arms are a better crown,
let them be your coronation.

ABSOLOM.   No, press your foot against my mouth.   510
Then to this favour add your word
that you will grace our shearing time
with your presence, since peace gives space
for relaxation and to me
a chance to set your mind at rest.   515

DAVID.   We should be a burden to you.
No, son, you enjoy your birthright
and let the state look after me
in my silver—haired old age.

ABSOLOM.   Since I can't persuade you in this,   520
I pray give leave that, in your stead,
Adonijah and Solomon
should see the honest love I bear them,
together with Amnon.   525

DAVID.   Amnon?
No, my son, no.   That cannot be.

ABSOLOM.   If he has melancholia,
the animals, the fields and rivers
will distract him from his sorrow.

DAVID.   What I fear's an act of madness   530
that will add to mine.

ABSOLOM.   I'm dismayed
how little trust you have in me.

DAVID.   The lessons of experience.
No rancour is more dangerous   535
than when it comes disguised as peace.

ABSOLOM.   The way I'll wine and dine him
shall testify to my good faith.
In that I'll be most scrupulous.   540

DAVID.   A little caution does no harm.

ABSOLOM.   If I harm the Prince, may Heaven
see me hanged from a gallows tree.[39]
I shall not rise up from your feet,   545
sire, until you give me Amnon.

DAVID.   It's he who's closest to my heart;

DAVID.   Del alma es la mejor prenda.
Pero en fe de que me fío
de ti, yo te lo concedo.

ABSALÓN.   Cierto ya de tu amor quedo.   550

DAVID.   (*Aparte*)   ¿De qué dudáis, temor frío?

ABSALÓN.   Voyle a avisar.

DAVID.   Hijo mío,
en olvido agravio pon.

ABSALÓN.   No temas.

DAVID.   Ay, mi Absalón,
lo mucho que te amo pruebas.   555

ABSALÓN.   Adiós.

DAVID.   Mira que me llevas
la mitad del corazón.   (*Vanse*)

*Salen Tirso, Braulio, Aliso, Riselo, Ardelio, ganaderos, y Tamar de
pastora, rebozada la cara con la toca.   Cantan.*

UNOS.   Al esquilmo, ganaderos,
que balan las ovejas y los carneros.

OTROS.   Ganaderos, a esquilmar,   560
que llama los pastores el mayoral.

UNO.   El Amor trasquila
la lana que le dan
·los amantes mansos
que a su aprisco van.   565

Trasquila la dama
al pobre galán,
aunque no es su oficio
sino repelar.

Trasquila el alcalde   570
al que preso está,
y si entró con lana
en puribus va.

Pela el escribén,

but, as a token of my faith,
I give my leave for him to go.
    ABSOLOM.   Now I feel certain of your love.   550
    DAVID.   *(Aside)* And I the chill of fear and doubt.
    ABSOLOM.   I'll go and tell him now.
    DAVID.   My son,
put hate behind you.
    ABSOLOM.   Have no fear.
    DAVID.   Oh, Absolom, my son, you try
the love I have for you.   555
    ABSOLOM.   Farewell. *(Exit)*
    DAVID.   You're taking half my heart with you.
Remember that, my son. *(Exit)*

*Enter Tirso, Braulio, Aliso, Riselo and Ardelio, a group of
farmhands, and Tamar, dressed as a shepherdess, with a wimple*[40]
pulled down over her face. They sing.

    FIRST GROUP.   It's shearing time, my likely lads,[41]
the sheep bleat in the pen.

    SECOND GROUP.   My likely lads, it's shearing time, 560
the master calls his men.

    SOLO VOICE.   Old Cupid shears the woolly backs
of shy and sheepish lovers.
They give him all the wool they've got
and run off to their mothers.   565

A lady who has scarce done more
than pluck her brows from habit,
will take a juicy lover man
and skin him like a rabbit.

The jailor fleeces those who lie   570
in prison all forlorn.
Though they came in all decked in fur,
they'll go out as they were born.

A scribe who writes with crooked pen[42]   575

porque escribanar 575
con pluma con pelo
de comer le da.

Pela el alguacil
hasta no dejar
vellón en la bolsa, 580
plata otro que tal.

El letrado pela,
pela el oficial;
que hay mil peladores
si pelones hay. 585
    TODOS. Al esquilmo, ganaderos,
que balan las ovejas y los carneros.
Ganaderos, a esquilmar,
que llama a los zagales el mayoral.
    TIRSO. Dichosas serán desde hoy 590
las reses que en el Jordán
cristales líquidos beben,
y en tomillos pacen sal.
Ya con vuesa hermosa vista
hierba el prado brotará 595
por más que la seque el sol,
pues vos sus campos pisáis.
¿De qué estáis melanconiosa,
hermosísima Tamar,
pues con vuesos ojos bellos 600
estos montes alegráis?
Si dicen que está la corte
doquiera que el rey está,
y vos sois reina en belleza,
la corte es ésta, no hay más. 605
La Infantica, entreteneos;
vuesa hermosura mirad
en las aguas que os ofrecen
por espejo su cristal.
    TAMAR. Temo de mirarme a ellas. 610
    BRAULIO. Si es por no os enamorar
de vos misma, bien hacéis,

can fleece as well as any.
He mars a figure here and there
and lives a life of plenty.

The constable will fleece your purse
and leave not a trace of fluff.   580
He'll clean you out of copper coins,[43]
if the silver's not enough.

The lawyer fleeces and the judge,
baillif, justice of the peace.
There will be a thousand fleecers
as long as there are lambs to fleece.   585
    ALL.   It's shearing time, my likely lads,
the sheep bleat in the pen.
My likely lads, it's shearing time,
the master calls his men.
    TIRSO.   From this day on, when they see you,[44]   590
even the cattle will be glad.
Though now they graze on salt wild thyme
and drink from Jordan's crystal stream,
when your beauty treads these pastures,
green grass will grow in the meadow,   595
no matter how the sun may burn.
Why are you so melanchronic,[45]
most beautiful Tamar? Those eyes   600
bring light to all the hills around.
If the court is where the king is,
as they say, and you're beauty's queen,
what I say is the court is here
and there's no two ways about it.   605
Don't be sad, my little princess.
Be happy; enjoy your beauty.
Come and look at its reflection
in the mirror of the waters.
    TAMAR.   I fear to see myself in them.[46]   610
    BRAULIO.   If you're afeard of being smitten
by yourself, then it's best you don't.

que, a la he, que quillotráis
desde ell alma a la asadura
a cuantos viéndoos están,   615
y que para mal de muchos,
el dimuño os trujo acá.
Mas asomaos con todo eso.
Veréis cómo os retratáis
en la tabla de este río   620
si en ella a vos os miráis;
y haréis un cuadro valiente,
que porque le guarnezcáis
las flores de oro y azul
de marco le servirán.   625
Honraldas, miraos a ellas.
    TAMAR.   Aunque hermosa me llamáis,
tengo una mancha afrentosa.
Si la veo he de llorar.
    ALISO.   ¿Mancha tenéis? Y aun por eso,   630
que aquí los espejos que hay,
si manchas muestran, las quitan,
enseñando acá amistad.
Allá los espejos son
sólo para señalar   635
faltas, que viéndose en vidrio
con ellas en rostro dan.
Acá son espejos de agua,
que a los que mirarse van
muestran manchas y las quitan   640
en llegándose a lavar.
    TAMAR.   Si agua esta mancha quitara,
harta agua mis ojos dan;
sólo a borralla es bastante
la sangre de un desleal.   645
    RISELIO.   No vi en mi vida tal muda.
Miel virgen afeita acá,
que ya hasta las caras venden
postiza virginidad.
¿Son pecas?
    TAMAR.   Pecados son.   650
    ARDELIO.   Cubrillas con solimán.

Faith, for you would raise a fever
as would burn the soul and vitals
of any man who sees you. 615
The Devil himself did send you
for the ruin of mortal men.
Still, all the same, you come and look.
Look at yourself and it'll make 620
the prettiest picture you ever saw.
And just to prettify it more,
here's some blue and golden flowers
to frame the handsomest portrait
as was painted in a river. 625
So do the water proud and look.
    TAMAR.   You call me beautiful and yet
I bear a dreadful mark, a stain.
The sight of that would make me weep.
    ALISO. Stains, you say? All the more for that. 630
Because the mirrors we've got here
show up the stains then take them off.
That's a lesson in good friendship.
At court, all a mirror's good for 635
is for bringing out your faults.
In glass you see them and they're thrown
back in your face. Here the water
shows them up, if all you do is look, 640
but cleans them when you stoop to wash.[47]
    TAMAR. If water could wipe out this stain,
my tears would be enough. But this
can only be removed by blood,
the blood of a traitor and a rat. 645
    RISELIO. No. Never seen no stuff like that.
Virgin honey's what they use here.[48]
Women nowadays even paint
virginity on their faces.
Freckles, is it?
    TAMAR.   It's for my sins.[49] 650
    ARDELIO. Use quicksilver or arsenic.
    TAMAR. It's not for want of that, shepherd.
My whole heart has turned to poison.[50]
    TIRSO. Some birthmark you're hiding, maybe? 655

TAMAR.   No queda, pastor, por eso.
Toda yo soy rejalgar.
    TIRSO.   ¿Es algún lunar acaso
que con la toca tapáis?   655
    TAMAR.   No se muda cual la luna,
ni es la deshonra lunar.
    TIRSO.   Pues sea lo que se huere,
pardiez, que hemos de cantar
y aliviar la pesadumbre,   660
que es locura lo demás.

Cantan.

Que si estáis triste, la Infanta,
todo el tiempo lo acaba.
Desdenes de amor
la ausencia los sana,   665
para desengaños
buena es la mudanza.
Si atormentan celos,
darlos a quien ama.
Para la vejez,   670
arrimar las armas.
Para mujer pobre,
gastar lo que basta.
Para mal de ausencia,
juegos hay y cazas.   675
Para escusar penas,
estudiar en casa.
Para agravios de honra,
perdón o venganza,
que si triste estáis la Infanta,   680
todo el tiempo lo acaba.

Sale Laureta con un tabaque de flores.

LAURETA.   Todas estas flores bellas
a la primavera he hurtado,
que pues de Amor sois el prado,
competir podéis con ellas.   685

TAMAR.   Like a birthmark, it will not change.[51]
Yet dishonour is no birthmark.
   TIRSO.   Well, whatever it is, by God,
we'll sing a little song for you
and drive away your sorrows.   660
There's nothing else that's worth a damn.

They sing.

Princess, if you're too sad to sing,
remember time cures everything.

Against a lover's rejection,
go away for protection.   665
For promises broken,
be fickle and wanton.
When on jealousy's rack,
don't give in, give it back.
When old age makes you frail   670
hang your sword on a nail.
When your woman is poor,
spend enough, but no more.
If your lover's away,
jousts and hunting all day.   675
To avoid trouble and strife,
stay at home all your life.
But for questions of honour
there's no one reaction.
You must either forgive
or have satisfaction.

Princess, if you're too sad to sing,   680
remember time cures everything.

Enter Laureta with a wicker basket full of flowers.

   LAURETA.   All these lovely flowers I've stolen
from springtime's garden, my lady.   685
My basket's full of them — fresh herbs,
the finest flowers, jazmin, roses,

Lleno viene este cestillo
de las más frescas y hermosas
hierbas, jazmines y rosas
desde el clavel al tomillo.
Aquí está la manutisa, 690
la estrellamar turquesada,
con la violeta morada
que Amor, porque huela, pisa.
El sándalo, el pajarillo,
alelíes siete ramas, 695
azucenas y retamas,
madreselva y hisopillo.
Tomaldos, que son despojos
del campo, y juntad con ellos
labios, aliento y cabellos, 700
pechos, frente, cejas y ojos.
  TAMAR. Todas las que abril esmalta
pierden en mí su valor,
Laureta, porque la flor
que más me importa me falta. 705

Dale unas violetas, y póneselas Tamar en los pechos.

  TIRSO. Ya vendréis a divinar
sueños o cosas de risa,
que como sois fitonisa,
consolaréis a Tamar.
Laureta, diz que tratáis 710
con el diablo.
  ARDELIO.   Ya han venido
los Príncipes que han querido
honrarnos oy.
  TIRSO.   ¿Qué aguardáis?
  ARDELIO. Mientras el convite pasa
al soto apacible vamos, 715
y de flores, hierba, y ramos
entapicemos la casa.
  TIRSO. Ardelio, tenéis razón;
démonos prisa, pastores.
¿Pero qué ramos ni flores 720

carnations, thyme. Here's sweet William, 690
the sea plantain of turquoise leaf,
and there's the purple violet,
bruised by love to shed its fragrance. [52]
Bergamot mint and columbine,
lilies and broom and wallflowers
with seven branches on their stems,
honeysuckle and the hyssop.
But you can match this loveliness;
you are the meadow where Love casts [53]
its seed. Take these flowers of Nature
and join them with your own: your lips
and breath, your brow and golden hair, 700
your breasts, your eyebrows and your eyes.
    TAMAR. All the flowers that April paints
will wither when I touch them,
Laureta. I no longer have
the one that matters to me most. 705

*Laureta gives her some violets and Tamar places them in her
bosom.*

    TIRSO. We'll have you 'terpreting dreams next
and all that there hocus—pocus.
Being a fortune—teller and all, [54]
you'll be a comfort for Tamar.
You've got dealings with the Devil, 710
that be what they say, Laureta.
    ARDELIO. The princes who honour us today
are come.
    TIRSO. Then what are you waiting for?
    ARDELIO. While our guests arrive, let's go down 715
to the wood and decorate the house
with branches, greenery and flowers.
    TIRSO. Ardelio, you're right. Come on,
you lads, let's get a move on there!
But who'll want to look at flowers 720

hay como ver a Absalón?

Vanse los pastores.

TAMAR. Vámonos de aquí, Laureta.
LAURETA. ¿Para qué? Bien disfrazada
estás.
TAMAR. Di mal injuriada.
LAURETA. Olvida, si eres discreta.   725
TAMAR. Bien dijo, aunque ése es buen medio,
un ingenio singular,
'El remedio era olvidar,
y olvidóseme el remedio'.

Salen Amón, Absalón, Adonías y Salomón

AMÓN. Bello está el campo.
ABSALÓN.   Es el mayo,   730
el mes galán, todo flor.
ADONÍAS. A lo menos labrador,
según ajirona el sayo.
AMÓN. Oid, que hay aquí serranas,
y no de mal aire y brío.   735
ABSALÓN. De mi hacienda son, y os fío
que envidien las cortesanas
su no ayudada hermosura.
AMÓN. Bien haya quien la belleza
debe a la naturaleza,   740
no al afeite y compostura.
ABSALÓN. Esta es mujer tan curiosa,
que de lo futuro avisa.
Tiénenla por fitonisa
estos rústicos.
SALOMÓN.   ¿Y es cosa   745
de importancia?
AMÓN.   De esta gente
hacer caso es vanidad.
Tal vez dirá una verdad
y después mentiras veinte.
¿Mas quién es la rebozada?   750

now that prince Absolom is here?

The shepherds go off.

TAMAR.   Let's go, Laureta.
LAURETA.   Why, what for?
You are well enough disguised.
TAMAR.   Ay, well disguised and badly used.
LAURETA.   If you were wise, you would forget.   725
TAMAR.   It's good advice, but nonetheless,
a very wise man once said:
'The remedy was to forget,
and I forgot the remedy'.⁵⁵

Enter Amnon, Absolom, Adonijah and Solomon.

AMNON.   How lovely nature looks today!
ABSOLOM.   A gallant month, the month of May,   730
all flattery and flowers.
ADONIJAH.   A peasant month more like, all rags.
Look how it's torn my clothes to shreds!⁵⁶
AMNON.   Well, here we have some peasant girls
and not bad—looking either.   735
ABSOLOM.   They are from my estate.   I vow
there's not a lady at the court
who is not green with envy
of their unassisted beauty.
AMNON.   Blesséd are those who are endowed   740
by Nature, not by cosmetics!⁵⁷
ABSOLOM.   That woman there is very strange.
She tells the future, so they say;
the locals here think she's a witch.
SOLOMON.   Is that serious?   745
AMNON.   It's folly
to pay these people too much heed.
For every truth she guesses,
she'll invent you twenty lies.
But who's the one who hides her face?   750

ABSALÓN.   Es una hermosa pastora
que injurias de su honra llora
y espera verse vengada.
AMÓN.   Ella tiene buena flema.
¿No la veremos?
ABSALÓN.   No quiere,   755
mientras sin honra estuviere,
descubrirse.
AMÓN.   Linda tema.
(*A Laureta*)
Ahora bien con vos me entiendo;
llegaos, mi serrana, acá.
LAURETA.   ¿Su Alteza?   Pretenderá   760
y después iráse huyendo.
AMÓN.   Bien parecéis adivina;
llena de flores venís.
¿Cómo no las repartís,
si el ser cortés os inclina?   765
LAURETA.   Estos prados son teatro
do representa Amaltea.
Mas porque no os quejéis, ea,
a cada cual de los cuatro
tengo de dar una flor.   770
AMÓN.   ¿Y esotra serrana es muda?
Quita el rebozo.
LAURETA.   Está en muda.
AMÓN.   ¿Mudas hay acá?
LAURETA.   De honor.
AMÓN.   ¿Y hay honor entre villanas?
LAURETA.   Y con más firmeza está,   775
que no hay príncipes acá
ni fáciles cortesanas.
Pero dejémonos de esto,
y va de flor.
AMÓN.   ¿Cual me cabe?
LAURETA.   (*Aparte a cada uno*)   Esta azucena süave.   780

ABSOLOM.   A shepherdess, pretty one too,
in mourning for some injury
to her honour.   She's sworn to see
herself avenged.
AMNON.   She's a cool one,
I must say.   Won't she show her face?
ABSOLOM.   Not till her honour is restored.   755
AMNON.   A peculiar obsession.
(*To Laureta*)
Well, I'll address myself to you.
Come, my girl.   Come here.
LAURETA.   Your Highness?   760
Would you pay me court then run
and leave a girl behind?
AMNON.   In that,
at least, she seems to read my mind.[58]
You're so laden down with flowers,
why not give one to each of us,
if you would be so courteous?   765
LAURETA.   There's plenty in the fields.   They grow
like fruits from Amaltheia's horn.[59]
Still, I don't want complaints, so here,
I'll give four flowers, one to each.   770
AMNON.   This other peasant, is she dumb?[60]
Take off this thing!
LAURETA.   A bird in moulting
will not sing.
AMNON.   What, lost her feathers
or her tongue?
LAURETA.   Her honour, my lord.
AMNON.   Do peasants prize their honour so?
LAURETA.   With more resolve than you would know,   775
my lord.   There are no princes here
or ladies of easy virtue.
But please let us leave all this
and get on with our flowers.
AMNON.   So which one have you got for me?
LAURETA. (*Aside to each in turn*)
This smooth white lily.   780

Dale una azucena con una espadaña.

AMÓN.   Eso es picarme de honesto.
LAURETA.   Yo sé que olella os agrada,
pero no la deshojéis,
que la espadaña que véis
tiene la forma de espada.   785
Y aquesos granillos de oro,
aunque a la vista recrean,
manchan si los manosean.
Porque estriba su tesoro
en ser intactos, dejaos,   790
Amón, de deshojar flor
con espadañas de honor;
y si la ofendéis, guardaos.
AMÓN.   Yo estimo vuestro consejo.
Demonio es esta mujer.   795
SALOMÓN.   ¿Qué os ha dicho?
AMÓN.   No hay que hacer
caso; por loca la dejo.
ADONÍAS.   ¿Qué flor me cabe a mí?
LAURETA.   Estraña
espuela de caballero.

Dale una espuela de caballero que es una flor azul.

ADONÍAS.   Bien por el nombre la quiero.   800
LAURETA.   A veces la espuela daña.
ADONÍAS.   Diestro soy.
LAURETA.   Si lo sois, alto.
Pero guardaos, si os agrada,
de una doncella casada.
No os perdáis por picar alto.   805
ADONÍAS.   No os entiendo.
ABSALÓN.   Yo me quedo
postrero. Id, hermano, vos.
SALOMÓN.   Confusos vienen los dos.
Si acaso obligaros puedo,
más conmigo os declarad.   810

She gives him a lily together with a pointed reed.[61]

AMNON.   This must be
to advertise my purity!
LAURETA.   I see you like to smell its scent.
Mind you don't knock off the petals;
the pointed reed you see with it
is shaped just like a sword and those   785
little specks of gold, so pleasing
to the eye, will stain if they are touched.
Their value lies in being intact.   790
Never depetal a flower,
Amnon, which has a sword to guard
its honour.   If you offend it,
then you must look to yourself.
AMNON.   I appreciate your good advice.
(Aside)   This woman's the very devil.   795
SOLOMON.   What did she tell you?
AMNON.   Pay no heed.
I left her; the woman's quite mad.
ADONIJAH.   Which flower is mine?
LAURETA.   The larkspur.[62]
A flower of great mystery.

She gives him a larkspur, a blue flower.

ADONIJAH.   Larkspur.   I like it for its name.   800
LAURETA.   A spur can do a lot of harm.
ADONIJAH.   I'm a good horseman.
LAURETA.   If you are,
I say no more.   But take good care.
Beware of a certain young wife,
if she should take your fancy.[63]
Don't overreach yourself and fall.   805
ADONIJAH.   I don't know what you mean.
ABSOLOM.   I'll stay
till last, brother.   You can go next.
SOLOMON.   The other two seem quite confused.
Could I prevail upon you, please,
to be more explicit with me?   810

LAURETA. Esta es corona de rey,
flor de vista, olor y ley.
Sus propiedades gozad,
que aunque rey, seréis espejo,
y el mayor de los mejores;   815
temo que os perdáis por flores
de amor, si sois mozo viejo.
AMÓN. Buena flor.
SALOMÓN.   Con su pimienta.
ABSALÓN. ¿Cábeme a mí?
LAURETA.   Este narciso.

Dale un narciso.

ABSALÓN. Ese a sí mismo se quiso.   820
LAURETA. Pues tened, Absalón, cuenta
con él, y no os queráis tanto,
que de puro engrandeceros,
estimaros y quereros,
de Isräel seréis espanto.   825
Vuestra hermosura enloquece
a toda vuestra nación;
Narciso sois Absalón,
que también os desvanece.
Cortaos esos hilos bellos,   830
que si los dejáis crecer,
os habéis presto de ver
en alto por los cabellos. (*Vase*)
ABSALÓN. Espera. Fuese. Si en alto
por los cabellos me veo,   835
cumpliráse mi deseo;
al reino he de dar asalto.
¿En alto por los cabellos?
Mi hermosura ha de obligar
a Isräel que a coronar   840
me venga loco por ellos.
AMÓN. Confuso os habéis quedado.
ABSALÓN. Príncipes, alto, a comer.
(*Aparte*) Sobre el trono me han de ver

LAURETA. Here's a kingcup, a noble flower,[64]
fine to look at and sweet to smell.
Take delight in its properties
and note them well, for you will be
a model king, the greatest
and the best. Yet in ripe old age,   815
this taste for posies and bouquets,
for gentle blandishments of love,
may well, I fear, lead you astray.[65]
    AMNON. Nice flower.
    SOLOMON.   But with a nettle's sting.[66]
    ABSOLOM. Which one is mine?
    LAURETA.   This narcissus.

Gives him a narcissus.

    ABSOLOM. He was the one who loved himself.[67]   820
    LAURETA. Then learn from his example, prince,
and love yourself a little less.
All Israel will reel from your pride,
your vanity and ambition.   825
The nation's infatuated
with your beauty, and so are you.
You are Narcissus, Absolom,
and vanity clouds your judgement.
Cut off these handsome locks, this pride.   830
As long as you will let them grow,
they will raise you up on high.[68] (*Exit*)
    ABSOLOM. Wait! She's gone. If I'm raised on high
by virtue of my hair, my wish   835
comes true. I'll seize the kingdom then.
'They will raise you up on high'
can only mean one thing: Israel,
infatuated by my looks,
will feel compelled to crown me king.   840
    AMNON. You seem perplexed.
    ABSOLOM.   Enough of this,
princes! Let us go in and dine.
(*Aside*) They shall see me on my father's

de mi padre coronado. 845
Muera en el convite Amón,
quede vengada Tamar,
dé la corona lugar
a que la herede Absalón.

Sale un Criado.

CRIADO. La comida que se enfría 850
a vuestras Altezas llama.
AMÓN. De aquesta serrana dama
ver la cara gustaría.
Idos, hermano, con ellos.
ABSALÓN. No nos hagáis esperar. 855
(*Aparte*) Reinando vengo a quedar
en alto por los cabellos.

Vanse si no son Amón y Tamar.

AMÓN. Yo, serrana, estoy picado
de esos ojos lisonjeros
que deben de ser fulleros, 860
pues el alma me han ganado.
¿Queréisme vos despicar?
TAMAR. Cansaráos el juego presto,
y en ganando el primer resto
luego os querréis levantar. 865
AMÓN. Buenas manos.
TAMAR.   De pastora.
AMÓN. Dadme una.
TAMAR.   Será en vano
dar mano a quien da de mano
y ya aborrece, ya adora.
AMÓN. Llegaréosla yo a tomar, 870
pues su hermosura me esfuerza.
TAMAR. ¿A tomar? ¿Cómo?
AMÓN.   Por fuerza.
TAMAR. ¡Qué amigo sois de forzar!
AMÓN. Basta, que aquí todas dais
en adivinas.

throne with his crown upon my head.   845
Amnon shall perish at the feast,
Tamar shall be avenged and the crown
shall wait till Absolom succeeds.

Enter a servant.

SERVANT.   Dinner awaits, Your Highnesses.   850
I fear the food is getting cold.
AMNON.   Do go in with your guests, brother.
I'll follow.   I should like to see
the face of this lady—peasant.
ABSOLOM.   Don't keep us waiting. *(Aside)* So be it.   855
My hair's my fortune, that's well known
and that shall raise me to the throne.

All leave with the exception of Amnon and Tamar.

AMNON.   I'm most displeased with you, my girl.
Those fascinating eyes of yours   860
have pierced my heart and won my soul.
They must have seen my cards and those
who cheat must give satisfaction. [69]
TAMAR.   You'd soon tire of the game, my lord,
and leave when you had won a hand.   865
AMNON.   Yours are very fine.
TAMAR.   Peasant hands.
AMNON.   Give me one of them.
TAMAR.   Give a hand
to one who would deny his heart,
who would adore me, then hate me?
No, not I.
AMNON.   Then I must take it.   870
Its beauty will not be denied.
TAMAR.   Take it?   How?
AMNON.   By force, if need be.
TAMAR.   You are a man who likes his way.
AMNON.   Enough of that!   I see you've all
turned fortune teller here today!

TAMAR.　Queremos   875
estudiar cómo sabremos
burlaros, pues nos burláis.
   AMÓN.　¿Flores traéis vos también?
   TAMAR.　Cada cual humilde o alta,
busca aquello que le falta.   880
   AMÓN.　Serrana, yo os quiero bien.
Dadme una flor.
   TAMAR.　　　Buen floreo
os traéis; creed, señor,
que a no perder yo una flor
no sintiera el mal que veo.   885
   AMÓN.　Una flor he de tomar.
   TAMAR.　Flor de Tamar diréis bien.
   AMÓN.　Forzaréos. Dalda por bien.
   TAMAR.　¡Qué amigo sois de forzar!
Pero tomad si os agrada.   890

Dale las violetas.

   AMÓN.　¿Violetas?
   TAMAR.　　　　　Para alegraros,
porque yo no puedo daros,
Amón, sino flor violada.
   AMÓN.　Eso es mucho adivinar.
Destapaos.
   TAMAR.　Apártese.   895
   AMÓN.　Por fuerza os descubriré.

Descúbrela.

   TAMAR.　Qué amigo sois de forzar.
   AMÓN.　¡Ay, cielos, monstruo tú eres!
Quién los ojos se sacara
primero que te mirara,   900
afrenta de las mujeres.
Voyme, y pienso que sin vida,
que tu vista me mató.
No esperaba, cielos, yo
tal principio de comida. (*Vase*)   905

TAMAR.   We study ways to pay you back   875
for all the tricks you play on us.
    AMNON.   You've been picking flowers as well?
    TAMAR.   Peasant or prince, each of us seeks
what satisfies our needs.   880
    AMNON.   Dear girl,
I am your friend, I love you well.
Give me a flower.   A token.
    TAMAR.   A token, like your empty words. [70]
Yet the loss of a flower brought
the grief I now feel in my heart.   885
    AMNON.   Come, girl, the flower.   I will have it.
    TAMAR.   It's not mine to give. [71]
    AMNON.   Then it's mine
to take.   So give it with good grace.
    TAMAR.   You are a man who gets his way!
Take them if that is what you want.   890

She gives him the violets.

    AMNON.   Violets?
    TAMAR.   Yes, that should please you.
It's all I have to give, Amnon:
a bruised and violated flower.
    AMNON.   This divination goes too far.
Show me your face!
    TAMAR.   Away from me!   895
    AMNON.   Then by force, if it has to be!

He uncovers her face.

    TAMAR.   You are a man who gets his way!
    AMNON.   By God, so it's you, you foul harpy!
I'd rather have torn out my eyes
than let them light on you again!   900
You defile the name of woman!
I'll quit the sight of you, because
your very sight is death to me!
God knows I was not expecting
such a way to start a banquet!   *(Exit)*   905

TAMAR.   Peor postre te han de dar,
bárbaro, crüel, ingrato,
pues será el último plato
la venganza de Tamar.   (*Vase*)

Salen los pastores con ramos cantando.

TODOS. (*Cantan*)   A las puertas de nuesos amos   910
vamos, vamos,
vamos a poner ramos.
    UNO.   A Absalón bello
alamico negro,
cinamomo y cedro,   915
y palma ofrezcamos.
    TODOS.   Vamos, vamos,
vamos a poner ramos.
    OTRO.   Al mozo Adonías,
de las maravillas,   920
rosa y clavellinas,
guirnaldas tejamos.
    TODOS.   Vamos, vamos,
vamos a poner ramos.
    UNO.   Al Príncipe nueso,   925
de ciprés funesto
y taray espeso,
coronas tejamos.
    TODOS.   Vamos, vamos,
vamos a poner ramos.   930
    OTRO.   Salomón prudente
ceñirá su frente
del laurel valiente
que alegres cortamos.
    TODOS.   Vamos, vamos,   935
vamos a poner ramos.

TAMAR. Then wait and see what's for dessert!
You cruel beast! You animal!
Revenge à la Tamar, so sweet,
is the last dish you'll ever eat! *(Exit)*

Enter shepherds carrying branches and flowers. They sing.[72]

[ALL.] Come bring flowers, come bring branches;   910
hang them round our prince's door.

FIRST VOICE. To Absolom the fair,
Sweet cinnamon and cedar's pride;   915
we'll weave palm leaves of triumph
with black poplar boughs beside.[73]

ALL. Come bring ... etc.

SECOND VOICE. We'll weave of fresh wild flowers
for young Adonijah bold   920
garlands of youth and passion:
dog rose, pinks and marigold.

ALL. Come bring ... etc.

FIRST VOICE. For prince Amnon, King David's heir,   925
we'll weave a solemn wreath
of cypress leaves and tamarisk[74]
and place his name beneath.

ALL. Come bring ... etc.   930

SECOND VOICE. But we shall weave a hero's crown
of laurel leaves instead[75]
for Solomon the prudent
to place upon his head.

ALL. Come bring... etc.   935

Gritan de dentro, y hacen ruido de golpes y caerse mesas y vajillas, y luego salen huyendo Salomón y Adonías.

ABSALÓN.   La comida has de pagar,
dándote muerte, villano.
AMÓN.   ¿Por qué me matas, hermano?
ABSALÓN.   Por dar venganza a Tamar.   940
AMÓN.   Cielos, piedad.   Muerto soy.
SALOMÓN.   Huye.
ADONÍAS.   Oh bárbaro sin ley,
todos los hijos del key
por reinar perecen hoy.   (*Vanse*)
TIRSO.   Oste puto, esto va malo.   945
ARDELIO.   Huyamos, no nos alcance
algún golpe de este lance.
BRAULIO.   ¡Mirad qué negro regalo
de convite!
TIRSO.   Oh mi cebolla,
más os quiero que Absalón   950
sus pavos.
ARDELIO.   Tirso, chitón,
que mos darán en la cholla.   (*Vanse*)

Descúbrense aparadores de plata, caídas las vajillas, y una mesa llena de manjares y descompuesta, los manteles ensangrentados, y Amón sobre la mesa asentado, y caído de espaldas en ella con una taza en la mano y un cuchillo en la otra, atravesada por la garganta una daga; y salen Absalón y Tamar.

ABSALÓN.   Para ti, hermana, se ha hecho
el convite; aqueste plato,
aunque de manjar ingrato,   955
nuestro agravio ha satisfecho;
hágate muy buen provecho.
Bebe su sangre, Tamar,
procura en ella lavar
tu fama hasta aquí manchada.   960

*From within comes the noise of shouting and blows, of crockery
being smashed and tables overturned. Solomon and Adonijah later
enter as if fleeing from the scene.*

ABSOLOM. The banquet must be paid for, slave!
My bill is your death.
AMNON.   Why, brother?
Why kill me?
ABSOLOM. To avenge Tamar.   940
AMNON. Mercy! For God's sake!
SOLOMON.   Run for your life!
ADONIJAH. Now there is no law. From this day
the throne of David will be stained
with the blood of all his sons![76]

Solomon and Adonijah leave.

TIRSO. God save us! This looks very bad!   945
ARDELIO. Come, let's get out of here, or else
some blow is bound to come our way.
BRAULIO. Look what they've left us from the feast!
TIRSO. I'll stick to onions. Absolom   950
can keep his peacock pie![77]
ARDELIO.   Tirso!
Hold your tongue or we'll lose our heads! (*They leave*)

*A curtain is drawn aside revealing cabinets of fallen silver and
china, a table laden with food in disarray, tablecloths stained with
blood and Amnon lying face upwards on the table with a goblet in
one hand and a knife in the other. There is a dagger through his
throat.*
Enter Absolom and Tamar.

ABSOLOM. This banquet was prepared for you,
my sister. With this humble dish,
though distasteful to the palate,   955
we can count honour satisfied.[78]
Here's wishing you good appetite.
Drink his blood, Tamar; wash that stain
from your hitherto polluted

Caliente está la colada,
fácil la puedes sacar.
A Gesur huyendo voy,
que es su Rey mi agüelo, y padre
de nuestra injuriada madre.   965
   TAMAR. Gracias a los cielos doy,
que no lloraré desde hoy
mi agravio, hermano valiente.
Ya podré mirar la gente,
resucitando mi honor,   970
que la sangre del traidor
es blasón del inocente.
Quédate, bárbaro, ingrato,
que en buen túmulo te han puesto.
Sepulcro del deshonesto   975
es la mesa, taza y plato.
   ABSALÓN.   Heredar el reino trato.
   TAMAR.   Déntele los cielos bellos.
   ABSALÓN.   Amigos tengo, y por ellos,
como dijo la mujer,   980
todo Isräel me ha de ver
en alto por los cabellos.

Vanse y encúbrese la apariencia.

Sale el Rey David solo.

   DAVID.   ¿Amón?   ¿Príncipe?   ¿Hijo mío?
Si eres tú, pide al deseo
albricias, que los instantes   985
juzga por siglos eternos.
Gracias a Dios que a pesar
de sospechas y recelos
con tu vista restituyo
la vida que sin ti pierdo.   990
¿Cómo vienes?   ¿Cómo estás?
¿Podré enlazando tu cuello
imprimir lirios en rosas,

reputation. The bleach is hot,[79]
it won't be hard to wash it out.
For myself, I'll flee to Geshur
where the king is my grandfather,
father of your mother and mine
who was dishonoured just like you.[80]

TAMAR. I'll not weep for my dishonour.
Not from today. Thanks to Heaven
and to you, my gallant brother.
Now that my honour is restored,
I can look people in the eye.
The banner of the innocent
is the blood of the offender.
So there you lie and there you stay.
The perfect tomb for a lecher
and a glutton: a table laid
with a wine goblet and a plate!

ABSOLOM. You know I intend to take the throne.

TAMAR. Then may sweet Heaven grant your wish.

ABSOLOM. I have my friends who'll see to that.
It's these locks. That's the reason why.
As the woman said, all Israel
shall see them raise me up on high.

They leave and the discovery curtain is closed.

Enter David alone.

DAVID. Is it the prince? Amnon? My son?
If it's you, then my longing heart
has made you come and will reward
you generously. The seconds
have seemed like centuries to me.
Thank God I've seen you once again,
though I feared I never would.
You restore my life; without you
I have none. How are you, my son?
May I embrace your neck and press
my pale lilies to your rosy cheeks?

960

965

970

975

980

985

990

Va a abrazar el viento.

guarnecer oro en acero?
Dame los amados brazos.   995
Ay, engaños lisonjeros.
¿Porqué con burlas pesadas
me hacéis abrazar los vientos?
Como la madre acallando
al hijo que tiene al pecho,   1000
¿me enseñas la joya de oro
para escondérmela luego?
Como en la navegación
prolija, en celajes negros
fingidos montes me pintas,   1005
siendo mentiras de lejos?
Como fruta de pincel,
como hermosura en espejo,
como tesoro soñado,
como la fuente al enfermo,   1010
burladoras esperanzas,
¿engañáis mis pensamientos
para acrecentar pesares,
para atormentar desvelos?
¿Amón mío, dónde estás?   1015
Deshaga al temor los hielos
el sol de tu cara hermosa;
remoce tu vista a un viejo.
¿Si se habrá Absalón vengado?
¿Si habréis sido, como temo,   1020
hijo caro de mis ojos,
de sus esquilmos cordero?
No, que es vuestro hermano, en fin;
la sangre hierve sin fuego.
Mas ay, que es sangre heredada   1025
de quien a su hermano mesmo
vendió, y llorará David
como Jacob en sabiendo
si a Josef mató la envidia,
que a Amón la venganza ha muerto.   1030
Absalón, ¿no me juró

He goes to embrace the air.

Inlay your gold on my grey steel?
Give me your arms, I beg of you!   995
False! Why do these sweet delusions
toy so cruelly with my mind
and make me embrace the empty air?
Like a mother who soothes a child
by giving him an empty breast?   1000
You let me glimpse the precious jewel
and then take it away from me?
As to one on a long sea voyage,
you represent in the distant clouds
the simulated hills of home?   1005
Like painted fruit, like beauty
in a mirror, like a treasure
in a dream, like cool spring water
to lips that thirst, you mock my hope!   1010
You delude my thoughts and increase
the torment of my sleepless nights!
Amnon, my son, where are you now?   1015
Oh, that the sun of your fair face
would melt away this icy fear
that grips my heart! Come back to me,
and make this old man young again.
But what if Absolom should take
revenge? What if you have fallen   1020
like a lamb to the shearer's knife?[81]
Oh, light of my eyes, I fear it's so.
But no, he is your brother still;
blood may boil, but he would not kill.[82]
And yet, he has the blood of those   1025
who sold their brother as a slave.[83]
David shall weep for Amnon like
Jacob wept for Joseph. One killed
by envy, the other by revenge.   1030
But Absolom, did he not swear

no agraviarle? ¿De qué tiemblo?
Pero el amor y el agravio
nunca guardan juramentos.
La esperanza y el temor   1035
en este confuso pleito
alegan en pro y en contra;
sentenciad en favor, cielos.
Caballos suenan; ¿si son
mis amados hijos éstos?   1040
Alma, asomaos a los ojos;
ojos, abríos para verlos.
Grillos echa el temor frío
a los pies, cuando el deseo
se arroja por las ventanas.   1045

Salen muy tristes Adonías y Salomón.

¿Hijos?
    ADONÍAS.   ¿Señor?
    DAVID.   ¿Venís buenos?
¿Qué es de vuestros dos hermanos?
¿Calláis? Siempre fue el silencio
embajador de desgracias.
¿Lloráis? Hartos mensajeros   1050
mis sospechas certifican.
Ay, adivinos recelos,
¿mató Absalón a su hermano?
    SALOMÓN. Sí, señor.
    DAVID.   Pierda el consuelo
la esperanza de volver   1055
al alma, pues a Amón pierdo.
Tome eterna posesión
el llanto, porque sea eterno,
de mis infelices ojos,
hasta que los deje ciegos.   1060
Lástimas hable mi lengua;
no escuchen sino lamentos
mis oídos lastimosos.
Ay, mi Amón, ay mi heredero,
llore tu padre con Jacob diciendo,   1065

he would do him no harm? He did.
So what is there to fear? That love
and vengeance keep no promises.   1035
The case goes on. Hope advocates
what fear denies. Only Heaven
can judge. Please God, it's for the best.
What's that? The sound of horses' hooves!
It must be my beloved sons.   1040
Come back, my soul, to these old eyes.
Eyes, open wide and dare to look!
Cold fear puts shackles on my feet,
though my heart flies through the windows!   1045

Enter Adonijah and Solomon with great sadness.

My sons?
   ADONIJAH. My lord?
   DAVID.   All's well with you?
Well, what news of your two brothers?
Speak to me! Silence always was
the harbinger of misfortune.
You weep? That's messengers enough   1050
to confirm my premonitions.
Did Absolom kill his brother?
   SOLOMON. He did, my lord.
   DAVID.   Then no more hope.
Amnon's gone, so there is no more.   1055
No more consolation either.
Let these poor eyes fill up with tears
and weep for ever till they're blind,   1060
my tongue speak nothing but sadness,
my ears hear nothing but despair.
Oh, my Amnon, my son, my heir!
Your father shall mourn like father
Jacob for his child and curse   1065

hijo, una fiera pésima te ha muerto.

ADONÍAS.   Y de Tamar la historia prodigiosa
acaba aquí en tragedia lastimosa.

Fin de la comedia.

the evil beast that took your life![84]

    ADONIJAH.   Tamar's revenge is done, all passion's gone.
The pity and the tragedy live on.[85]

THE END

King David Repentant

NOTES

Full details of references abbreviated in these notes will be found in the bibliography. References to Tirso de Molina, *Obras dramáticas completas* (ed. Blanca de los Ríos) list only volume and page numbers.

ACT I

1. **dressed for travelling:** with the convention of the open stage and daylight performance in the *comedia*, costume was an important way of establishing the situation, status of characters, time of day, etc. Amnon would probably be wearing more or less contemporary dress suited to the circumstances and his royal status.

Jonadab: although portrayed as a servant in the play, Jonadab was in fact the son of Shimea, David's brother, and therefore Amnon's cousin. (See 2 Samuel xiii 32).

Hebrew costume: *hebreos* in the Spanish probably refers to the costume the actors would be wearing rather than the nationality of the characters. Their loose—fitting robes would immediately classify them as servants in the minds of the audience as well as conveying a biblical atmosphere.

2. **never left his side:** from the beginning we are alerted to the differences and similarities between David and his eldest son, Amnon. Here we are concerned with their different attitudes to war. Comparisons in amorous activities come later and this prepares us for Amnon's entry into his father's seraglio, which echoes David's seduction of Bathsheba.

3. **the city of the idolatrous Ammonite:** the reference is to the siege of Rabbah first mentioned in 2 Samuel xi.

4. **war machines:** this appears to be some sort of siege tower.

5. **Post horses:** an example of Tirso's use of anachronistic detail.

6. **griddled trout:** literally 'sections of salmon'.

7. **walls of love:** Absolom establishes the equivalence between military and amorous conquest, a well—worn literary metaphor in the poets of the palace song—books or *cancioneros* and the work of Jorge Manrique. In the Old Testament plays of Tirso the pursuit of military glory and amorous success are often related to the same moral failing: vanity and self—indulgence.

8. **Eros is the son of Mars:** Tirso in fact uses the term *Amor*, though the fact that the word is capitalized clearly refers to the god Eros or Cupid. Eros is commonly thought to have been the son of Aphrodite (or Venus). As to his father, there is no settled agreement between the claims of Ares (Mars), Zeus or Hermes. In *La mujer que manda en casa* Tirso makes Jezabel refer to the love between Mars and Venus, an idea based on a story told by Homer in *The Odyssey* viii 266—327.

9. **for you to sell it:** there is no basis for this in Scripture, which refers only to the weight of hair cut off in Absolom's annual haircut. 'And when he polled his head, (for it was at every year's end that he polled it: because the hair was heavy on him, therefore he polled it:) he weighed the hair of his head at two hundred shekels after the king's weight' (2 Samuel xiv 26). The popular notion that Absolom sold his hair comes from the interpretation of 'shekel' as a unit of price rather than weight. In his edition of *La venganza de Tamar*, Alan Paterson quotes from the commentary of the seventeenth—century scholar, Cornelius a Lapide, who rejects both the weight and the price as improbable (Paterson, pp.131—2). Here Amnon is suggesting that Absolom pays for his women by giving them locks of his hair.

10. **heads like garlic:** the garlic was frequently used in popular speech as an image of baldness (e.g. *Cabeza de ajos*, 'garlic head').

11. **Love's menu:** *minuta* literally means 'list' or 'inventory', but in view of the dominance of food imagery in the play, 'menu' seems appropriate.

12. **Greasy as a lump of lard:** this represents an expansion of the original version which uses simply 'espesa'. The word literally means 'thick', but is used here in the seventeenth−century sense of 'dirty', i.e. 'thick with grime or grease'.

13. **Josephus of Isacar:** a name presumably invented by Tirso.

14. **You're not your father's son in that:** Eliazer deliberately misunderstands Amnon's remark here. Amnon clearly means that he feels sorry for married men because they are burdened with a wife, whereas Eliazer is implying that David never felt sorry for married men since he took their wives away from them.

15. **Nabal's woman:** the reference is to Abigail. See note 25 in Act II.

16. **guards them so close:** this detail appears to be taken from Josephus who writes '...Amnon fell in love with her (Thamara) but, since he could not obtain his desire because of her virginity and because she was closely guarded, he became very ill...' (*Jewish Antiquities*, p. 449).

17. **I'll have the lot:** see 2 Samuel xvi 21−2. In the power struggle against Absolom, David was temporarily forced to flee from Jerusalem, leaving his palace in the keeping of 'ten concubines'. On the advice of Ahithophel, Absolom slept with his father's concubines as a symbolic act of irrevocable defiance to his father's rule. In this we have an excellent example of the link which Tirso will subsequently explore between Absolom's sexual appetite and his political ambition.

18. **absurd predictions:** from Amnon's response, it is clear that he takes this as a challenge to his rights as eldest son.

19. **I'm feeling curious today:** the idea of curiosity still had strong moral connotations in the seventeenth century. Curiosity was seen as the principal reason for Eve's fall from grace, an unjustified prying into things that did not concern her, into matters relating to God's providence. All the examples of usage quoted in the *Diccionario de Autoridades* give a negative and pejorative sense to this word. It is signficant that Tirso precedes this phrase by a build−up of a dark, hot, sensual atmosphere which will dominate the following scene.

20. **My purpose is to do my will:** the word *gusto* denotes a total surrender to selfish appetite. The comments made by Eliazer a few lines later confirm that this obstinacy in pursuit of his own ends is typical of Amnon's behaviour.

21. **I'll use it as a ladder:** the situation here appears to be a conscious echo of *La Celestina*: the high garden wall, the ladder and later the dialogue between mistress and maid.

22. **four dozen preachers:** literally 'fourteen preachers'. No particular significance is attached to the figure.

23. **such heat as this?:** the enclosed garden had been a popular emblem since the Middle Ages. To the medieval imagination, the garden represented a harmonious retreat away from the dangers of the world, a place of innocence but, like its archetype, the Garden of Eden, it was also a place of temptation. Gradually this latter idea began to predominate and the garden became associated with the sensual attractions of the world (see Dawn L. Smith's edition of *La mujer que manda en casa*, pp.38−45). In this as in other garden scenes in his plays, Tirso evokes a highly sensual atmosphere in which the darkness and the stifling heat are conducive to Amnon's bewitchment by love. Tamar's skittish and coquettish behaviour is far from suggesting the innocence of Eden. The garden is charged with the passion of her love−sickness before Amnon enters.

24. **bake the bread:** Dina's metaphor and Tamar's reply represent the first unequivocal appearance of the association between passion and hunger in the play.

25. **I stumble over everything:** the moral overtones of this speech are clear. Amnon's moral blindness is ritualized in his stumbling progress in the unfamiliar territory of the garden. The whole scene is conceived in moral and emblematic rather than physical or psychological terms.

26. **female conversation:** this refers back to Amnon's previous line '...to see what conversation/entertains the ladies of the court'.

27. **evergreen plumage:** green was the traditional symbol of hope in the seventeenth century in Spain. For a full treatment of Tirso's colour symbolism, see S.G. Morley, 'Color Symbolism in Tirso de Molina', *Romanic Review*, 8 (1917), 77−81.

28. **and come straight back to me:** the refrain comes from a popular song of Tirso's own time (see Angel López, *El cancionero popular en el teatro de Tirso de Molina*, p.31). This song as it appears here is a shortened form of a longer version printed in Tirso's miscellany *Los cigarrales de Toledo*, published in 1624, which has led scholars to speculate that *La venganza de Tamar* was probably written before that date (see Paterson, pp.27−8).

29. **serpent's face:** the image is a clear allusion to the archetypal emblem of temptation derived from the Book of Genesis, although here it seems to be mingled with that of the siren.

30. **infant god:** i.e. Cupid.

31. **another artist such as he:** literally 'an illustrious musician'. Apollo, the sun god, was also the god of poetry and music.

32. **Bound by the force of unseen laws:** Amnon's imagery suggests that he has become the slave of his passions.

33. **divil take it:** the rustic speech that Amnon adopts in the original was known as *sayagués*, which was in fact the name of a real dialect from the Sayago region in the province of León. This conventional literary form of rustic speech, however, bore little relation to the actual language of the region.

34. **music and fair young ladies:** the Spanish contains a pun on the single word *mosicas* which is a hybrid form of *músicas* ('music') and *mocicas* ('young girls').

35. **I'm bad at recognitions:** the original, literally translated 'I am uncouth in my knowledge', almost certainly contains the sexual connotation of 'carnal knowledge'.

36. **a present of fruit and flowers:** compare the episode in Act III in which Amnon demands and receives a flower from the disguised Tamar. Such details as this suggest a conscious symmetry in the Amnon — Tamar relationship.

37. **to kiss her hand:** it is not clear whether Amnon is intended to make another attempt to kiss Tamar's hand at this point. The dialogue seems to refer to the previous occasion.

38. **Fooled you!:** the Spanish phrase *mamóla* comes from the verb *mamar* ('to suck') with *la* presumably referring to the *teta* ('teat'), literally 'you sucked it!' in the sense of 'you fell for it'. There is an identical usage of the verb in *La mejor espigadera* in which the shepherd Gomor comments on the ease with which his friends have been deceived with the phrase *mamáronla* ('they've sucked it') (I, 1027). The *Diccionario de Autoridades* explains that the expression is usually accompanied by a gesture with all five fingers of one hand under someone's chin.

39. **it's not all flowers ... love:** the original alludes to a proverb, *todo es flor, y al fin de azar*, which relies for its double meaning on the similarity between the pronunciation of *azar* ('chance' or 'fate') and *azahar* ('orange blossom'). The sense of the proverb would be roughly 'life is all flowers and orange blossom (or fickle fate)'. See Gonzalo de Correas, *Vocabulario de refranes y frases proverbiales*, p.481.

40. **not in black, but red:** the literal sense of the original runs as follows: 'cast the die not in white (i.e. 'blank' or 'to no purpose'), but in red'. The gaming image is taken up again later in the play.

41. **his thoughts are nonetheless on you:** it is possible that some veiled irony is intended here, especially since Adonijah mentions Bathsheba and Abigail in his next speech. Both of these had been married women when David met them and love of the wife had always been associated with armed hostility to the husband. See notes 25 and 26 in Act II.

42. **ready to leave tomorrow:** ten days appear to have elapsed since line 65 in which Absolom speaks of a ten—day truce that David has granted to the Ammonites.

43. **old silver hairs:** literally 'the cold silver which he combs'.

44. **Leave me:** although there is no stage direction, it seems clear that Eliazer and Jonadab go off at this point.

45. **with my own imagination:** seventeenth—century philosophy tended to regard the human imagination as a source of error rather than of inspiration. The word was frequently used in the pejorative sense of a false apprehension of something or judgement which had no basis in reality.

46. **The dice of fate:** this picks up the gaming imagery previously used in line 568.

47. **to climb the wall of tyrant Love:** this phrase of Amnon underlines the emblematic and abstract significance of the walled garden.

48. **How can the falcon flee?:** the specific meaning of *sacre* is 'saker hawk'. The comparison of the lover to a hawk or falcon was a very common one in the seventeenth century. It contained both the notion of hunting and aggression associated with the bird of prey and that of docile subservience to its master or mistress. Amnon is alluding here to his enslavement by his own passion, but, as Paterson points out in his note (p.135), he is also unwittingly suggesting the destructive potential of that passion which will be released in Act II. Tirso also uses the analogy in *La mujer que manda en casa* (Act I, 25—37) when king Ahab expresses his jealousy of the hawk perched on Jezabel's hand.

49. **They talk of the singer and the dolphin:** all the mythological allusions in this speech concern unnatural love affairs to which Amnon compares his incestuous passion. Tirso would have had a wide variety of published anthologies of classical lore and mythology to draw from. Paterson claims

that the first three examples appear in Pero Mejía's popular miscellany, *Silva de varia lección*, first published in Seville in 1540, and the last one in Ravisius Textor, *Officinae*, Tomus Primus, Lyons, 1560, p.218.

The first is probably a reference to the story of Arion, a Greek poet and master of the lyre of the seventh century B.C. Arion was invited to compete in a music festival at Taenarus (Sicily) in which he won all the prizes and was showered with rich gifts. On the return voyage to Corinth, the sailors plotted to rob and kill him. Before he was thrown overboard, he requested permission to sing a last song and one of a school of dolphins, attracted by his music, carried him on its back to Corinth. The dolphin, it is said, subsequently refused to be parted from Arion and accompanied him to the court where it succumbed to a life of luxury (see R. Graves, *The Greek Myths*, Penguin Books, vol. 1, pp.290—91).

The second example is probably a reference to Xerxes, or Ahasuerus in the Bible (hence 'Persian king' in the translation), although the original refers only to 'the Persian'. One of the legends linked with this highly irrational king is that he fell in love with a plane tree.

The vague allusion to 'one who loved a statue' could be a reference to the Pygmalion myth, but Paterson mentions another story widely popular among seventeenth—century collectors of classical lore of an anonymous Athenian youth with an amorous attachment to a statue.

In the last example, the Spanish speaks only of 'the most brazen Assyrian woman', which is probably a reference to Semiramis. Originally associated with orgiastic fertility rites in ancient Syria, the figure of Semiramis later became confused with an Assyrian queen, Sammuramat, who lived around 800 B.C. Pliny, in his *Natural History*, Book VIII, chapter 64, stated that her lust was such that she had intercourse with a horse.

Chronologically, most of these allusions seem to date from a period later than the reign of King David, normally thought to have been between about 1000 and 960 B.C.

50. not just reason, but composure: Amnon's frequent changes of mind in this scene are symptomatic of the irrational behaviour attributed to those suffering from melancholy (see note 1 in Act II). At this stage, however, he still remains conscious of his obligations and tries to resist his instinctive desires.

51. seasoned love: the phrase suggests that Tirso is deliberately placing Amnon's encounter with Tamar against the background of a wedding in order to emphasize the contrast between his sudden passion and mature love which keeps within the bounds of reason.

52. They take their seats: if this refers to the guests in general, a previous stage direction already has them sitting down. Possibly it refers only to the royal party and the bride and groom.

53. Cruel sister ... between us!: I have taken the liberty of transposing these two lines, since it seemed illogical to speak of obstacles after fate had provided an opportunity of making contact with Tamar.

54. The place beside her: literally: 'The place of my impossible tyrant is unoccupied'. Since Tamar is clearly in her place at this point, Tirso presumably means that there is no one next to her or guarding her.

55. and have my way: again the streak of self—centred single—mindedness is stressed by Tirso as one of Amnon's dominant characteristics. The same trait is picked up in Act III when Amnon and Tamar meet again under different circumstances.

56. Kill him, I say!: Tamar's violent over—reaction to the gesture of the hand—kiss is a calculated detail designed to indicate the violence latent in Tamar's character. It stands in contrast to her previous somewhat coquettish response in the garden scene and anticipates her later state of mind when she becomes obsessed with revenge. Josephus's concluding remark underlines this point for the audience.

ACT II

1. melancholy: Amnon's state of mind would have been seen as physical in origin. Melancholy, according to Renaissance medical theory, was one of the four primary 'humours' that constituted our physical make—up, the other three being blood, choler and phlegm. Melancholy is described in *Autoridades* as the 'residue' or 'dregs' of the blood which nourishes the parts of the body which share its properties, such as the spleen and the bones. A predominance of melancholy over the other humours could thus produce a natural tendency towards 'melancholic' behaviour in the individual and this could be considerably exacerbated by an excess of passion. This acute state of melancholy was described as 'melancholy adust', which is clearly the condition in which Amnon now finds himself. The best known contemporary treatises on the subject are R. Burton's *Anatomy of Melancholy* and, in Spain, Huarte de San Juan's *Examen de ingenios*. A convenient general account of melancholy as reflected in Spanish literature may be found in Otis H. Green, *Spain and the Western Tradition* (Madison and Milwaukee, 1967, vol. 2, pp.147−50).

montera: headgear defined by Covarrubias as 'having a round crown made up of four segments, so that they could be easily joined and sewn, with a wide brim that could be used to cover the forehead and the ears'. It was usually worn by hunters, but in Tirso's day was also fashionable in the cities. The dramatic point is that this is blatantly inappropriate for indoor use, especially so soon after rising from his bed, and that it serves as an emblem of Amnon's unbalanced state of mind, of which he gives many indications during the course of this scene. The detail is obviously anachronistic.

2. **hundred crowns:** the Spanish uses the word *escudos*, so called because of the royal coat of arms on the coin. They were minted in both gold and silver. The silver *escudos*, which are most probably being alluded to here, consisted of eight *reales de plata* (silver *reales*). In view of what Eliazer says later in his anecdote about doctors (line 69), i.e. that their average income was some 50 *escudos* a week, we may gather that this is a considerable sum of money. The unit of currency is again an indication of Tirso's disdain for historical accuracy. See also note 11 on 'two hundred reals'.

3. **amber:** used to make a perfume which was applied to clothing.

4. **kill more men ... with their swords:** i.e. by writing their prescriptions. During the sixteenth and seventeenth centuries writers treated the medical profession with scant respect. References to the lethal ignorance of doctors, their pretentiousness, wealth and ostentatious dress, etc. are commonplaces of Golden Age literature. The details that occur most frequently are those of the amber−perfumed gloves, handsome mule, bejewelled fingers, bearded features and shelves well−stocked with unread volumes. Tirso himself makes numerous satirical references to the profession (e.g. in *El amor médico*, Act I, 145−224).

5. **like full−time executioners:** literally 'without being executioners'.

6. **I do my gambolling in bed:** Paterson notes that lines 85 to 124 in the original only appear in the MS version of the play and not in any of the printed versions. He suggests that this provides an interesting insight into the extent of bawdry that was tolerated on the stage, though not in the printed text. If we imagine the impact of this salacious account on Amnon's state of sexual frustration, it perhaps goes some way towards justifying what might seem to be a long and irrelevant speech.

7. **the vapours:** this is the equivalent suggested by Paterson for *opilaciones*, which is defined as an obstruction or chlorosis in the ducts through which the humours circulate (Covarrubias), a condition thought to be caused by lack of exercise and commonly found in young ladies.

8. **The adage simply isn't true:** Paterson suggests that the adage Tirso had in mind was probably 'honra y provecho no caben en un saco' ('honour and profit cannot fit into the same sack'). See Gonzalo de Correas, *Vocabulario de refranes y frases proverbiales*, p. 247.

9. **côtes de veau:** the original version suggests a satirical reference to affected and pretentious usage (*vaquita* instead of the usual word for veal, *ternera*). Clearly, if contemporary satire is intended, the allusion is anachronistic. Hence the translation is likewise.

10. **cups:** this refers to the practice of 'cupping' used by surgeons to draw blood from an inflamed part of the body or as an alternative means of blood−letting to leeches. The air inside the 'cup' or 'cupping glass' was first heated and the cup was then firmly applied to the skin. When the air cooled, a partial vacuum was formed and the blood was thus drawn from the neighbouring parts to the skin under the cup. Sometimes, as in this case, small incisions were made in the skin before applying the cup. The Espasa Calpe *Enciclopedia Universal Ilustrada* states that a maximum number of cups that could be safely applied was eight. Fourteen would presumably have placed the patient in considerable danger.

11. **Two hundred reals:** with eight *reales de plata* to an *escudo*, this would make twenty−five *escudos*. The earlier estimate of their income at fifty *escudos* a week thus seems rather conservative.

12. **How can you find so much to say?:** the ironic contrast with Amnon's earlier line 'Why so silent, Eliazer?' confirms Tirso's comic emphasis in this scene.

13. **Little birds that welcome:** this seems to be an adaptation of a type of popular song known as *cantares del alba* or 'dawn songs' (see A. López, *El cancionero popular en el teatro de Tirso de Molina*, p. 81).

14. **Give me the black foil:** the *espada negra* was the fencing foil and the *espada blanca* the real sword. The Spanish contains a play on the word *blanco* in the double sense of 'white' or 'blank'. The literal sense of the original is: 'Give me the black foil; although since my nevergreen hope remains white (i.e. 'blank' or 'unfulfilled'), I might as well use the white sword rather than the black one'. In the traditional colour symbolism of Golden Age literature, green represented hope.

15. **late—lamented freedom:** i.e. he has become a prisoner of his senses.

16. **twelve illustrious tribes:** the original twelve tribes of Israel, descended from the sons of Jacob, were Reuben, Simeon, Judah, Issachar, Zebulun, Benjamin, Dan, Naphtali, Gad, Asher, Levi and Ephraim and Manesseh. These last two were counted as one, except in parts of the Bible where either Levi or Simeon is omitted from the list.

17. **the fall of great Goliath:** a reference to the way in which the women of Israel celebrated David's triumphal return after killing Goliath: 'And it came to pass as they came, when David was returned from the slaughter of the Philistine, that the women came out of all cities of Israel, singing and dancing, to meet king Saul with tabrets, with joy, and with instruments of musick. And the women answered one another as they played, and said, Saul hath slain his thousands, and David his ten thousands' (1 Samuel xviii 6—7).

18. **David speaks:** the general tone of this scene is one of great pomp and solemnity. David's speech is outrageously boastful and its style almost ludicrously convoluted. In view of Tirso's well—known dislike of this brand of euphuism and distorted syntax associated with the poet Góngora and in view of the fact that no other speeches in the play even remotely approach the syntactical complexities and density of allusions displayed here, one can only assume that Tirso is caricaturing the pomp and circumstance of David's return to Jerusalem. The turgid and inflated language of the speech is deliberately undermined by the bathos of his last sentence: 'How are you all?' The conditional clauses introduced in the first half of the speech are not resolved until line 313 with 'then I wish ... '. A rough paraphrase of the sense would be as follows: 'If, after the many trophies won and deeds accomplished in my prime, my glory is now reduced to this small trifle (the Ammonite crown) and for this one crown my valour is rewarded with no fewer than four (constituted by the eight arms of Michal, Abigail, Bathsheba and Tamar), then I wish I could grow three other heads to reciprocate the honour that you do me.' David appears to be saying that he places greater value on the loving welcome of his family than on the trophies of war, that love has triumphed over war. Another occasion on which Tirso expresses pride and vanity through linguistic affectation is the speech by Tisbea in the first Act of *El burlador de Sevilla (The Trickster of Seville)*.

19. **victories over Assyrians, Midianites, Philistines, over Gath and Canaan:** a convenient summary of David's military campaigns is provided in 2 Samuel viii (see Map). Whereas it is clear that David finally broke the power of the Philistines, took the Philistine city—state of Gath to the south—west of Jerusalem (see 1 Chronicles i) and incorporated most of the city—states of Canaan into the state of Israel, there is no recorded encounter between David and the Assyrians or Midianites. The limits of David's empire fell well short of Assyria to the north and the Land of Midian to the south—east. John Bright in *A History of Israel* (Philadelphia, 1981) describes the composition of that empire as follows: 'The Canaanites of Palestine had been incorporated in the state, the Philistines restricted to a narrow strip along the southern coastal plain, while Moab, Edom and Ammon, under one arrangement or another, yielded tribute. All of southern and central Syria was embraced in the empire, apparently under provincial administration' (p. 204). David's conquests in Syria, chiefly in retribution for Syrian intervention in the war against the Ammonites, are described in 2 Samuel viii 3—8. It is possible that Tirso confused the words *sirios* (Syrians) and *asirios* (Assyrians) but, in any case, the conflict with Syria almost certainly came after the events recorded in the play.

20. **Libyan lion:** the youthful David's victories over the lion and the bear are narrated in 1 Samuel xvii 34—7. The reference to the laurel leaves being transformed into vines is a figure of speech meaning that the victory was celebrated with wine.

21. **shapeless bear:** the victory over the bear is expressed in a complex conceit of the dead bear becoming clothing and adornments for David's body. The bear becomes 'shapeless' once it is reduced to a skin.

22. **loaned to it in gold:** i.e. now that time has turned his golden hair to grey.

23. **Bellona:** normally represented as a companion (though possibly a wife or sister) of Mars, Bellona had a celebrated temple in Rome near the gate of Carmenta. The priests of Bellona were chosen from amongst the gladiators.

24. **Michal:** the daughter of Saul given to David in marriage by her father in exchange for two

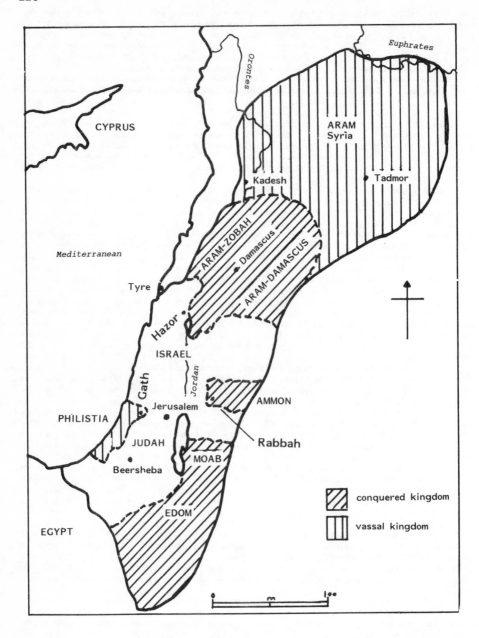

David's empire

hundred foreskins of the Philistines killed in battle (1 Samuel xviii 20−27). According to the version of Josephus (p. 267) David presented the heads of six hundred Philistines to Saul. Later, when Saul attempted to have David killed, Michal helped her husband to escape (1 Samuel xix 11−17). During David's period of wandering exile, Saul re−married Michal to Phalti (1 Samuel xxv 44), but David subsequently recovered her as his wife through the agency of Saul's general, Abner (2 Samuel iii 14). The 'unworthy possessor' referred to is evidently Phalti and the vengeful envy seems to refer to Saul's action in giving Michal a second husband. The 'deception' and 'tales of scandal' are less clearly documented in Scripture, although there are signs of tension between David and Michal in 2 Samuel vi 20−23. The statement that Michal 'had no children until the day of her death' (contradicted, apparently in 2 Samuel xxi 8) seems to indicate that David did not sleep with her after this disagreement.

25. **Abigail:** before her marriage to David, Abigail had been the wife of Nabal, a rich and ill−mannered farmer from Mount Carmel. Abigail had given food and hospitality to David and his men when her husband, despite being under an obligation to David, had refused to do so. David married Abigail when Nabal died shortly after this incident (see 1 Samuel xxv and Josephus pp. 313−21).

26. **Bathsheba:** the Bible story (2 Samuel xi) relates how David slept with Bathsheba, the wife of Uriah, the Hittite, after seeing her washing herself from the roof of his palace. The 'mortal hurt' committed against Uriah was that David engineered his death by arranging with Joab to have him placed in the front line of battle during the siege of Rabbah. The penitential psalm referred to is psalm 51.

27. **the prince ... Ark of the Covenant:** i.e. Solomon.

28. **in the form of a cloud:** God's presence is said to have taken this form at the dedication of the temple built to house the Ark of the Covenant (2 Chronicles v 13−14).

29. **Ophir ... Tarshish its silver:** towns of the ancient world famous for their trade in gold and silver (see 1 Kings x 11 and 22).

30. **Hiram:** the king of Tyre who provided Solomon with the fir and cedar wood for the Temple in return for wheat and olive oil (1 Kings v). He was also a craftsman in his own right and carried out extensive brass work on the Temple (1 Kings vii).

31. **a talent in weight:** the weight, though not the value, of the crown is mentioned in the Bible (2 Samuel xii 30) and Josephus (pp. 445−6).

32. **the enemy's water supply:** these details relating to the siege and capture of Rabbah indicate Tirso's familiarity with Josephus's account (pp. 445−6).

33. **Give me your arms, my lord:** although this line is given to Solomon in the Spanish text, it seems more likely that it would be spoken by Adonijah.

34. **resolved to see me die:** the change from the arrogant to the pleading, self−pitying tone characterizes the erratic and contradictory temperament of the ageing David.

35. **in Latin:** in the original there is no reference to Latin, which is introduced simply as an attempt to render the word play on the two names.

36. **conscript in Love's army:** like David in his homecoming speech, Amnon depicts the triumph of love over war. The feeling contained in this speech is ambivalent, in part conveying a sense of love's moral superiority and in part depicting the enslavement of the mind by the senses.

37. **with pagans and idolaters:** a passage in Deuteronomy chapter seven urges Israel to have no truck with other nations of different religion: 'And when the Lord thy God shall deliver them before thee; thou shalt smite them, and utterly destroy them; thou shalt make no covenant with them, nor show mercy unto them. Neither shalt thou make marriages with them; thy daughter thou shalt not give unto his son, nor his daughter shalt thou take unto thy son' (verses 2 and 3).

38. **holy Deuteronomy:** in direct contradiction to the passage in the previous note, the law of Moses does admit exceptions: 'When thou goest forth to war against thine enemies, and the Lord thy God hath delivered them into thine hands, and thou hast taken them captive, And seest among the captives a beautiful woman, and hast a desire unto her, that thou wouldest have her to thy wife; Then thou shalt bring her home to thine house; and she shall shave her head, and pare her nails; And she shall put the raiment of her captivity from off her, and shall remain in thine house, and bewail her father and her mother a full month; and after that thou shalt go in unto her, and be her husband, and she shall be thy wife' (Deuteronomy xxi 10−13).

39. **heard of hungry men:** see Introduction for a discussion of the food imagery.

40. **have come to speak with you:** for purely stylistic reasons, I have transposed this phrase which in the Spanish, appears in the second line of Amnon's speech.

41. my tragic face: the word *figura* in the original may mean simply a character in a play or, more specifically, according to the *Autoridades* definition, 'a pompous individual who affects gravity in his actions and words'. The burlesque tone of the speeches that follow clearly indicates that Tirso is indulging in a parody of a conventional love scene here.

42. My Heaven: literally 'zone' (*zona*) of the celestial sphere, equivalent to one of the five zones of the terrestrial sphere. Each zone was divided into twelve segments presided over by a sign of the Zodiac. Tirso has Amnon appeal to the pagan and deterministic science of astrology to justify his desire and response to Tamar's beauty.

43. kneeling down: literally 'this position', though it seems reasonable to deduce from the context that Amnon might be kneeling at this point.

44. precious jewel: the dialogue resumes its tone of comic parody up to the exit of Amnon.

45. Jebusites: this refers to the capture of the citadel in Jerusalem from the Jebusites by David's army shortly after he became king of Israel. David promised the command of his troops to the first man to reach the citadel and Joab was the first to make the climb (see 1 Chronicles xi 4–6 and Josephus pp. 391–3). There is a suggestion of discreet comedy in the slightly priggish tone of Joab's speech.

46. kisses her hand and leaves: see Introduction for a discussion of the hand–kiss motif. Although this reconciliation scene between Tamar and Joab involves some repetition from the previous scene, it is perhaps dramatically justified by Tirso's need to give the eavesdropping Amnon that extra degree of motivation (jealousy and revenge) to turn his obsession into violent action.

47. your twice–kissed hand ... to that: literally: 'your kissed hand will give you the lie, since, in order to do so, it sought two months'.

48. dissembling words: Tamar has now realized that Amnon is disguising the true object of his passion and that his feelings are for her.

49. inconstant–as–the–sea Tamar: the Spanish contains an untranslatable pun on Tamar and *mar* ('sea'). Literally: 'fickle Tamar, you end in 'sea', since you are a sea in your inconstancy'. This word–play contrasts in tone and meaning with the punning on Tamar's name at the beginning of this scene.

50. like attracting like: the idea that love consisted in the attraction, not of opposites, but of like for like was a commonplace of seventeenth–century philosophy. Paterson (p. 139) quotes supporting evidence from J. de Aranda's book of commonplaces, *Lugares comunes* (Madrid, 1613). On the moral question of incest in biblical times there is some contradiction. The law of Moses (Leviticus xviii) clearly prohibits marriage with a half–sister on the father's side and yet Tamar's words in 2 Samuel xiii ('I pray thee, speak unto the king, for he will not withhold me from thee') seem to indicate the contrary. Rabbis reconcile this contradition by explaining that Tamar's mother had given birth to her before being converted to Judaism and that consequently Tamar was not strictly speaking a blood relation of Amnon according to Jewish law. Some biblical commentators even claimed that the mother had been pregnant with Tamar before being brought captive to Jerusalem (see Serge Maurel, *L'Univers dramatique de Tirso de Molina* p. 493).

51. Adam's children: Amnon rationalizes his passion by referring to the marriage of Cain. Genesis iv records that Cain 'went out from the presence of the Lord, and dwelt in the land of Nod', where he 'knew his wife'. The orthodox explanation of this marriage was that Cain had a sister not mentioned in the Bible and it was justified on the grounds that, at this early stage in human society, survival of the species necessarily had to prevail over moral law. Amnon, however, is arguing for a more general priority of the law of Nature over man–made ethical codes.

52. supposed to soothe me: this short transition scene provides a brief and uneasy lull before the climactic and highly charged confrontation between Tamar and Amnon. The gentle lyricism of the song interacts dramatically with the mounting violence of Amnon's feelings.

53. since I know your humour: the original is ambiguous and could refer to the humour of the king. Since it is Amnon's mood that is relevant here, I have opted for this interpretation and adapted the punctuation accordingly.

54. to provide the seasoning: this biblical episode supplies the whole basis for the sustained food metaphor in the play. Here Tamar plays on the double meaning of *sal* ('salt' or 'wit') and *sazonado* ('tasty' or 'witty'). The dish she brings will have no taste because she herself is not in the mood to serve it.

55. I am your blood: Tirso suppresses any reference to Tamar's request (2 Samuel xiii 13) that Amnon should ask David for her hand in marriage. Given Tirso's habitual scrupulousness in his use of biblical sources, this omission must have been to underline the unnatural character of the crime, parallel to Absolom's subsequent willingness to commit parricide. Interestingly, Calderón, who adapted the material of Tirso's second Act for the first Act of his *Los cabellos de Absolón*, does not omit this plea.

ACT III

1. **basilisk:** allegedly hatched by a serpent from a cock's egg, the basilisk was a serpent with a diadem—shaped crest on its head and white patches on its body. Though no more than a hand's span in length, the basilisk was reputed to be capable of killing by its breath or a look from its eyes, according to the Covarrubias dictionary.

2. **fruit of Sodom:** a reference to the apples of Sodom or Dead Sea Fruits which were reputed to grow on the shores of the Dead Sea and contain the burnt—out ashes of the city. Although their external appearance was attractive, they would dissolve into smoke and ashes on being plucked (see Josephus, *Jewish War*, bk. IV, Loeb Classical Library, vol. III, p. 143).

3. **you do me greater wrong:** although Tirso omits Tamar's plea that Amnon should request her hand from the king, he follows the biblical source in making Amnon's subsequent rejection a greater injury than the act of rape or incest. It is clear that Tamar's later desire for revenge is based more on offended pride than the breaking of a taboo.

4. **This dress:** Tirso is thinking of the 'garment of divers colours' mentioned in 2 Samuel xiii 18. According to the biblical source, this multi—coloured dress was symbolic of purity: 'for with such robes were the king's daughters that were virgins apparelled'. Josephus (p. 453) adds the details that it was a long—sleeved tunic which reached down to the ankle.

5. **gambled with my honour:** the gaming imagery that Tirso puts into Tamar's mouth in this speech (and also later in this Act) denotes that the stable and permanent values of love have been abandoned for the vagaries of passion and appetite. The parallel that Tirso is implicitly drawing between gaming and passion is the inherent uncertainty and instability of both.

6. **winner's generosity:** Tirso uses the word *barato*, which was the tip that the winner usually gave to servants or bystanders after the game.

7. **the serpent that torments:** an indication of the tone in which Tirso intended Tamar's last speech to be delivered. Evidently, he envisaged a shift from raging fury in the first speech to icy, contained anger, possibly with a touch of sarcasm, in the second.

8. **would stand in pools of purple dye:** literally: '(Your veins) would clothe my feet in purple'. Purple alludes both to the colour of blood and the colour traditionally associated with royalty.

9. **if Amnon dies:** this scene between Absolom and Adonijah establishes the fact that their ambition is stimulated by Amnon's apparent illness. It is also necessary to establish Absolom's ambition dramatically before he can be seen to use Tamar's revenge as a pretext to advance it.

10. **golden hair:** the original specifies *oro de Ofir*. See note 29 in Act II.

11. **A monarch's crown ... dainty head:** literally: 'you offend against your delicacy and your softness'.

12. **A noble form ... ugliness:** Paterson suggests possible sources for these commonplaces: 1. the Latin proverb, *exteriora indicunt interiora* ('outward appearances reveal inner realities'). 2. The line from Virgil's *Aeneid* V 344: *gratior et pulchro veniens in corpore virtus* ('virtue is more pleasing when it comes in a beautiful form'). 3. Seventeenth—century commonplace books which told the story of the philosopher Diogenes who once remarked on seeing a man whose handsome features contrasted with his depraved mind: 'A fine house but an evil tenant'.
The origin of these aphorisms is, however, less important than Tirso's use of them to reveal Absolom's vanity. Absolom consistently draws on such philosophical *dicta* to bolster his own vain and selfish designs, usually distorting their meaning in the process.

13. **as your name implies:** according to 2 Samuel xii 25, Solomon was also called Jedidiah, which in Hebrew means 'beloved of Yah' (see Josephus, p. 445, note c.)

14. **it shall be written on Israel's throne:** Tirso gives David a clear premonition that Solomon will eventually rule over the kingdom of Israel, although, as we have seen, he still regards Amnon as his heir at this stage.

15. **dressed in mourning:** an emblem of Tamar's lost virginity. Tirso underlines the transformation of Tamar from carefree young girl to vengeful harpy with the visual device of a change of costume.

16. **descendant of the lion:** the lion is the emblem of the tribe of Judah which, in fulfilment of

Jacob's dying prophesy, became the royal house of David. Judah, son of Jacob and founder of the tribe, is described in the following terms: 'Judah is a lion's whelp: from the prey, my son, thou art gone up: he stooped down, he couched as a lion, and as an old lion; who shall rouse him up?' (Genesis xlix 9).

17. covered with ashes: this detail is taken from 2 Samuel xiii 19. Ashes in the Old Testament were symbolic of penitence and mourning. In the next four lines Tirso extends the metaphor to embrace burnt—out passion (alluding to Amnon's lust) and ashes as a traditional method for removing stains.

18. substantial broth: the original contains a pun impossible to translate into English. Tirso uses the word *sustancia* which means both 'broth' and 'substance' in the philosophical sense of the essential property of a thing. In the Spanish, the philosophical metaphor continues by saying that the 'substance' may be rendered ineffectual by the *accidentes* or the presence of other 'accidental qualities', in this case the degraded state of Amnon's appetite. The literal sense would be: 'but the substance is of no avail if there are accidents of inclination (taste) opposed to it'.

19. city streets: this detail appears to be derived from Josephus (p. 453) in whose account Tamar deliberately calls public attention to the outrage done to her.

20. Do not leave as your successor: here Tamar provides Absolom with the means to link her revenge with his own ambition, by claiming that a man guilty of incest is not worthy to succeed to the throne.

21. raised his knife against his child: see Genesis xxii.

22. tearing lions limb from limb: see 1 Samuel xvii 34—6.

23. same mother: the mother of Absolom and Tamar was Maacah, the daughter of Talmai, king of Geshur (see 2 Samuel iii 3 and 1 Chronicles iii 2).

24. by taking from you Israel's crown: neither Scripture nor Josephus hints at any political motive of ambition behind Absolom's adoption of Tamar's cause. Both attribute it to simple vengeance.

25. As brother to the princess: although he is given very few lines in the play, Solomon is sharply characterized by Tirso. This speech reflects his essentially judicial attitude, balanced though ultimately unhelpful.

26. is moved on seeing him: in the Spanish this stage direction appears after 'How are you?' in the next line, but in production David's change of attitude would almost certainly have to precede this enquiry.

27. for adultery and murder: the allusion is, of course, to David's seduction of Bathsheba and the murder of her husband Uriah, narrated in 2 Samuel xi. David's agony can be seen as the working out of a divine punishment, since he is placed in the same situation vis à vis his son as God was vis à vis David. From this point onwards, the focus of dramatic interest is on David's response to his children's actions and, in particular, on the conflict between justice and mercy in his mind. The psalms of David constantly return to the theme of mercy but seldom suggest any moral conflict between justice and mercy. Tirso, however, clearly sees the incompatibility between them in David's situation.

28. 'Father I have sinned': this appears to be an echo of psalm 51, which David composed after Nathan rebuked him for his sin with Bathsheba.

29. retribution ... forgiveness in my right: this could be a reference to a seventeenth—century emblem recorded by Sebastián de Covarrubias in his *Emblemas morales* (Madrid, 1610), Centuria iii, Emblema 82, in which a king is depicted with a garland in his right hand and a sword in his left. The verse exhorts the king to emulate God, as far as he can, in mercy and magnanimity, claiming that his name will be greater by this than by the execution of rigorous justice.

30. power of love: here for the first time in the play Amnon uses *amor* in the sense of Christian charity rather than Eros or desire. The force of David's compassion momentarily touches Amnon's heart but, as we see later, makes no lasting impression on him. At this stage, however, Tirso engineers a shift in audience sympathy by revealing this strain of humanity in Amnon and, immediately afterwards, by underscoring the opportunist ambition in Absolom.

31. Here is his chamber: since the context makes it obvious that Absolom has not yet seen David approaching, I take the phrase *Aquí está* to refer to David's room rather than his physical presence.

32. serves me up a dish: the food imagery ('dish', 'succulent', 'morsel') clearly links Absolom's appetite for power with Amnon's appetite for the flesh. There is no mention of this episode in either the Bible or Josephus. Paterson suggests that Tirso may have derived it from an old Jewish legend relating to Adonijah, who, it was said, tried on the crown of David and found that it did not fit him. This, according to the legend, demonstrated that he was destined not to succeed to the throne, since the crown had the remarkable property of always fitting the legitimate heir (see Louis Ginzberg, *The Legends of the Jews*, Philadelphia, 1913, vol. IV, p. 118). The story probably had a European—wide circulation since a similar version appears in Holinshed's *Chronicle* from which Shakespeare derived his scene in *Henry IV, Part II.*

33. a baser metal: the original pun on the word *yerro* ('iron' or 'error') is untranslatable. The literal version would be: 'he who dishonoured Tamar was a) made of iron b) an aberration of nature'.

34. next to mine: Absolom is referring to his hair. Literally: 'although you may be exalted to that height, you will fear being dazzled by the gold of my hair'.

35. He kneels: Absolom's action in kneeling before the king underlines the parallel with the previous scene in which Amnon had knelt before David. David's reaction to Absolom's unscrupulous hypocrisy in this scene highlights the vulnerability of his merciful nature. In making the comparison between the two brothers, the audience shifts the bulk of its moral condemnation on to Absolom.

36. a good talent: the weight of the crown is specified in 1 Chronicles xx 2 as 'a talent of gold' and there is no mention of its value. Here Tirso is punning on 'talent' in the general sense of 'gift' or 'aptitude' and as a unit of money.

37. hence your anger against Amnon: David characteristically misjudges Absolom's motives.

38. between the earth and sky: this reference to Absolom's eventual fate would not have been lost on Tirso's audience. 'And Absolom rode upon a mule, and the mule went under the thick boughs of a great oak, and his head caught hold of the oak, and he was taken up between the heaven and the earth; and the mule that was under him went away' (2 Samuel xviii 9). Absolom was killed by Joab while still hanging by his hair from the branches of the tree.

39. gallows tree: another unwitting allusion to the manner of his own death.

40. wimple: a form of head—covering made of light material which was worn over the head and around the neck and chin by women, especially in the late medieval period.

41. It's shearing time, my likely lads: the translation of the song is necessarily freer than that of the dialogue in order to accommodate the rhyme. In both languages, however, it is based on the dual sense of such words as 'to fleece' and 'skin', satirizing the mercenary habits of women and officials of the law. The purpose of the song and of the following scene in general is to emphasize the contrast between the corrupt values of the court and the city and the simple truths of country life, very much a theme of Tirso's own time.

42. with crooked pen: the sense of the original depends on the association of *pelar* ('to pluck', 'crop' in the sense of 'to rob') and *pelo* (the 'hair' on the tip of a quill pen which mars the writing). Marring the writing seems to imply sharp practice here.

43. He'll clean you out of copper coins: the sense of 'fluff' and 'copper coins' are both contained in the word *vellón*. This is an allusion to the debased copper coinage that was introduced in the early part of the seventeenth century and was the object of much public protest and literary satire.

44. Tirso: Tirso often introduced himself as a shepherd in his plays, e.g. *La república al revés.*

45. melanchronic: there is a deliberate malapropism in the original Spanish. Tamar's melancholy attitude parallels that of Amnon in Act II.

46. I fear to see myself in them: Tirso seems to imply that Tamar's fear of looking at her reflection is not just that of contemplating her dishonoured image, but of confronting the change within herself.

47. when you stoop to wash: the contrast between the corrupting artificiality of the court and the salutary effect of a life in harmony with nature was a commonplace of seventeenth—century literature in Spain. The circumstances of Tirso's life had given him a highly developed distaste for the vanities of court life and his allusions here are more relevant to his own contemporary situation than to biblical times. Nevertheless, there are also more general Christian overtones of the waters of baptism and the remission of sins.

48. Virgin honey's what they use here: 'virgin honey' is a literal rendering of *miel virgen*, which, according to the dictionary of Covarrubias, was honey that had been distilled rather than boiled. Honey was commonly used as a basis for cosmetics and, by painting their faces with pure unadulterated honey, Riselio claims, women are advertising a purity they do not possess.

49. It's for my sins: the pun on *pecas* ('freckles') and *pecados* ('sins') is unfortunately untranslatable in English.

50. has turned to poison: quicksilver and white arsenic were used for the removal of skin blemishes. Tamar claims that the remedy would be of no avail in her case, as she had already absorbed so much poison.

51. birthmark ... will not change: Tamar's reply is deliberately enigmatic and calculated to mystify her rustic audience. The Spanish text puns on the words *lunar* ('mole' or 'spot') and *luna* ('moon') with all the latter's associations of mutability. Literally: 'It will not change like the moon'.

52. bruised by Love ... fragrance: in the traditional colour code of the Golden Age, violet was the colour of love. Tirso himself gives us a reasonably comprehensive list of associations in *La república al revés*, II viii. More specifically, both the flower and the colour were associated with the *wound* of love and here, as later in the scene, the connotations of bruising and violence are uppermost in the author's mind.

53. But you can match ... seed: this corresponds to the third and fourth lines of Laureta's speech in the original which, for stylistic reasons, have been transposed in the translation.

54. fortune—teller: the Spanish text uses the word for 'pythoness' or priestess of the temple of Apollo. According to Covarrubias, these were generally credited with powers of divination and the word was commonly used as a synonym for *hechicera* or 'sorceress'.

55. 'The remedy was to forget, etc.': refrain of a popular song found in many Golden Age plays (see E.M. Wilson and J. Sage, *Poesías líricas en las obras dramáticas de Calderón*, London, 1964, pp. 58—9).

56. torn my clothes to shreds: *ajironar* can have the meaning of 'to trim with braid', although the other sense of 'to tear into strips' seems more likely in the context. A pun appears to be intended here.

57. not by cosmetics: possibly a sly allusion to Absolom.

58. she seems to read my mind: the tone of Amnon's dialogue in this scene strongly suggests that he has dismissed the Tamar incident from his mind and has now become a conventional court gallant, more or less in the style of Absolom in Act I.

59. Amaltheia's horn: literally: 'These meadows are the theatre where Amaltheia performs'. In Greek mythology Amaltheia was the name of the goat said to have suckled the young god Zeus with her milk or, in some versions, of the nymph who nursed him with goat's milk. The goat's horn was the original cornucopia or 'horn of plenty' which had the property of refilling itself inexhaustibly with whatever food or drink its possessor wished for. In Golden Age literature, Amaltheia became a common literary symbol for abundance.

60. is she dumb?: the ensuing dialogue contains a complex and untranslatable pun on the different seventeenth—century meanings of the word *muda*. In the original question ('...*es muda?*') *muda* has its literal sense of 'dumb'. Laureta's reply (*Está en muda*) means 'She's in moulting', a metaphorical phrase often used of a person who is silent in a conversation, by analogy with the bird which does not sing during the moulting season. Amnon picks up the word and, by using it as a plural noun, changes the meaning to 'ointment' or 'lotion'. The literal sense of his line would be 'Do they have cosmetics here?', possibly referring back to Absolom's previous comment about the local women's 'unassisted beauty'. Laureta's answer is that, in the country, women are more concerned with their honour than with their faces or appearance. Unfortunately, it was difficult to preserve all these levels of meaning in the English translation and it was necessary to change the sense of Amnon's question, *¿Mudas hay acá?*

61. a lily together with a pointed reed: in the following scene Tirso uses Laureta's distribution of flowers to David's sons to make some pertinent comments on their character and the fate that lay in store for them. The dictionary of Covarrubias describes the lily as a symbol of chastity for its whiteness and of good reputation for its scent. A broken lily was a common emblem for lost chastity (see Sebastián de Covarrubias, *Emblemas morales* (Madrid, 1610), Centuria i, Emblema 5).

62. The larkspur: the Spanish name (literally 'gentleman's spur'), in addition to the phallic shape of this flower, unequivocally conveys its sexual associations. The sexual innuendo is continued in the dialogue that follows. It is curious that Tirso should have been so explicit about the colour. Possibly this was because blue was the traditional colour of jealousy.

63. if she should take your fancy: see 1 Kings ii 15—25. The reference is to Abishag the Shunammite whom Adonijah requested for his wife. This request was made shortly after Solomon had ascended to the throne and was interpreted by the latter as a manoeuvre to usurp his position. As a result Solomon had Adonijah killed.

64. kingcup: the flower in the Spanish text (literally 'king's crown') is given the botanical name of *melilotus* or *sertula campana* by the *Diccionario de Autoridades*. Apart from the obvious regal associations of its name, I have been unable to discover any other emblematic significance. The literal English equivalent is 'large birdsfoot − trefoil'.

65. **lead you astray:** Laureta is predicting Solomon's love for 'many strange women' in his old age who 'turned away his heart after other gods' and caused him to reject the covenant and statutes of the Lord (see 1 Kings xi).

66. **nettle's sting:** according to *Autoridades*, the phrase *tener mucha pimienta* ('to be very peppery') was used to signify that a certain commodity had too high a price. Solomon presumably means that there is a price to pay for his good fortune.

67. **the one who loved himself:** the story of Narcissus is told by Ovid in his *Metamorphoses* III, 339−510. He was the son of the river−god Cephisus and so vain that he was incapable of feeling love for anyone. After he had spurned the advances of the nymph Echo and other admirers, Narcissus was punished by the goddess Nemesis who caused him to conceive an insanely passionate love for his own reflection in a pool. He was so overcome with this passion and so distressed by the impossibility of its fulfilment that he languished and died, contemplating his own image. While his naiad−sisters and dryads were preparing the funeral pyre, his body disappeared, leaving in its place the flower that bears his name.

68. **raise you up on high:** see 2 Samuel xviii 9.

69. **They must have seen ... satisfaction:** although unaware that he is talking to Tamar, Amnon continues the gambling and card−sharping imagery that Tamar had previously used to describe his treatment of her at the beginning of the Act. It is clear from this imagery and from Amnon's imperious demands first for her hand and then for the flower that he has once again become the slave of his capricious appetite.

70. **A token like your empty words:** the Spanish involves a play on the words *flor* ('flower') and *floreo* which means the flourish at the beginning and end of a fencing bout, but is used here in the metaphorical sense of 'flattery' or 'pretty speeches'.

71. **It's not mine to give:** it has been necessary to change the sense in English as the original text contains an untranslatable pun on *tomar* ('to take') in the previous line and the name of Tamar. Literally the exchange runs: Amnon: 'I mean to take (*tomar*) a flower'. Tamar: 'The flower of Tamar, you mean'. Since Amnon does not apparently react to this last speech, one must assume that it is spoken as an aside.

72. **They sing:** again Tirso uses the technique of a song to convey an uneasy lull before a storm. Also, for purely practical reasons, it is introduced to give time for the preparation of the *apariencia* or tableau of Amnon's death. Paterson notes that the one song belongs to the same popular tradition as the one in Act I, the *versos de gaita gallega* (see Angel López, *El cancionero popular en el teatro de Tirso de Molina* p. 34).

73. **with black poplar boughs beside:** the shepherds decorate the princes' pavillions with branches and flowers possessing symbolic associations appropriate to the character and destiny of each of David's sons. I have tried to make these associations more explicit in the translation. In the case of Absolom, the cinnamon evokes suggestions of beauty (Song of Songs iv 14), cedar suggests strength but also unbending pride, the palm probably refers to his imminent triumph over Amnon, but the funeral associations of black poplar cast the shadow of his own death over this victory. According to Covarrubias, these associations came from the fact that the poplar tree bore no fruit.

74. **of cypress leaves and tamarisk:** the cypress is traditionally linked with death and sterility possibly because, when cut, it never grows again (Covarrubias). In Roman mythology the tree was dedicated to Pluto, god of the Underworld, and both Greeks and Romans reputedly put cypress twigs inside coffins for burial. In Spain, particularly, cypress trees have traditionally been associated with cemeteries. Cypress was also the wood, owing to its extreme durability, from which coffins in the ancient world and, according to legend, the arrows of Cupid were said to have been made. I have been unable to find any symbolic associations for tamarisk.

75. **laurel leaves:** in the ancient world laurel was associated with poetry and the spirit of prophesy, hence the custom of crowning the Pythoness or priestess of Apollo who delivered the oracles with laurel leaves and of placing them under one's pillow to summon up inspiration. Tirso probably had Solomon's proverbial wisdom in mind as well as his eventual success in inheriting the throne.

76. **the throne ... of all his sons:** a more literal version would be: 'today all the sons of the king perish by ruling'. A prophetic reference to the history of violence and bloodshed that was henceforth to be associated with succession to the throne of Israel.

77. **I'll stick ... peacock pie:** onions were traditionally the food of the poor, just as peacock was

the dish of royalty.

78. count honour satisfied: in the first four lines of this speech, I have adopted the text of Calderón's *Los cabellos de Absolón* where the punctuation seems to make better sense. Calderón reproduced this third Act almost word for word in the second Act of his play. Consult Gwynne Edwards' edition of *Los cabellos de Absolón* (Oxford, Pergamon, 1973).

79. The bleach is hot: the allusion is, of course, to Amnon's blood which is still warm.

80. dishonoured just like you: Absolom's grandfather was Talmai, king of Geshur (2 Samuel iii 13). I have been unable to find any source in Scripture or Josephus for the alleged dishonour of Maacah, mother of Absolom and Tamar. Paterson suggests that Tirso may have confused her with Queen Maachar, daughter of Abishalom and mother of Asa, who was deposed for making an idol in a grove (1 Kings xv 13). Alternatively, this may have been a touch added by Tirso in order to echo the historical repetition of the sins of the flesh through the generations.

81. like a lamb to the shearer's knife: in his Introduction to the play, Alan Paterson suggests that Tirso is implanting an analogy in the minds of the spectators between Amnon delivered to the slaughter by David and Christ sent as the sacrificial lamb by God the Father. He is careful to point out that he is not suggesting that Amnon is a 'Christ figure'. Tirso, he claims, is simply guiding the audience's imagination towards 'the day when justice, having exacted its final penalty in Christ's death, would be reconciled to mercy' (p. 25).

82. blood may boil, but he would not kill: the sense of the original is obscure here. The proverb *La sangre hierve sin fuego* ('blood boils without fire') usually refers to the ease with which the sexual appetite can be aroused. However, this does not seem appropriate in this context.

83. who sold their brother as a slave: i.e. the sons of Jacob who sold their brother Joseph into slavery (see Genesis xxxvii 28).

84. evil beast: this is a reference to the 'evil beast', mentioned in Genesis xxxvii 33, which Jacob's other sons claimed had devoured Joseph. It is possible that this refers generally to the phenomenon of human passion rather than to Absolom specifically in the play.

85. Tamar's revenge ... lives on: Golden Age plays almost always ended with a direct address to the audience, often requesting applause or indulgence for the play's deficiencies. This is consistent with the *comedia*'s disregard for illusionist realism (also illustrated in the uses of the discovery curtain). These endings are often omitted in contemporary productions of Golden Age theatre. I have opted for a very free translation here since the literal version ('And here the prodigious history of Tamar ends in pitiful tragedy') might well have broken, not merely the stage illusion, but the mood of the play for a modern audience.